The Cautious Diplomat

THE CAUTIOUS DIPLOMAT

Charles E. Bohlen
and the Soviet Union, 1929–1969

T. MICHAEL RUDDY

The Kent State University Press
Kent and London

The paper in this book meets the guidelines for permanence and durability of the Committee on Production Guidelines for Book Longevity of the Council on Library Resources.

Library of Congress Cataloging-in-Publication Data

Ruddy, T. Michael.
  The cautious diplomat.
  Bibliography: p.
  Includes index.
  1. Bohlen, Charles E. (Charles Eustis), 1904–
Views on the Soviet Union.   2. United States—Foreign
relations—Soviet Union.   3. Soviet Union—Foreign
relations—United States.   4. Diplomats—United States—
Biography.   I. Title.
E748.B64R83   1986   327.2'092'4   86-4705
ISBN 0-87338-331-1

For Joshua, Sarah, and Noah

CONTENTS

PREFACE

History involves much more than the chronicling of events. It entails understanding the causes and effects of these events, as well as the rationale which motivated the men instrumental in guiding them. When applying this principle to a historical study of the decision-making process in the United States government, one cannot clearly grasp how government policy develops without delving beyond the top-level policy makers and examining the thinking of those in the second echelon who also contributed to policy formulation.

In this context, a study of the career of Charles E. Bohlen provides a distinctive perspective for examining the evolution of American foreign policy. He was an insider, having served in the State Department as a professional Foreign Service officer from 1929 to 1969. He was a recognized authority on the Soviet Union. He attained positions of influence during and after World War II and was an informed observer who attended most of the wartime and postwar conferences in his capacity as both an interpreter and advisor. As such, he was in a unique position to report on and evaluate the successes and failures of American diplomacy. Only recently, particularly since the release of major portions of the State Department files covering the postwar years, have historians begun to appreciate Bohlen's role and recognize his contribution.[1] When historians noted his place previously, either they perceived him as primarily an interpreter for Franklin Roosevelt and Harry Truman or they peremptorily portrayed him as a classic cold warrior who mechanically espoused the cold war line and promoted a policy of confrontation with the Soviet Union. Such cursory descriptions, however, overlook the nuances in Bohlen's perceptions. They ignore the opportunities—both seized and missed—which Bohlen had to influence the direction of American foreign policy. Bohlen was a complex individual with a deep understanding of the Soviet Union and its people, which served as the starting point for his insights and advice during his four decades in government service.

As historians have come to realize, the State Department was not a monolith, devoid of contrasting opinions and policy options, during and after World War II. Rather, the consensus on American policy which seemed to emerge was the end product of some significant internal controversies and divergent viewpoints. Bohlen was one component of this diversity. Certainly he was a man of his times. He was, broadly speaking, of the cold war mentality. He saw the Soviet Union as a threat inspired not only by national interests, but also by the Communist ideology which permeated every aspect of its national life. Yet his outlook was not always in agreement with that of everyone else in the Department of State.

This study is not an effort to expose the complex and often confusing debates which filled the State Department during these pivotal years when the United States was coming to grips with its responsibilities as a great power. Rather, it studies only one of the figures involved in this debate, a diplomat whose thinking at times converged with, at times diverged from, the predominant direction of the policy makers. This biography is to a certain extent an intellectual history, an effort to discover the continuity and evolution in Bohlen's thought and how this affected the advice he offered on American relations with the Soviet Union.

Overall, this biography, in tracing both Bohlen's own role and his observations about Soviet-American relations, refutes the contentions of many revisionist historians who try to blame the coming of the cold war on the United States. These revisionists have often suggested that policy makers attempted to shape a postwar world conducive to the expansion of American capitalism. Exemplary of this point of view is the work of Joyce and Gabriel Kolko. They argue that the postwar American government was self-conscious of its strength and confident of its ability to direct world reconstruction along lines compatible with its goals. They describe these goals as essentially "to restructure the world so that American business could trade, operate, and profit without restrictions everywhere. On this," they assert, "there was absolute unanimity among the American leaders, and it was around this core that they elaborated their policies and programs."[2]

An analysis of Bohlen's views and how his advice coincided with the advice of others in government rebuts both the economic emphasis these revisionists maintain dominated American policy and their assertion that there was a unanimity of purpose among American leaders. Bohlen did acknowledge the importance of economic concerns and the part they played in the thinking of decision makers. But in his own mind, other factors, such as the quest for national security and the need to combat communism, assumed a more pivotal role. To him, the economic strength of the United States was more a means to an end than an end in itself. When Bohlen's judgments were applied to American policy, they were not always consonant with the judgments of colleagues. Disagreements abounded among the policy-making establishment before, during, and after World War II.

Furthermore, a study of Bohlen's career reveals many of the misconceptions and mistaken policies pursued during these years. Blame for the cold war could not rest solely on the United States, however; Soviet intransigence, paranoia fed by Communist distrust of the western capitalist powers, and aggression in Eastern Europe bore equal responsibility for the growing tensions between East and West.

In refuting the revisionist position, this work does not reinforce the more traditional orthodox historical viewpoint that the Soviet Union presented an irreconcilable threat which the United States had to counter at all points, an ideological threat which presented a dire and unending challenge to the very existence of the capitalist, western systems of government.[3] Bohlen, like most in the postwar State Department, was suspicious of the Soviet Union and never believed that normal relations were attainable. Yet he did not exaggerate the Soviet challenge. He constantly counseled the pursuit of negotiations, not confrontations. He was often the voice of moderation, urging a more restrained assessment of the Soviet Union.

Bohlen was a realist, a man rooted in the immediate moment. He tried to understand Soviet motives and to develop from this understanding an appropriate response for the United States. Although he held prominent offices in the foreign policy bureaucracy, he was sought more as an advisor than as a policy maker per se. As one author pointed out in describing Bohlen's elevation in 1947 to one of his highest posts, department counselor, Bohlen's duties entailed advising and assisting the secretary of state "in the *consideration* and *solution* of major problems of foreign relations."[4] The actual policy making was left to others. His superiors heeded or rejected his insights at their own discretion.

But even the rejected advice deserves consideration. Robert L. Messer, in discussing an analysis presenting an alternative course to containment, which Bohlen wrote in collaboration with Geroid T. Robinson at the end of 1945, remarked that "looking back at these paths not taken both illuminates the chosen route and reveals what factors were, and to some extent still are, important in determining this country's direction in foreign affairs."[5] In examining Bohlen's career, it is evident that he was certainly in a position to influence American decisions. At times, his advice made a marked difference, but more often it either went unheeded or was incorporated with the insights of others into a particular policy. Whatever the fate of his contribution to the process, that contribution merits consideration as one indication of the nuances surrounding American intentions.

This study will probe the roots of Bohlen's image of the Soviet Union and the evolution and growing sophistication of his perceptions. It will chronicle this insider's impressions of the historical events unfolding before him. It will, furthermore, examine the advice Bohlen proffered. The study thus aims not only to clarify Bohlen's place in the foreign policy bureaucracy, but also, more importantly, to raise some questions about and shed new light on the evaluation of American foreign policy during Bohlen's forty-year career.

ACKNOWLEDGMENTS

In the years that I have been researching and writing this biography, numerous individuals—colleagues, students, and personnel at the libraries and archives I visited—have been of enormous assistance. While I cannot thank them all individually, I am grateful for the help that all provided. There are, however, a few whom I would like to particularly thank. Foremost is Lawrence S. Kaplan of Kent State University—respected scholar, inspiring teacher, and concerned counselor—who contributed his expertise and support at every stage of my work. Also, thanks to José Sanchez and Daniel Schlafly, my colleagues at St. Louis University, who read early versions of my manuscript and offered valuable insights. In the preparation of the manuscript, I owe a debt to Barbara Mangogna and Carol Sullivan, who helped in the typing, and to Jeanne West and Laura Nagy of Kent State University Press, who contributed so much to the final form and readability of this work.

Finally, I am deeply thankful for my family. Eileen, my wife, has been part of my work from the beginning—typing, transcribing notes, reading the manuscript, and listening to my endless rambling until she knew more than she really cared to know about Charles Bohlen. My three children, to whom this book is dedicated, provided the needed diversion from my work, forcing me to realize that there is much more to life than the "ivory tower" world of a college professor.

1.

THE EDUCATION OF A DIPLOMAT

"The Soviet Union is like the act of love. You can read and memorize every page of all the literature about it. But you can't possibly tell what it's really like, until you've experienced it yourself."[1] So spoke Charles Eustis ("Chip") Bohlen, a man who by the end of his long diplomatic career had gained that experience. Through nearly forty years in the State Department, Bohlen encountered firsthand the changes and continuity, the crises and cooperation in American relations with the Soviet Union and grew to understand Russia's enigmatic nature.

In many ways Bohlen himself was an enigma. Although a member of the Ivy League establishment which dominated the State Department and Foreign Service of his time, he nonetheless had what many described as a common touch, was noted for his ruffled appearance, and did not always play the conventional diplomat's role. He was not one of the "striped-pants" crowd.[2]

He was also an enigma in his approach to the Soviet Union. From one perspective, his actions bespoke a hard-liner, suspicious of the Kremlin and doubtful of any really close relationship with it. But his toughness was tempered by a deep-rooted pragmatism and a deep-seated belief in the efficacy of the diplomatic process, especially personal diplomacy, which he practiced with considerable deftness. Wary of the U.S.S.R., he never totally despaired of the possibility of reaching limited accommodation. He was a man who survived the bureaucratic shifts and infighting within the State Department, leading at least one historian to describe him as an opportunist.[3] But he did not survive by avoiding controversy or failing to stand up for what he believed, as his response to Sen. Joseph McCarthy's attacks, which brought Bohlen to public attention in 1953, demonstrated. Experience created these apparent contradictions in him, and experience fostered his complex assessment of the Soviet Union.

Bohlen hailed from the American gentry, the East-coast Ivy League establishment. His grandfather, a member of a well-established German family, had emigrated to Philadelphia at the end of the eighteenth century.[4] His father, Charles, was a banker and an avid and accomplished sportsman. Celestine Eustis, his mother, came from a well-situated New Orleans family. A cosmopolite, she had traveled extensively in Europe. Her father, James B. Eustis, had been Grover Cleveland's ambassador to France. Eustis, a widower, had relied on his daughter to serve as hostess of the Paris embassy; there she developed an abiding admiration for France.

The resort town of Aiken, South Carolina was the family home, but Bohlen, the second of three children, was born in Clayton, New York on 30 August 1904, while the family was visiting its summer residence. When he was twelve, his family moved to Ipswich, Massachusetts, where he grew up in the elite Boston society.

Bohlen's mother proved to be the greatest influence on his early life. Beginning with a trip to Switzerland in the winter of 1912–13, when Bohlen was only eight, she instilled in him a love for travel and a deep appreciation for European culture, particularly that of France. By the time Bohlen reached maturity, he had visited nearly every country in Western Europe.[5]

As befitted the son of gentry, Bohlen entered St. Paul's School in 1917, and while at St. Paul's, extracurricular activities outshone his academic prowess. He made his reputation as a guard on the school football team where his "ability to suit his style of play to his immediate opponent" seemed to foreshadow his diplomatic finesse in future years.[6] He followed in his father's footsteps, entering Harvard in 1923, where once again sports and social life occupied much of his time, the hallmark being his membership in the Hasty Pudding Institute of 1770 and the Porcellian Club, often described as the club of "Boston's best." His affable and friendly personality inspired fellow members to dub him "Chipper," a nickname which in shortened form remained with him.[7] Bohlen enjoyed himself in the usual collegiate activities, exerting relatively little effort on preparing for a future career.

Graduating in 1927 with a degree in European history, Bohlen signed on as an apprentice seaman on a tramp steamer for a six-month trip around the world, hoping this diversion would help him sort out his goals and settle on a career. But it did not. Only when by chance a cousin introduced him to William R. Castle, the assistant secretary of state for European affairs, did Bohlen begin to determine his calling. His cosmopolitan childhood obviously increased the attractiveness of a diplomatic career to him. And since the 1924 Rogers Act had created a career Foreign Service, here was an honorable profession for a gentleman which appealed to him more than banking or finance, the career choices of most of his classmates. After passing the entrance exam, he entered the Foreign Service in March 1929.[8]

The traditional diplomat of this period was the generalist rather than the area expert who ·vould be so prevalent later in the State Department, but Robert Kelley, the head of the Division of Eastern European Affairs, recognized the need for specialization as early as the mid-1920s. In anticipation of America's inevitable recognition of the Soviet Union, a country he perceived as a potential threat, he established a program to train diplomats in the Russian language and culture.[9] Beginning in 1927, he selected two Foreign Service officers yearly for an intensive program of study.[10]

Before Kelley's program was discontinued because of the economic constraints of the depression, it produced seven Foreign Service officers skilled in the Russian language and Soviet affairs. George Kennan, who would become the other leading State Department Soviet expert, was in the first group chosen, while Bohlen was in the third. The two men eventually became close friends, but they served together only in William Bullitt's first delegation to Moscow. Bohlen respected Kennan's views, describing his discourses as some of the finest political commentary he had ever seen, but he suggested that Kennan had trouble putting his feelings out of the way in decision making, something Bohlen would strive to point out to him on numerous occasions. Kennan, while acknowledging his differences with Bohlen, declared that his friend was always open to his ideas and quick to knock unsound ones out of his head.[11]

The careers of these two men would converge and diverge from the late twenties on. During the wartime era, Kennan would criticize what he considered the naïve policies pursued by the Roosevelt White House. Bohlen, admitted to the White House inner circle by the 1940s, would be less pessimistic. Their debates continued in the immediate postwar years as both served in the State Department and contributed to the formulation of American policy.

The early training of both these professionals influenced their careers in at least two ways. First, their mentor, Kelley, was an avid anticommunist, a bias reflected in his program's curriculum. With many of the courses taught by Russian émigrés and with outside reading carefully chosen, the training had a definite anti-Bolshevik thrust. While the participants received grounding in Russian culture and language, study of Soviet politics, economics, and government was not an integral component. Bohlen, entering the program with few preconceived notions and little particular interest in Russian history—the 1917 Russian Revolution, which had impressed many in the United States, had neither positively nor negatively inspired him—was susceptible to such anticommunist influence. Second, besides Kelley's pessimistic assessment that ideology limited the possibilities for a deep and meaningful relationship with the Soviet Union, Bohlen was also swayed by a more pragmatic aspect of the training. Kelley emphasized the necessity of objective and accurate diplomatic reporting, of verifying every fact as completely as possible, so that Bohlen would often be overly cautious in some of his early reporting.[12]

Before beginning his formal studies, Bohlen was required to serve a probationary period in Prague, Czechoslovakia, during 1929. His duties as junior vice-consul were more routine than demanding, the most critical situation he faced being a dressmaker who was defaming the American flag by using it as a decoration on his "top-grade brassieres."[13] Such mundane conflicts allowed Bohlen's superiors to evaluate his competence. The young diplomat struck them as brusque and self-centered, not always conscientious, with a tendency to be careless when it came to detail. But his "stability of purpose," they were quick to interject, balanced out these shortcomings. He eagerly associated with Russian students and strove to learn their language, demonstrating a facility for languages that suited him well for Kelley's program.[14]

On the basis of these recommendations, Bohlen moved on to Paris in November of 1929 to begin his work at the École Nationale des Langues Orientales Vivantes. For two and a half years he availed himself of the cultural and social feast that the Paris of the early thirties laid out before him (at least until Franklin Roosevelt devalued the dollar and forced him into a more frugal existence) and studied the Russian language, culture, and politics. During summer vacations he traveled to Estonia, where he immersed himself in the Russian language, living at places like the pension of the Serebryakovy sisters in the resort town of Narva-Jõesuu. There, in the style of the tsarist aristocracy, late dinners were followed by hours of discussion of poetry, philosophy, and politics around the samovar—"like characters in the stories of Chekhov."[15]

Soon after Bohlen had completed his studies in 1933, the Roosevelt administration extended recognition to the Soviet Union.[16] The president appointed William Bullitt as the first ambassador, Bullitt chose Bohlen as part of his staff, and the delegation embarked for the Soviet Union on 27 February 1934.

A friend of the Soviets since the October Revolution, Bullitt was filled with great expectations about the future of U.S.-Soviet relations. He dazzled Bohlen and the other young Foreign Service officers with recollections of his 1919 fact-finding mission to the Soviet Union—how he met with Lenin and returned to the Versailles Conference carrying Lenin's recommendation for a cease-fire in the Russian civil war. The Lenin proposal called for all armies to maintain control over the territory they held at the time; a peace conference then would be held among all the contending Russian leaders. Bullitt believed that this plan offered the hope of improving relations between the Bolsheviks and the western powers. But President Woodrow Wilson and the other leaders at Versailles distrusted the Bolsheviks and repudiated the plan, and Bullitt's efforts to bring peace to the Soviet Union failed.[17]

Haunted by this failure for more than a decade, Bullitt was now determined to succeed. In the agreement accompanying diplomatic recognition, the Soviets had acceded to three American demands: they renounced their support for and direction of revolutionary activities against the American government; they agreed to negotiate for the repayment of money loaned to the provisional government at the time of World War I; and they guaranteed Americans in the Soviet Union the right to worship freely. In return, the American government made loans available to the Soviet Union.

As Bullitt discovered, however, it was one thing to conclude an agreement, another to implement it. One problem stemmed from the loan agreement, which was not clearly stated. The United States perceived the loans as credits to be expended within the United States, hoping this would increase American trade with Russia. Soviet Foreign Minister Maxim Litvinov, in contrast, saw the loans as money the Russians could spend any way they wished. In addition, Soviet reluctance to permit Americans to worship freely in the Soviet Union compounded the difficulties in implementing the diplomatic agreement. Finally, the Seventh Congress of the Communist International, which convened in Russia during the summer of 1935, violated—from the American standpoint—the promise to avoid fomenting revolutionary activity against the United States. This congress, while supporting a popular front to combat fascism, reaffirmed Communist intentions to undermine capitalist democracies. When Litvinov responded to Bullitt's queries about this reaffirmation by shrugging the conference off, arguing that Stalin had not even been aware that the meeting was taking place, the American ambassador lost hope.[18] Bullitt's attitude, according to Bohlen, was transformed once and for all.

While Bullitt was undergoing this metamorphosis, Bohlen was learning about the Soviet Union firsthand as he immersed himself in his embassy duties. His major political responsibility was analyzing Soviet intentions by preparing a daily summary of news reports from the official news agency, Tass.[19] But his informal contacts with the Russian people often proved more of an education than the daily news analyses. Bullitt encouraged fraternization between the Russians and the embassy staff, promoting such activities as teaching the Cossacks to play polo and baseball, or hosting receptions and parties for members of the Bolshoi Ballet. Furthermore, Bohlen learned much on his own as he traversed the city in search of coat hangers and French spices, or as he traveled by train across the Caucasus to hunt wild gazelles near Baku.[20]

These experiences nurtured in him a sensitivity to the Russian people. He admired their simplicity and lack of affectation, seeing them as primitives "in the best sense of the word." Contrary to the political system which dominated them, Bohlen saw "individualists" who accepted "with passivity harsh dictatorial authority over their lives." The specter of the police state permeated their society, yet Bohlen saw that they "built a wall between themselves and the authorities," separating their personal lives from the people in command.[21] Implicit in Bohlen's diplomatic style, especially later in his career, was a tendency to appreciate the personage he was dealing with. He enjoyed the give and take, the unofficial banter, which was so much a part of diplomatic negotiations. He even began to think like a Russian, understanding not only what was said, but also the intention *behind* what was said.

The Russia Bohlen first encountered was a police state, but the purge trials, the epitome of Stalin's brutality, still lay in the future, and the magnitude of the police state was not yet readily apparent. Bohlen's assignment was cut short before he was personally exposed to this terror. While on leave in the United States in 1935, Bohlen received word that he was being transferred. Evidently, his apparent "carefree" approach to his assignment in Moscow bothered some of his superiors. But many colleagues as well as visitors to the embassy were impressed by his abilities and his grasp of the Russian scene, ensuring that 1935 would not be his last sojourn in the Soviet Union.[22]

Bohlen was surprised and a bit disappointed by his transfer. Life in the Soviet Union had been an adventure. But his disappointment was eased by a budding romance with Avis Thayer, a member of a socially prominent family from Villanova, Pennsylvania. Bohlen had first met Avis several years earlier while visiting her brother George, a school chum from Harvard. Bohlen paid little attention to the young girl at that time. In 1934, however, when she came to Moscow with her sister and a friend to visit another brother, Charles, a colleague and fun-loving crony of Bohlen's in the embassy, Avis caught Bohlen's attention. He was particularly impressed with her interest in world affairs and Russian culture, an interest he obviously shared. Their romance moved from Moscow, where at one point the embassy staff had to rescue Avis from the Soviet police, who had arrested her for taking illegal pictures of the Kremlin, to a courtship "carried on in taxis and bars in New York." The two were married on 29 August 1935 and set up housekeeping in Washington.[23]

Bohlen's new State Department assignment was in the office of the undersecretary of state and later in 1936 in the Division of Eastern European Affairs. Here he could still observe and keep abreast of Soviet developments. Since Roosevelt had become president, however, a rift had been developing between the State Department and the White House. Robert Kelley, the head of the Eastern European Division, disagreed with the evaluation of the Soviet Union advocated by many Roosevelt advisors, including the president's confidante, Harry Hopkins, and the newly appointed ambassador to the Soviet Union, Joseph Davies. In this time of the popular front opposing the growing fascist threat, Kelley's caution and outward hostility was inconsistent with White House ideas of a new era of relations with the Soviet Union. In a bureaucratic power play, the Division of Eastern European Affairs was eliminated and incorporated as a desk in the new Division of European Affairs.[24]

Bohlen, still a junior officer, could only watch this controversy unfold. It would not influence him directly until World War II, at which time he would become chief of a revived and once more important East European section. For the time being, he occupied himself with his duties, including his first taste of international negotiations. In the spring of 1937, he served as secretary to the American delegation at an International Sugar Conference in London; in November another mission took him to the Nine Power Conference in Brussels, called to discuss Japan's invasion of Manchuria. While preparing for the latter, he received welcome news of his reassignment to Moscow.

The Moscow he returned to in 1938 had changed dramatically from the city he had left in 1935. Soviet-American relations had shown progress by 1935, but by 1938 the first two purge trials had left their mark, a third was beginning, and the effects were felt in diplomatic circles. Personal contact between Russians and foreigners, which Bohlen had profited from and relished in the earlier period, was now risky business. Furthermore, events increasingly underlined for Bohlen the predominance of the system over any ideological considerations in the Stalinist regime.

One of Bohlen's first major responsibilities was to attend sessions of the third purge trials as translator for Davies, the new ambassador. A wealthy corporate lawyer and political supporter of Franklin Roosevelt, Davies had his own naïve view of the growing Stalinist oppression. Bohlen found him "sublimely ignorant of even the most elementary realities of the Soviet system and of its ideology." He "never even faintly understood the purges," gullibly accepting the official Soviet version. Nevertheless, Bohlen, a junior officer, dared not discuss his own impressions with the ambassador directly—impressions which, although somewhat muddled, were much more critical of the Soviet actions than Davies's were.[25]

Bohlen observed the sham trial manipulated to vindicate Stalin's cold-blooded restructuring of the government and the party bureaucracy. Twenty-one party members, most notably Nikolai Bukharin, appeared before the Soviet court. All had the right of counsel, but they seldom conferred with their lawyers; all listened to the state's charges, mechanically admitted their guilt, and pleaded for "proletarian mercy."

It took Bohlen years to fathom the full meaning of these events. He finally decided that Stalin was trying to deflect blame for the five-year plan's failure from himself by exploiting the traditional Soviet myth that the people were surrounded by terrible enemies working to destroy the country. By eliminating his party opposition, he could prevent a revolt against the policies he even then saw would be necessary if the Soviet system were to survive. Bohlen suspected that Stalin, aware of his society's internal weakness and external vulnerability, was not acting out of a blind commitment to the Communist cause. Rather, the dictator was being brutally realistic.

Stalin's machinations aside, the purges left a long-term legacy that troubled Bohlen. Many of the most competent Bolsheviks—those influenced by the "humane values of Western Christian civilization"—were purged from the party. Those remaining around Stalin hailed from a different Russian tradition with a different attitude toward humanity and society. They were more ruthless, less capable rulers.[26]

A new constitution promulgated in 1936 further contributed to entrenching Stalin's authority. When the Supreme Soviet convened in January 1938, Bohlen had the opportunity to observe what this document really meant in practice. It was no surprise to him that the sessions were, as he called them, a "farce." Stalin dominated the proceedings, and the representatives of the workers and peasants, who seemed of a "considerably higher stratum" than most of their class, along with the representatives of the various nationalities—who were hampered by the fact that no effort was made to translate the proceedings into their native tongues—docilely ratified all that was placed before them. Bohlen concluded that the whole purpose of the reforms aimed at eliminating duplication in the system and entrenching party control not exercised "in its own name but through its members placed in key positions in the government machinery."[27]

While far from a novel conclusion, this assessment, merged with other insights, led Bohlen to reconsider ideology's role in the Soviet program. At the same time he was observing this blatant political power play, however, other evidence indicated that it was too early to concede the demise of ideology. Communist doctrine still had its place, influencing the attitudes of the leadership, shading their perspective toward the capitalist West, and serving as a useful tool to expand their control.

For instance, Bohlen reported on a June 1938 speech in which M. I. Kalinin, a member of the Politburo, singled out the United States as an adversary to be watched since it was still stronger than the U.S.S.R. Bohlen noted that Kalinin played upon the Communist fear of capitalist encirclement as a rationale to support strengthening both Soviet defenses and world socialism.[28]

This declaration complemented an address by the same Politburo member a month earlier. Published by the Commissariat for Defense under the title "Be True to the Cause of Proletarian Internationalism," Kalinin asserted that "the international proletariat looks upon the final victory of socialism in the Soviet Union as the beginning of socialism in the entire world and that therefore the realization of the international tasks and obligations incumbent on the Soviet people is an integral part of the creed of every Communist and, in the Soviet Union, even of every honest citizen."[29] This to Bohlen was indeed consistent with Stalin's portrayal of the Soviet Union as the vanguard of international socialism.

The drive to entrench the Stalinist system under the pretext of ideology not only influenced domestic developments, but also international relations, an area of increasing importance for Bohlen as the political reporter for the embassy. After Davies was transferred to Brussels, leaving Chargé d'Affaires Alexander Kirk as ranking officer, Bohlen assumed primary responsibility for intelligence gathering. Forced to rely principally on the Soviet press, government pronouncements, and limited personal contacts, Bohlen had to keep his analyses tentative.[30] Even so, he could not help but be uneasy about Soviet activities.

During the summer of 1938, Hitler's interest in Czechoslovakia triggered Bohlen's increasing interest in the Kremlin's position vis-à-vis Germany's ambitions. At first he accepted, though uncomfortably, the prevailing opinion of the embassy staff that there was little chance of a reconciliation between Hitler and Stalin, given the fact that nazism was so opposed to communism.[31] But the matter lacked certainty. Stalin's record of political maneuvering had convinced Bohlen that the Soviet leader's personal interests and those of his country took precedence over ideological considerations. France, England, and the other countries opposing Nazi Germany were hostile capitalists, and thus all were ideological anathemas to Stalin. Thus Bohlen began to suspect that, if it suited Stalin's purposes to switch his allegiance, he would not let doctrinal differences stand in his way.

Soviet policy through the mid-1930s had been dominated by the concept of collective security. This approach had fostered improved relations with the capitalist democracies in an attempt to combat cooperatively the growing fascist threat. But Bohlen, with foresight, began to see signs of movement in another direction. In February 1938 he catalogued a series of earlier incidents which, when considered individually, were of minor significance, but as a whole posed an "impressive array of evidence," showing the recurrence of the "two hostile worlds" theory of the Soviets, which postulated the inevitable antipathy between the socialist and capitalist worlds, and which had been written into the preamble to the 1923 constitution. Movement away from collective security might possibly portend movement closer to Germany, he speculated.[32]

Among the incidents Bohlen cited to substantiate his suspicions was a speech Stalin made in 1937 to the Central Committee. In it, Stalin made no distinction between "friendly or democratic countries" and "fascist aggressors." This inspired an antiforeign campaign, the closing of many foreign consulates, and a purge of the Soviet foreign office and diplomatic service, "resulting in the replacement of many of the most-skilled Soviet diplomatists by persons who, as far as can be ascertained, have had little or no experience in international affairs."[33]

Compounding Bohlen's concern were remarks made by other officials and reprinted in the Soviet press, most notably an address by Maxim Litvinov at the one-hundredth session of the League of Nations. Litvinov denied any Soviet "moral guilt" for the League's weakness, since his country had had no role in its establishment, and he contended that of all the powers, the Soviet Union needed the least help in defending its borders, having joined the League only because of "devotion to the principles of peace." Litvinov concluded with the implied warning that "the Soviet Union will support the League of Nations as long as there is the faintest hope that it will act as an impediment to the aggressors." The implication, from Bohlen's viewpoint, was that whenever the Soviet Union decided that membership in the League was no longer useful, it would "feel free to withdraw."[34]

Adding further to Bohlen's uneasiness were certain remarks by Stalin stressing that the U.S.S.R. was subjected to a hostile world state system in which the Soviets could depend only on the international working class and the Soviet armed forces. Of particular interest to Bohlen, Stalin made no mention of collective security. Bohlen was certain this was no oversight.[35]

He realized that Soviet self-interest seen in the light of Communist ideology explained Soviet actions, and that this was an integral part of the Soviet reaction to the developing Czechoslovakian crisis. Despite a 1935 nonaggression pact between Czechoslovakia and the Soviet Union, Stalin, Bohlen believed, probably would not aid the Czechs in the event of a German attack, especially if France remained indifferent.[36] Czechoslovakia stood as the test of whether Stalin was moving away from collective security and toward a rapprochement with Germany. The French and British held the key to Soviet policy toward Germany. To Bohlen, the 1938 Munich pact, which capitulated to German demands and granted the Sudetenland to Hitler, aggravated Soviet paranoia about isolation from the rest of the world. The Kremlin was now inclined to watch the response of other countries cautiously before making a commitment.[37] Bohlen's unease grew as he began to detect Stalin, who had lost confidence in Western Europe, pragmatically repositioning himself.

In March 1939, for example, Stalin appeared before the Eighteenth Congress of the Soviet Communist Party to analyze political developments. He argued that the Soviet Union wanted peace. Refuting rumors of German intrigues in the Ukraine, he maintained that most of Hitler's attention was directed westward. While Bohlen noted Stalin's remark that the Soviet Union was not going to enter a war "to pull somebody else's chestnuts out of the fire," he avoided reading too much into the words, judiciously suggesting only that the dictator wanted to foster good relations with any country that did not threaten Soviet security, and that now included Germany.[38]

Maxim Litvinov's removal as foreign minister in May 1939 also disturbed Bohlen. Litvinov, an advocate of collective security, was replaced by Vyacheslav Molotov, whom Bohlen depicted as Stalin's toady. Yet Bohlen still hesitated to jump to conclusions. He could see that while the appointment might serve as a step toward establishing relations with Germany, it might also prove a diplomatic ploy to pressure England to move more rapidly toward an anti-Nazi coalition.[39]

By mid-May, however, Bohlen's uncertainties were erased. While relaxing at an American-owned dacha outside Moscow, Bohlen received some discomforting information. Hans Herwarth, a friend of Bohlen's on the staff of the German embassy and in private an opponent of Nazi policy, took Bohlen aside and informed him that the German ambassador, Werner von der Schulenberg, had made a brief visit to Berlin during his return from a trip to Iran. In Berlin Joachim von Ribbentrop, the German foreign minister, had notified Schulenberg that "no ideological barrier remained between Germany and Russia," and that overtures to ease hostility were in order.

Bohlen, cautiously protecting the identity of his source, reported this to the embassy, and the embassy in turn relayed the information to the State Department.[40] Bohlen's subsequent contacts with Herwarth detailed the unfolding German-Soviet rapprochement. Herwarth's early information confirmed that Germany was willing to negotiate outstanding issues between the two countries, including Poland's future and a new economic relationship with the U.S.S.R. But Molotov's first reaction was apparently noncommittal. When queried about resuming economic negotiations, for example, Molotov responded that matters first had to be put on a "political basis," an indication to Bohlen that Molotov was holding out for a definite proposal, which was not immediately forthcoming from Schulenberg.[41]

Discussions proceeded slowly until Schulenberg again journeyed to Berlin in late June. Upon his return, during a 28 June meeting, he told Molotov that Germany had no aggressive intentions and broached the possibility of a nonaggression pact, an idea which Molotov did not immediately reject. Meanwhile, despite supposedly being well-informed by the State Department, the British and French made these German initiatives even more attractive to the Russians by their diplomatic incompetence. Their low-level delegations, sent to Moscow by a slow boat, did not even arrive until 10 July.[42] By then, the Germans had made substantial progress in their negotiations with the Soviets. British and French foot-dragging also led the Soviets to question the sincerity of their intentions to reach an accord to protect Soviet interests.

Judging from Herwarth's information, Bohlen sensed that Germany by its actions could determine the course of the negotiations. Stalin realized the potential benefit of a treaty with Hitler, but he was still suspicious of Hitler's intent. During a meeting at the beginning of August, Molotov questioned German assertions that it had no aggressive intentions toward the Soviet Union, citing the Anti-Comintern Pact, Germany's encouragement of Japan in the Far East, and Hitler's refusal to attend any meetings with the Soviet Union as reasons for his distrust. Schulenberg, obviously coached by Berlin, retorted that Germany no longer considered communism a threat. The Anti-Comintern Pact, he explained, was aimed primarily against England. The Soviet Union would be a target only if it joined with England and France. Molotov responded that his country's primary concern was defense against aggression. Herwarth now warned Bohlen that the possibility of agreement existed, but the intense distrust between the two countries foreshadowed extended negotiations.[43]

That prediction proved overly optimistic. On 15 August, Herwarth approached Bohlen during a party at the German embassy with the disconcerting news that Germany and Russia had reached an agreement. Schulenberg had presented Molotov with a direct communication from Hitler declaring that Germany was prepared to negotiate any matters, including Eastern Europe, and that a high-level official would be sent to Moscow for that purpose. Molotov, now more certain of Germany's serious intent, agreed to negotiate.[44]

A week later, Ribbentrop arrived. And on 24 August, Herwarth apprised Bohlen that a late-night meeting with Stalin had produced results: a ten-year nonaggression pact; a secret protocol recognizing eastern Poland, Estonia, Latvia, Lithuania, and Bessarabia as Soviet spheres, and western Poland as the German sphere; German guarantees of compensation for any territorial changes between Germany and the Soviet Union; and finally the mutual guarantee that neither party would join groups directed against the other, thus negating the German-Japanese alliance as well as the Anglo-French negotiations with the Soviet Union.[45]

"The fate of the Soviet system," remarked Bohlen later, "was more important than the fate of Russia itself."[46] Stalin was intent upon deflecting any threat to the Soviet Union. British-French complacency had driven him into the German camp. In reaching an accord with the Nazis, Bohlen believed that Stalin was cold-bloodedly and realistically trying to avoid drawing his country into war.

The revelations produced by Bohlen's contact were initially greeted with skepticism in Washington. But upon conclusion of the pact, Washington commended the Moscow embassy for its role, even though information relayed about the pact did little for the American government other than to lessen the shock of the official announcement. The British and French governments, which Washington had also kept informed, could have influenced events, but they did not. While the reasons for this inaction remain something of a mystery, Bohlen later was told by Anthony Eden, that time British Foreign Secretary, that a Communist in the code room had held up information on the pact until it was too late.[47]

Seven months after the accord was consummated and World War II had begun, Bohlen was further convinced of Stalin's intentions and motives. He saw even more clearly a devious Stalin, shrewdly playing realpolitik to serve his and his nation's interests. Ideology remained, but was twisted. The capitalist nations were still hostile, but Stalin had chosen to collaborate with the one which provided the most advantages in a marriage of convenience, not an alliance of mutual trust. Stalin fostered this precarious relationship, but Germany was the key to its survival.

Fear of involvement in a major war and the inevitability of an attack by the western capitalist powers, Bohlen pointed out, had been prime influences on the Soviet decision to enter the agreement in the first place. It was further reinforced by the realization that, despite advances in recent years, the Soviet Union could not stand the economic, military, or political strain such a conflict would require without severe risk to the Stalinist regime. The agreements were working, not because they were made by allies seeking common ends, but because of the mutual self-interest that dictated their continuation.

Additionally, Germany was a geographic barrier to Western Europe. The "aggressive and dynamic" National Socialists potentially posed the greatest military threat as well as the greatest protection. Hostility between Germany and the Soviet Union, Bohlen argued, had been fanned primarily by Hitler. Only this hostility had forced Stalin to move closer to Western Europe and collective security. Collaboration neutralized the German threat and seemed a realistic alternative once Stalin concluded that France and England could not be depended upon. Bohlen's observation of Stalin's machinations and his realization of the advantages Germany offered prompted him to doubt whether Stalin had even taken seriously the possibility of an agreement with France and England.

The association with Germany provided further immediate advantages. Germany acceded to Soviet expansion in Eastern Europe. Economically, Germany provided a "natural" and "more profitable" trading partner than the countries to Germany's west.

For Stalin's part, Bohlen predicted that the situation would remain static. Stalin did not want to expand the relationship with Germany, for this would risk involvement in war with France and England. In addition, a quick German victory would free Hitler to move against the U.S.S.R. In Bohlen's estimation, the "cautious" and "opportunistic" Stalin had no ulterior motives or long-range plans; he simply wanted to avoid war while securing as many advantages as possible. The Soviet Union would not shift until it was "physically impossible" or "nationally suicidal" for Germany to invade Russia. Hence Germany would determine the future of the relationship. Since at the time Germany also gained from this state of affairs—the elimination of an eastern front, the acquisition of needed raw materials, and the establishment of diplomatic collaboration in Eastern Europe and the Balkans—Bohlen anticipated that the status quo would continue.[48]

In the midst of these developments, Bohlen was notified in late 1940 of his transfer to Tokyo, where Ambassador Joseph Grew had requested a Soviet expert to keep him abreast of developing Japanese-Soviet relations. Since Bohlen had sent his now pregnant wife back to the United States to receive proper medical care, he had to make the gloomy trek across Siberia alone. Despite an uncomfortable mid-winter trip to Vladivostok, with "nothing to see except snow which is very similar wherever it is," Bohlen plunged into his new assignment eagerly, particularly since American relations with Japan were "going from bad to worse and a complete break [was] freely predicted for this spring [1941]."[49]

The change of scene did little to alter his outlook on the Soviets. Watching Soviet moves from his new post, he wrote as late as 16 June 1941 that Stalin's desire to avoid war insured that the German-Soviet relationship would survive. The Soviet leader would go to great lengths to appease Germany. Bohlen predicted that Stalin's concessions might include acquiescing to German attempts to dictate Soviet economic or political development. He would probably agree to increase grain and oil shipments in order to ease the strain the British blockade had imposed on Germany, or he might even condone German moves in the Far East. Bohlen, however, felt that Stalin would balk at a more active Soviet role and would continue to resist any pressure to join the tripartite pact, since this would entail abandoning Soviet neutrality.

But unfortunately, as Bohlen had noted earlier, the future of the relationship did not hinge on Stalin. In the 16 June letter Bohlen concluded that the possibility of a Soviet-German conflict depended "almost entirely upon decisions reached in Berlin." Still, he saw only one basis upon which a German attack would be predicated, "that Hitler has abandoned any hope of victory over England this year [1941], which, in essence means for the future also, and is therefore faced with the prospect of a long war necessitating the organization of the entire continent of Europe, including the granaries of the Ukraine, and the oil fields of the Caucasus to resist successfully an Anglo-American blockade."

Bohlen confidently predicted that facts mitigated against Nazi military action against Russia. Such an attack would mean postponing a

German invasion of England and curtailing air strikes, which would give England a chance to rebuild, swinging the battle of the Atlantic in Britain's favor. More significantly, sources Bohlen regarded as quite reliable estimated that it would take two years from the time of a successful campaign against Russia for the Germans to rebuild a supply line that could carry as much material as Germany was already receiving by its agreement with the Soviets. Bohlen, therefore, argued that not only would Stalin work to appease Hitler, but, barring Hitler's abandonment of hope for victory in the West, Germany would also continue to keep its demands within acceptable limits.[50]

Bohlen was so convinced of the stability of the pact that he was genuinely surprised when word arrived that Germany had invaded the Soviet Union on 22 June. Bohlen was sure that Hitler had made a fatal mistake. "Hitler lost the war," one colleague recalled Bohlen declaring when their lunch was interrupted by word of Germany's attack.[51] Hitler had made the same mistake other leaders had made in the past; he thought he could subdue Russia.

Events now unfolded rapidly. When Japan attacked Pearl Harbor on 7 December, the United States plunged into the conflict, and Bohlen found himself interned in Tokyo for six months along with the rest of the embassy staff. Whiling away their time playing golf, studying foreign languages, and other diversions, the diplomats waited to be exchanged for American-held Japanese, while beyond the confines of the embassy compound the war intensified.

These early years in the Foreign Service laid the foundation for Bohlen's insight into the Soviet psyche. Ideology, he had seen, was important to policy decisions. But like other young diplomats stationed in Moscow, Bohlen was striving to fathom the true role of Communist doctrine in the actions of Soviet leaders. The purge trials, Stalin's intrigues, and the Russo-German pact, among other factors, at first confused Bohlen, then tilted him away from the obsession with the role of ideology as fostered in Kelley's training program, and more toward a belief that the "system" was at the root of Soviet actions—both in the sense that Stalin's dictatorial structure had to be preserved and that the security of the U.S.S.R. took precedence over idealistic Communist goals. Ideology still formed the backdrop for diplomatic activity, but ideology was manipulated to conform to the needs of the leadership.[52] This was the foundation of Bohlen's outlook once he returned to the State Department to deal with the complexities of working with the Soviet ally during World War II.

2.

INTO THE INNER CIRCLE

Exchanged for Japanese diplomats and civilians, Bohlen and the other Americans departed from Japan on 17 June 1942 and arrived in the United States on 25 August. The return voyage aboard the Japanese ship, *Asama Maru*, and then the American vessel, the *Gripsholm,* was at times tense, at times humorous. Delegated to assign cabin space, Bohlen occasionally erred, once moving a Catholic nun into quarters with an American sailor. But buoyed by a thriving black market in scotch and American cigarettes, he survived the ordeal.[1]

After a brief leave to recuperate from his detainment in Tokyo and to spend some time with Avis and their infant daughter, also named Avis, he returned to the Eastern European desk in the State Department, succeeding to the position of assistant chief of the European Affairs Division.[2] The rift between the White House and State Department was still as prominent as it had been in the mid-1930s when Bohlen had last served in Washington. President Roosevelt was now directing all of his energy toward prosecuting the war, which required close collaboration with the Soviet Union. In contrast, the longer-range view of many State Department personnel was more pessimistic about Soviet-American relations than the president's; their outlook was interpreted as "foot-dragging" by the White House.[3]

Bohlen conceded the need to address the exigencies of war, yet he, too, worried about the ultimate fate of Soviet-American relations. He even doubted Soviet trustworthiness for the duration of the European war. In June of 1943, responding to the question of Soviet reliability, he voiced the perspective of the State Department, a perspective with which he concurred. "The Department," he noted, "has no evidence of any kind to lead to the conclusion that the Soviet Union will not remain an active member of the United Nations until the military defeat of Germany. However, it is too strong to state that the State Department is 'convinced' of this fact if only for the reason that a dictatorship responsive in the last analysis to the views of one man is of necessity unpredictable." While there was no immediate indication that the U.S.S.R. would conclude a separate peace, the possibility could not be ignored.[4] For Bohlen, Stalin's past actions were ample proof that he would ruthlessly pursue those options that were in the Soviet Union's best interest. He had done so in the 1939 pact with Germany, and he might do so again.

Stalin's actions during the war, from Bohlen's viewpoint, did little to allay suspicions. In February 1943, Stalin issued an order of the day on the occasion of the twenty-fifth anniversary of the Red Army in which he intentionally ignored the congratulations of the allies and expounded the Soviet war aims as the liberation of "Soviet soil and peoples (in which he includes Latvians, Lithuanians, and Estonians) from the German invasion." Irked by the absence of a second front, Stalin failed to credit the allies with aiding in the effort against Germany and maintained that the Soviet army alone was bearing the brunt of the war. Bohlen wondered if this might spark a new campaign "with all its attendant bitterness" against the United States and Great Britain. To Stalin, the war was a Russo-German affair, which by implication divested him of any obligation to the allies for assistance rendered.[5]

Throughout 1943, Bohlen realized that Soviet and American attitudes conflicted in many areas of mutual concern. Even lend-lease aid, which had been extended to the Soviet Union in November of 1941, was a constant bone of contention. The United States was determined to aid the Russians, but at the same time American industry had to supply other allies as well. Bohlen was caught in this dilemma as a participant in the negotiations for the Third Protocol, the agreement for lend-lease aid during the third year of the program. Russian demands so far exceeded American ability to deliver that this a protocol could not be concluded by the time it was to go into effect. Nevertheless, Bohlen agreed with most in the department that the lack of a protocol should not hinder shipments of essential aid to the beleaguered Soviets.[6]

Lend-lease aid was imperative to the war effort and consistent with American self-interest. Bohlen was eager to aid the Soviet Union; he wanted the Soviets to make specific what they expected from the United States, however. And he hoped that for its part the United States could convince them that it had no intention of constructing a *cordon sanitaire* around the Soviet Union. He also thought the United States had to recognize that there were limits to what it could expect or demand from the Soviets. Like it or not, there was little chance that the Baltic states would exist in the postwar world except as part of the Soviet Union.

Asked to comment on an analysis written by Samuel Cross, a Harvard professor and Roosevelt's interpreter during Molotov's 1942 visit, Bohlen had the opportunity to interject his own opinion that the United States had to come to grips with these realities and let the Soviets know that it was tired of "diplomatic shadow-boxing." He agreed with Cross's assertion that the United States should "help them to victory by any means within [its] power and play ball with them in the establishment of as lasting a peace as possible." He concurred with the Harvard academic's advice that America inform its ally that it regarded "the present policy of even apparent mystification as something less than the present world-crisis demands, and should reserve absolute freedom of action after victory if it were to continue." Cooperation was possible, but only if the United States struck the proper balance between firmness toward the Soviet Union and willingness to recognize its legitimate concerns. The question was whether the United States was capable of adapting to Stalin's realpolitik. Bohlen believed that the "basic underlying difficulty" in American relations with the Soviet Union was whether the United States was "prepared to abandon certain traditional American principles in regard to territorial adjustments on a power politics basis in the hope of obtaining real cooperation from the Soviet Government in the postwar world."[7] The tension between satisfying Soviet security concerns and American principles would be crucial to the postwar diplomatic settlements.

But for the time being, the exigencies of war took precedence over these differences. While opening the second front so desperately requested by Stalin was delayed, the military situation improved for the allies during 1943. Success in North Africa, Sicily, and Italy coincided with Russian counterattacks which prepared the way for an advance into Poland. Reinforced by these military victories, the foreign ministers of Great Britain and the Soviet Union, Anthony Eden and V. M. Molotov, respectively, and Secretary of State Cordell Hull met in Moscow from 19 to 30 October to prepare the way for a December summit meeting at Teheran. Bohlen accompanied Hull as his interpreter and advisor on Soviet affairs.

Bohlen was still a relative unknown both within government circles and publicly. *Time* magazine, reporting on Hull's delegation, referred to Bohlen as "Charles L. ('Chick') Bohlen." Unbeknownst to Bohlen, however, the post was a test for greater responsibilities—translating for the president. Cross, who had served as Roosevelt's translator in the past, had indiscretely entertained friends at cocktail parties with the details of the president's 1942 meeting with Molotov. Roosevelt, therefore, demanded that Harry Hopkins and Undersecretary of State Edward R. Stettinius find a more reliable interpreter. Stettinius narrowed his search to Bohlen and G. Frederick Reinhardt, also a Russian expert.[8]

The political climate in Moscow during this period exuded friendliness. The Russians agreed to the establishment of a European Advisory Commission to arrange surrender terms for Germany and in principle supported the establishment of a United Nations after the war. Stalin further assured Hull of Russian assistance in the Pacific conflict once the war had ended in Europe.

While interpreting for Hull, Bohlen first met W. Averell Harriman, the American ambassador to the Soviet Union. Harriman had been pressing the State Department for months to assign him someone well-versed in Soviet affairs. Since Robert Kelley's training program had been short-lived, Soviet experts were scarce items. Harriman now became more specific, requesting the services of Bohlen. But because Bohlen's seniority in the Foreign Service precluded his appointment as embassy counselor, the post Harriman wanted to fill, and because the State Department required Bohlen's services in Washington, he was only temporarily assigned to Moscow for two months following the conclusion of the conference. To assuage Harriman, arrangements were made for George Kennan, who was then assigned to the European Advisory Commission, to replace Bohlen.[9]

This solution was amenable to all sides, so Bohlen remained with Harriman, helping him with arrangements for the upcoming Teheran conference as well as a scheduled meeting in Cairo where Roosevelt and Churchill were to discuss the status of the Pacific war with Chiang Kai-shek. Bohlen also helped facilitate lend-lease shipments, which were still a bone of contention between the U.S. and the U.S.S.R.[10]

In late November, Bohlen accompanied Harriman and several other Americans and Britons on the flight to Cairo aboard the ambassador's plane, a converted B-25 bomber. As the plane approached Stalingrad, it developed engine trouble, forcing Harriman's group to spend the night as unexpected, but welcome, guests of the local Communist party leadership. Just like the early days immediately after Roosevelt had recognized the Soviet Union, Bohlen and the others fraternized with their Russian hosts as vodka flowed freely at a sumptuous banquet. Caught up in the revelry, Bohlen topped off the evening by offering a spirited rendition of "Stenka Razin," a traditional Russian folk song, to the delight of his hosts.[11]

The next morning, barely recovered from the previous evening, the diplomats proceeded on to the Cairo meeting (22–26 November 1943). Bohlen at this point did little but tour the city while the leaders met. But when the meeting shifted to Teheran (28 November–1 December 1943), where Stalin joined Roosevelt and Churchill, Bohlen was at the center of activity, interpreting for the president and keeping the conference minutes. He was initially nervous and stumbling as he tried to grasp the nuances of the language and convey the proper meaning in the translation, but he quickly adjusted to the demands made of him.[12]

This conference may have stood as the "highwater mark" of allied cooperation from Bohlen's perspective, but the exchanges anticipating postwar arrangements made him uncomfortable. Stalin's soft-spoken and considerate facade made Bohlen even more suspicious. When he tried to summarize his apprehensions, he found an eager listener in Ambassador Harriman, who shared his concerns. Bohlen wrote that the Soviet Union was intent upon securing its own interests, which included becoming "the only important military and political force on the continent of Europe." If the Soviets had their way, "the rest of Europe would be reduced to military and political impotence."

Bohlen doubted that Soviet and American postwar goals coincided. Although Stalin had agreed to an international organization, he downplayed the potential effectiveness of such a body, feeling that bases and strategic points should be kept in the hands of the Big Three. On the issue of how to deal with Germany after the war, Bohlen even at this time suspected that Stalin wanted a permanent rather than temporary division; Stalin apparently felt there was no adequate guarantee against Germany's rising again.

Soviet designs in Eastern Europe, particularly in Poland, especially worried Bohlen. Not only were Soviet territorial demands—the Curzon line in the East with Poland being compensated in the West at the expense of Germany—a problem, but Stalin was determined to prevent another *cordon sanitaire*. The Kremlin's view that the Polish exile government in London was illegitimate and composed of Nazis implied further difficulties.[13]

Bohlen, like many of his colleagues in the State Department, was not as enamored with the possibility of postwar Soviet-American cooperation as the Roosevelt White House appeared to be.[14] Bohlen's skepticism would persist through the war, but an association with Harry Hopkins beginning at Teheran exposed him to the rationale and insights of those around Roosevelt, ultimately modifying some of his perceptions. Hopkins had first met Bohlen at a dinner party in 1942. On that occasion, Hopkins had been curt with Bohlen's wife and then proceeded to discuss Soviet relations with Bohlen by asking if he was one of the "anti-Soviet clique" in the State Department.[15] Hopkins personally had little regard for members of the Foreign Service, whom he described as "cookie-pushers, pansies—and usually isolationists to boot."[16]

However, at Cairo and Teheran Hopkins changed his mind about Bohlen. Impressed with Bohlen's defense of the Foreign Service, Hopkins listened attentively as Bohlen explained the handicaps under which diplomats were forced to function. The resulting close friendship directly affected Bohlen's career.[17] His status was then in a state of flux with his temporary assignment to Moscow nearing an end. Harriman wanted him to remain, since the original plans for Kennan to be transferred to Moscow had temporarily gone awry; Ambassador John G. Winant was adamant that Kennan was needed on the European Advisory Commission. Furthermore, Kennan's services were denied everyone for several months when he was incapacitated by an ulcer. But Hopkins was determined to get Bohlen, and with Hopkins's support the department prevailed. Bohlen was reassigned to Washington in January 1944 as chief of the Division of Eastern European Affairs.[18]

Harry Hopkins wanted more than Bohlen's return to the State Department. He envisioned Bohlen as an assistant to the secretary of state in charge of White House liaison. Secretary of State Cordell Hull, who should have performed this function, was not close to Roosevelt. From early 1944, therefore, Bohlen served unofficially as liaison, and the post was formally created in December after Hull, who had jealously protected his intermittent contacts with the White House, resigned and was replaced by Stettinius.[19]

Why Hopkins proposed these liaison duties is a point of conjecture. One author has speculated that Bohlen could be used "to monitor and prod" the State Department machinery. When Undersecretary of State Sumner Welles resigned in August of 1943, Roosevelt's link to the department had been severed. Now it could be reestablished.[20]

Bohlen's explanation, however, seems more plausible. He observed that by 1944 the war was moving rapidly to a close, meaning that political issues affecting the postwar world would become increasingly important. The department had been isolated from the wartime diplomacy, the map room in the White House having served as Roosevelt's personal "state department," where decisions were made and communications with foreign countries transmitted—many of which never made their way to the State Department. Hopkins, in appointing Bohlen, hoped to tap the expertise in the department so that intelligent decisions could be made regarding postwar political arrangements.

Although Bohlen continued to be intimately involved in Soviet affairs, he now regularly met at the White House with Admiral Leahy, Roosevelt's chief of staff, and Hopkins, and at times with Roosevelt himself. He kept both the White House and State Department apprised of what the other was thinking.[21] Dividing his time between offices in the State Department and the Executive Office Building, Bohlen no longer was an unknown. He had come a long way from 1943 when reporters misnamed him "Chick." He and his wife were often included on the White House guest list for social functions.

Bohlen eagerly embraced his new responsibilities, working long hours and weekends engrossed in deciphering the Soviet Union. Saturdays often found him presiding over informal meetings at a Washington seafood restaurant where State Department personnel exchanged ideas and information with those in other agencies who were involved in Soviet-American relations.[22] Wearing two hats, one as White House liaison and the other as head of the Eastern European Division, not only put Bohlen in a position to influence policy, but also led him to appreciate the White House perspective. The result was more an evolution and sophistication, rather than a rejection, of his past interpretation of policies and events.

The rebuff of German forces, the advances of the Soviet armies, and the D-Day invasion of 6 June 1944 occasioned increasing conflicts between the two powers over postwar political arrangements. Bohlen blamed the growing rift on "the nature, structure, and methods of the Soviet state." Begun as a revolutionary dictatorship, this regime was premised on irreconcilable hostility with the capitalist nations, a legacy of Communist ideology which, while modified, had not been destroyed. For revolutionary purposes, the Kremlin had organized Communist parties throughout the world.

But ideology in itself only partially explained Soviet designs. As the state developed, national interests began to prevail over revolutionary aims. Stalin's dictatorship in a disguised fashion used the parties, originally instruments of revolution, to further Soviet national aims, complicating relations between the Soviet Union and other nations.

Bohlen was now concerned about America's response to this increasingly apparent state. He realized that the United States had always tried to promote "friendly, cooperative relations." Even after the Nazi-Soviet Pact, Washington refused to recognize the seizure of the Baltic states and other areas, but continued to facilitate Soviet commerce with the United States. Granting that America's vital interests dictated cooperation with the Soviet Union in order to defeat Hitler, Bohlen still questioned whether America had been firm enough in negotiations with its allies, especially now that the war was ending. Although he recognized real advances in Soviet-American relations during the war, he foresaw problems in integrating the U.S.S.R. into the family of nations. The United States would certainly have to play a leading role in that integration by using a "skillful combination of friendliness and firmness."[23] So often in the past, Bohlen had pointed to Stalin's caution and pragmatism. The U.S. government had to stand up to this pragmatic dictator, forcing him to be more malleable and compromising; otherwise he would take advantage of the political situation created by wartime. Bohlen's restrained pessimism was his contribution to White House policy making.

Bohlen's cynicism reflected much of what he had observed through 1944. In March, he had listed the "current problems" hampering relations between the U.S. and the U.S.S.R.: Soviet domination over the Baltic states; the growing conflict over Poland's eastern boundary and recognition of the Polish government-in-exile; and the Soviet unilateral exchange of representatives with the Italian government of Marshal Badoglio. Although he saw no other "major crises" at the time, and although he still believed that satisfactory solutions were possible, he conceded that other issues would undoubtedly arise as the war drew to a close. The United States, he warned, had to uphold its principles while convincing the Soviet Union of the value of accommodation. "The chief aim of this Government," he believed, "should be to continue to endeavor to bring the Soviet Government to the realization in its own interest and for the peace and stability of the world of the advantages of cooperative rather than unilateral action in the discussion and resolution of political problems arising out of the prosecution of the war."[24]

In light of the growing rift between East and West, Bohlen refused to take Soviet concessions at face value and cynically attributed Soviet moves to ulterior motives intended to create postwar advantages. When the Kremlin in early 1944 announced that each of its sixteen republics would henceforth be allowed to maintain diplomatic relations and have its own army, Bohlen discounted this apparent evidence of Soviet internal liberalization, asserting that the move did not portend greater decentralization of control from Moscow. It did not alter the constitution. Control was exercised through the Communist party, not through the government apparatus. The supposed liberalization was simply a useful tool which fit neatly into Soviet plans. Internally, the change might alleviate growing discontent among national minorities who were becoming alarmed at the Great Russian chauvinistic nationalism which, during the war, had promoted Russian nationalism at the expense of the nationalism of the minorities. Externally, annexation of the Baltic states would be more palatable to the world since they would at least on paper be semi-independent. Reincorporation of areas of eastern Poland, White Russia, and the Ukraine into the Soviet Union would be facilitated because they would be united with Ukrainian and White Russian areas rather than outwardly coming under the control of Moscow. But as befitted his cautious demeanor, Bohlen rejected the conclusion that the Soviets were planning to seize other territories. The affected areas were well-Sovietized, and to expand elsewhere would spawn charges of imperialism.[25]

In July, the formation of a Council for the Affairs of Religious Cults also evoked Bohlen's suspicion. Attached to the Council of Peoples' Commissars, it was designed as a liaison between the Soviet government and the leaders of several religious groups, excluding the Orthodox Church, which Bohlen described as enjoying a privileged position as virtually the state religion. This new council was to consult on questions related to these religions and requiring government action. Bohlen granted that the creation of the council gave these religions a degree of recognition and coincided with a more tolerant governmental attitude evident since the outbreak of the war. But he argued that it also forced them to conform more to Soviet policy. In the long run, he could envision the council as a vehicle for handling questions involving the Catholic population in eastern Poland, soon to be incorporated into the Soviet Union.[26]

Clearly, as Bohlen saw it, the Soviets were preparing for the war's end. The growing indications that they were not committed to postwar cooperation, combined with rapidly developing events on the battlefront that portended imminent victory, made it imperative that the United States step up planning for the postwar world. Responsibility for such preparation fell to several State Department committees.[27] The fate of Poland stood out as the major obstacle to postwar peace and the issue most responsible for the rift which became so characteristic of the cold war. The Polish issue prompted two contradictory answers to the question of how the United States should proceed. The hopeful supported a United Nations organization, whereas the more pessimistic contended that to approach the postwar situation realistically one should concede Poland and Eastern Europe as a part of the Soviet sphere, reserving Western Europe as America's domain.

Russian military advances into Poland in January 1944 confronted the American government with some pivotal decisions. Not only did Soviet demands for Polish territory as far as the Curzon line raise the question of compensation for Poland at Germany's expense, but Stalin's recognition in early 1945 of a pro-Soviet government based in Lublin rather than the government-in-exile in London also pointed to future problems over the structure of a postwar Polish government.

In the spring of 1944, Bohlen had not completely discounted the possibility that Stalin might be willing to compromise. Nothing was certain, but in a May memorandum to Stettinius, he suggested that, as was the case throughout the war, Stalin's government still refused to deal with the government-in-exile. Yet Bohlen's involvement with those around Roosevelt may have led him to see Soviet actions as portending possible positive developments in the future. The Soviet commander in Vohynia, for example, had reached an operational agreement with the Polish underground. Military expediency dictated this move, but at least it was something. Polish divisions in the Red Army, despite indoctrination, still were not rejecting the Polish exile government. An American priest had returned from a trip to Moscow with the news that Moscow was prepared to return the cities of Vilna and Lwow to Poland and to deal with a reorganized Polish government in London. All of this information was unconfirmed or circumstantial, but, as Bohlen wrote to Stettinius on 16 May, Stalin, "with his great sense of realism," might have revised his estimations about the feelings of the Polish people:

> Previously the Soviet thesis was that the great majority of Poles, both at home and abroad, supported the Soviet thesis in regard to Poland and were violently opposed to the "reactionary" Government-in-exile. It is quite likely that with the entry of the Red Army into Poland and an examination of the feelings of the Polish soldiers in the Red Army Stalin has come to realize that there is not such a great degree of difference between the views of the moderate members of the Polish Government-in-exile and the Polish people as a whole, and that any attempt to force down the throats of the Poles a government of Soviet selection or too arbitrary a solution of the border problem would result in a unified and hostile Poland on the frontiers of the Soviet Union.

Bearing these possibilities in mind, Bohlen urged that the United States government be prepared "to consider most carefully our attitude towards any new developments in the Soviet-Polish dispute."[28]

Bohlen's attitude as expressed in this memorandum coincided with Roosevelt's. At the same time that the president wanted to offer hope to the exiled Polish government, he did not want to abandon the possibility of Soviet collaboration on this and other matters. In early June, the president invited the representative of the Polish government-in-exile, Prime Minister Stanislas Mikolajczyk, to Washington. The meeting itself produced very little. Mikolajczyk expressed his determination to press for an independent Poland and sought a postponement of political and territorial settlements, despite Roosevelt's efforts to persuade him to rearrange his government into a form more amenable to the Soviet Union. The only result of consequence was America's tender of its good offices to arrange a meeting between the Soviets and the exiled Polish leaders in Moscow.[29]

Bohlen endeavored behind the scenes to insure that the proper interpretation emerged from these discussions. He tried even before they began to defuse any Polish involvement in domestic politics. Public sympathy in America, which ran high for the cause of the Poles, could prove disastrous for Soviet-American relations.[30] Furthermore, he attempted to guarantee that Stalin would not be misled by the way Mikolajczyk's group interpreted the talks. Having examined the Polish records of the conversations, Bohlen and Elbridge Durbrow, another member of the Eastern European Division, met with Mikolajczyk and Stettinius on 13 June. Conceding that the record was accurate, they nonetheless proposed one alteration. Rather than stating that the Poles had the president's moral support in their effort to reach a settlement with the Soviet Union, Bohlen and Durbrow suggested that the record might read that the "president's moral support would be given towards their efforts to reach a solution mutually satisfactory to Poland and the Soviet Union." This shrewd diplomatic turn of phrase would more accurately convey the president's stance, avoiding the implication that the United States was taking a positive stand against the Soviet Union. The time and the exact form of this moral support would be left up to Roosevelt and would not be rigidly defined.[31]

One way of imposing that support to encourage an eventual solution was Roosevelt's idea of arranging a meeting between Mikolajczyk and Stalin. At first leery of this plan, Bohlen now thought the president could use his talks with Mikolajczyk to pave the way for some beneficial discussions with Stalin. The president, Bohlen thought, could send Stalin a message with his impressions of the meeting, in the process allaying "any suspicions that the Soviets might have had that some sort of deal was being cooked up."[32] His personal sympathy for the exile government's plight was clearly tempered by his realistic perceptions of America's best interests.

Encouraged by both Bohlen and Stettinius, Roosevelt wrote to Stalin on 19 June, assuring Stalin that he had no intention of interfering in the dispute and that his talk with Mikolajczyk had been a frank discussion with no specific plans or proposals being considered. Roosevelt then asked Stalin to receive this "sincere" and "reasonable" man in

Moscow. Stalin agreed to see Mikolajczyk, but showed no signs of yielding on the composition of a future Polish government and recognition of the Curzon line.[33]

Stalin's unbending posture foreshadowed the tenor of the meetings. While Mikolajczyk was heading to Moscow in July, the Kremlin established the Polish Committee of National Liberation in Lublin. Stalin then pressed the Polish leader to accept the Soviet territorial arrangements, suggesting only that some of the London Poles might possibly be incorporated into the Lublin government. Stalin even tried to arrange a meeting between the two Polish groups, all the time clearly placing his support firmly behind the pro-Soviet regime.[34]

Stalin's stance underlined the need for the United States to adopt a clear and coherent policy toward Eastern Europe. Almost from its inception the postwar planning committee in the State Department had been wrestling with this need. Participating in these deliberations, Bohlen had tended to be cautious, intent upon avoiding alienation of the Soviet Union, and committed to finding a realistic and workable solution. During a March meeting of the committee he had argued that since Soviet policy in Eastern Europe was not yet clear, all proposals had to be quite tentative. But he perceived a "minimum program" which might involve alliances between Eastern Europe and the Soviet Union "under which the sovereignty and independence" of these countries "would not be impaired." To him such an arrangement between a large nation and lesser nations on its borders would not constitute a threat to American interests and would coincide with Soviet security wishes. Since the Soviet Union would face a massive program of reconstruction following the war, he doubted that it would venture beyond this minimum program, although the United States had to bear in mind that the Soviet definition of a friendly government differed from the western view. Bohlen believed that the key point was whether the Soviet Union was "prepared permanently to abandon its missionary spirit so far as its relations with neighboring countries were concerned." If the minimum program were the case, the possibility of collaboration with the West remained.

Here was an indication of Bohlen's realistic acceptance of a divided world, but a world divided in spheres which served the interests of both the Soviet Union and the United States. Only time would tell if the Kremlin would be content to accept such terms. The test of whether such an arrangement were possible would not be Poland—which he did not consider "representative" in view of "past history and feeling"— but Czechoslovakia, where President Benes was seeking friendship with the Soviet Union at all cost.[35]

Poland may not have been the typical case in Eastern Europe; still, it did become the barometer of Soviet intent. Despite his personal sympathies for the Polish cause, Bohlen constantly strove to present advice which would keep America's options open and lead to a policy which would serve its best interests. His efforts continued even after Soviet recognition of the Lublin regime made Stalin's intentions for Eastern Europe clearer. During a meeting of the policy committee in October of 1944, Bohlen remarked that the United States had not yet conveyed to Great Britain and Russia what responsibilities it was willing to assume in Eastern Europe. Since the Soviets tended to act on an *ad hoc* basis and often failed to understand clearly the implications of their actions, he speculated that a well-defined American plan might influence them to act more in line with American desires. But, as he later told Ambassador Ciechanowski, the representative of the London exile government, America had to avoid a stance on the Polish government which contradicted the basic American principle of self-determination promulgated in the Atlantic Charter. How to reconcile American sentiments and its adherence to such principles with legitimate Soviet security concerns was the dilemma.

Bohlen also argued that, if an international organization were established, it would have to make decisions based on world security needs. He concurred with the American tilt toward the exile government, yet cautioned against leaning so far in that direction to preclude compromise.[36]

If Stalin was playing realpolitik, Bohlen was trying hard to promote a firm but fair and realistic response to a challenge complicated by the fact that the United States had to cope not only with Russia's self-interest, but also with Britain's. Churchill, committed firmly to Mikolajczyk's government and eager for a solution in Eastern Europe which might also shore up the declining British Empire, decided to travel to Moscow in October 1944. Before Churchill left, Bohlen received an urgent call from Harry Hopkins on 3 October. Hopkins had intercepted messages from Roosevelt to Stalin and Churchill which left the implication that the British prime minister while in Moscow would be speaking on behalf of the president.

Bohlen was as concerned as Hopkins. It was dangerous to permit Churchill to speak for the United States. Further, if the meetings were held without an American representative present, the Europeans might conclude that "the United States had washed its hands of European political problems." Bohlen could only speculate on topics to be discussed, but he anticipated one of two results: a "first class British-Soviet rowe [*sic*] over European problems" or a division of Europe into spheres of influence. If this meeting had to take place, he proposed that Ambassador Harriman be present as Roosevelt's observer to insure that the United States was not committed even by inference to any policies it did not want.[37]

Hopkins, who had been ill, had temporarily lost touch with the Roosevelt policy. Uncertain that the president would even heed his warnings, he nevertheless had Bohlen draft more satisfactory presidential communications. To Hopkins's relief, when he approached Roosevelt in his dressing room and voiced his warning, the president readily agreed and approved Bohlen's drafts.[38]

Bohlen's and Hopkins's concerns were well-founded. At this October meeting, Churchill and Stalin discussed a percentage division of Eastern Europe and the Balkans. Bohlen personally questioned how much the two leaders actually agreed upon, but the implication was certainly there.[39] And Bohlen and Hopkins prevented the United States from being locked into a policy which conflicted with its own interests.

Churchill and Stalin were willing to settle the problems of Eastern Europe by mutually beneficial spheres of influence. Within the American foreign policy establishment, however, was a diversity of views on this tactic. Some did espouse spheres of influence, but the official stand remained supportive of the United Nations, a Wilsonian internationalist approach to world problems. To its proponents, it was an alternative to such power political solutions as spheres of influence.

From 21 August to 7 October, the allies met at Dumbarton Oaks out-side Washington to flesh out this postwar international body. Bohlen was characteristically skeptical of such an organization's potential usefulness, but he conceded that no one knew if something would work unless it was tried, an attitude undoubtedly inspired by his close contact with the Roosevelt White House. The precedent of cooperation between the U.S. and U.S.S.R. had been established during the war. Perhaps this cooperation might continue into the postwar period. Besides, he laid his doubts aside for the time being because he could not produce any concrete evidence to support his "instinctive feeling that trouble lay ahead."[40]

Bohlen attended the conference as advisor on Soviet matters, splitting his time between these meetings and his regular duties at the State Department and White House. The basic framework of the United Nations took shape. Left unsettled, however, were the Soviet demand that all sixteen Soviet Republics be represented, a request which Roosevelt persuaded the Soviets to put aside for the time being, and the issue of the veto power for permanent members of the United Nations Security Council.

The Security Council was to be composed of eleven members with the Soviet Union, United States, France, Great Britain, and China as permanent members. All concerned agreed that permanent members should have a veto power to safeguard their interests. At issue was the extent of the veto, the Soviet Union demanding an all-inclusive veto, the United States and Great Britain proposing that parties to a dispute abstain from voting, and opposing the extension of the veto power to block diplomatic discussions. While the American position reflected an idealistic perception of what this organization should be, Bohlen could also understand Soviet concerns. The Soviet representatives were "absolutely determined to safeguard their sovereignty, to prevent any mechanism of an international or other character from ever placing the Soviet Union in a position of being overridden on its policies and desires by the weight of the opinion of other countries."[41]

On this issue, even Roosevelt's vaunted personal charm failed to overcome Soviet determination. When a deadlock was apparent in September, Stettinius, who was intimately involved in the U.N. negotiations, took Hull's and Hopkins's advice and arranged a bedroom meeting between the president and Soviet Ambassador Andrei Gromyko. They thought that Roosevelt could broach the possibility of a personal appeal to Stalin. Concurring in this maneuver, Stettinius assigned Bohlen to draft a proposed message. Bohlen, who agreed with this approach, was by now familiar enough with Roosevelt's thinking that he was able to capsulize the White House position with only a few modifications by the president. Bohlen pointed out that American public opinion, the United States Senate, and numerous nations around the world would object to great powers voting in the Security Council on disputes in which they were involved. "They would most certainly see in that an attempt on the part of the great powers to set themselves up above the law." Roosevelt added only an analogy during the meeting with Gromyko, pointing out that an American tradition held that parties to a dispute never voted on their own fate, as when a husband and wife appeared before a judge. The letter was then sent on to Stalin, who was unswayed by this rational appeal, thus leaving in doubt the future of an international organization.[42]

If, as seemed a possibility, this international organization could not work, one of the few viable alternatives remaining for postwar peace and security was spheres of influence. Bohlen understood the appeal spheres held. In fact, when he spoke of the Soviet Union's "minimum program" for Eastern Europe, he was not denying that Soviet security requirements were real and that great powers could not help but exercise a predominant influence over small nations on its border, something he felt that the United States could realistically live with. But many factors—American principles and political considerations being most prominent—intervened to make it unrealistic for the United States to participate in such a blatant division of the world.

His colleague George Kennan, who had been back in Moscow since the summer of 1944, was less certain that the United States should delay facing the issue head on. Whereas Bohlen's White House experience had tempered his pessimism, Kennan's experiences in Moscow had reinforced his cynical view of Soviet-American relations. In January of 1945, he wrote Bohlen that he thought it necessary that the United States dissociate itself from the Russian political programs. He granted that Soviet military help was necessary to win the war, but he worried that Russian policy had to "find its rewards at the expense of other peoples in eastern and central Europe."

Sure now that he understood Russian intentions, Kennan asserted that American policy was confusing to its friends and to the Russians as well because it failed to advance a positive and constructive program for the future organization of the European continent. His idea of a positive program was to "divide Europe frankly into spheres of influence." A commitment to an international organization would only link the United States to a "swollen and unhealthy Russian sphere of power." So the United Nations, he suggested, should be buried "as quickly and as quietly as possible." And the United States should write off Eastern and Southeastern Europe unless it was willing "to go whole hog" in challenging the Soviet Union there. Finally, it had to accept that Germany would be partitioned and then to begin negotiations with Great Britain and France to set up a Western European federation which would include the West German states.[43]

Bohlen, busy with the Yalta conference, found time to answer only briefly. Like others close to the Roosevelt White House, including Averell Harriman, Bohlen, despite his suspicions, was not yet prepared to abandon efforts to solicit postwar Soviet cooperation. He took a wait-and-see attitude, observing that a number of factors militated against implementing Kennan's proposal at the moment. He agreed with a number of Kennan's concerns and granted that the government was pursuing a current policy of "no small risks." But he described Kennan's "constructive" suggestions as "naïve" to a degree. They were good in the abstract, but as practical suggestions were "utterly impossible" and could only be implemented in a totalitarian state, not in a democracy. At no time during the war, Bohlen argued, could the United States have acted any differently; to defeat Germany, for example, Soviet armies had to be allowed in Eastern Europe. Bohlen therefore urged Kennan to be realistic. He was perplexed as to "why a piece of paper that you did not get should be regarded as so much more real than those you did get. Isn't it a question of realities and not of bits of paper? Either our pals intend to limit themselves or they don't. I submit, as the British say, that the answer is not yet clear."[44]

Bohlen believed that Kennan had overlooked some crucial factors in accepting the spheres of influence view. In the abstract, it was easy enough for the United States to divide the world in two, but this would arouse the Slavic minorities, who constituted a part of the American electorate and who would not docilely stand by and let the United States openly abandon their homelands. Not only would such a blatant move damage America's moral standing in the world and arouse significant political opposition at home, but also it would not solve the problem of Soviet tendencies toward expansionism. Implicit in Bohlen's comment to Kennan was the role played by ideology and party, which Bohlen would later take note of in a discussion of Kennan's correspondence. Kennan seemed to have forgotten that the Soviet Union was both an ideological and a national movement. Nothing would prevent the Kremlin from utilizing the Communist parties around the world for its own purposes by fomenting revolutions beyond its own sphere while the government denied that it was violating any agreements.[45]

Bohlen had certainly succumbed to the optimism within the White House. But this optimism was countered by doubts about the future he shared with so many in the State Department. His reply was a result of these competing forces. From Bohlen's standpoint, Kennan's error in supporting spheres of influence was mainly in his timing. The Soviet Union had not yet shown that it would resist cooperation. Also, the political climate in the United States was not yet conducive to such a maneuver. He understood Kennan's anxiety, but could see that his colleague was not realistically considering the domestic political situation which was the context for such a decision.

This outlook was characteristic of Bohlen during 1944. He brought into the State Department a bit of the White House optimism about the ability of the United States to reach limited accords with the Soviet Union and found the opportunity in the White House map room to voice his doubts and reservations about Soviet actions. Periodically, he had at least an indirect influence on the decisions and pronouncements of Roosevelt himself.[46]

His White House contacts, however, did not obliterate his suspicion of Soviet intentions. While ideology could not be completely discounted, it became increasingly apparent that national interest and realpolitik motivated the Soviet Union under Stalin. On the one hand, if the Soviet Union did act more like a nation than a cause, it would increase the possibility that diplomacy might produce results. On the other hand, Bohlen could not ignore evidence of impending problems. Communist fear of capitalist encirclement was reinforced by the fact that Soviet national interest had a plan for postwar Europe which contrasted with that of the United States. Bohlen was not ready to abandon hope, especially since his assessment of Soviet intent was still based on circumstantial evidence. But when Roosevelt, Churchill, and Stalin met for the last time at Yalta, political differences would assume major proportions and Bohlen's pessimism would be confirmed.

3.

YALTA TO POTSDAM

The Yalta conference, the most notable of the wartime summit meetings, convened on 4 February 1945. For a week, Churchill, Roosevelt, and Stalin tackled issues destined to have a long-range impact on the postwar world. From the perspective of domestic American politics, the decisions made, the manner in which Roosevelt concluded them, and the way in which they were or were not implemented eventually made Yalta the target of conservatives, isolationists, and Republicans, culminating in the hysteria of McCarthyism during the 1950s.

Not only was this summit of moment for world affairs, but also it was personally significant for Bohlen. He had proven his reliability in 1944 and was now in a position of importance within the Roosevelt administration, serving as interpreter, liaison, and resident expert on Soviet affairs.[1] He proffered advice, and as interpreter he was present at meetings where some of the most crucial decisions were made. This Yalta connection would later provide ammunition for his opponents when Eisenhower nominated him as ambassador to the Soviet Union.

Roosevelt and most of his close advisors sailed to this pivotal encounter with Stalin and Churchill aboard the cruiser *Quincy*. Bohlen, however, was assigned to accompany Hopkins on a preconference fact-finding mission to London, Paris, and Rome. They left by air soon after the president was inaugurated in January and caught up with Roosevelt's entourage on 2 February at Malta, where the president and Churchill held preliminary discussions. Bohlen then flew on to Yalta with the rest of the presidential party.[2]

When Bohlen boarded the *Quincy* to meet with the president, he was shocked at how "frail" and obviously ill the president appeared, how much his health had deteriorated in only two weeks. But Bohlen was encouraged that the president regained some of his vigor by the time they arrived at Yalta.[3] Bohlen was aware of the president's physical infirmities, but his impressions of the conference notably paid little attention to this as a major factor in the negotiations and the agreements reached.

At Yalta, the American delegation was housed in the old tsarist summer residence, the Lividia Palace, which also served as the main conference headquarters. The president had spacious quarters, but Bohlen and many others in the delegation doubled up in small, newly white-washed rooms on the floor above the presidential suite. Bohlen's situation was made more pleasant, however, when he met a Russian waiter who had been a servant in the American embassy during the 1930s. The Russian immediately recognized Bohlen and made sure that he had ample supplies of caviar, vodka, and other necessities throughout the conference.[4]

At the time the Yalta conference took place, Bohlen was still clinging to some hope for postwar Soviet-American relations. Only when the real Soviet attitude toward these accords emerged in the aftermath of Yalta did Bohlen begin to despair. As he recalled in his memoirs, "Hope dies hard . . . in the American diplomatic breast, and for the next few years I found myself traveling back and forth across the Atlantic in a vain quest for an understanding with the Kremlin."[5]

In his assessment of the conference, he understood Roosevelt's motivations and the limitations on his actions. He also acknowledged the shortcomings of the agreements. He judged that on certain topics a more determined American position could possibly have yielded more modification in Soviet demands. But these were technical errors in the negotiations that may or may not have made a difference. Bohlen chose to stress the positive side, the goals which Roosevelt sought. For the most part, Bohlen blamed the Soviet Union for Yalta's ultimate failure. In this respect, his analysis was consistent with his previous experience with and attitudes toward the Soviets. His defense of Yalta at the hearings to confirm him as ambassador to the Soviet Union in 1953 was essentially the same as his assessment during and immediately after Yalta.

The Yalta conference convened at a critical point in the war. By February of 1945, German forces were retreating as the allied armies approached Berlin from both east and west, and it was only a matter of time before Germany surrendered. But Europe was not Roosevelt's sole concern. There was still the Pacific theater, where Soviet participation, if it materialized, could make a difference. Roosevelt was determined to guarantee this Soviet help. Bohlen saw a president at Yalta who was confident that the rapport he had nurtured with Churchill and Stalin would stand him in good stead, a president so confident that he often ignored the briefing books and data provided by the State Department and relied on personal diplomacy, an approach which often led to issues being handled in a haphazard fashion. This tendency worried Bohlen.[6]

Roosevelt's personal approach was particularly significant given the important topics being discussed—obstacles to a United Nations; France's participation in the German occupation; the German reparations issue; and the fate of Poland. Finally, with Germany near defeat and Japan still a threat in the Pacific, it remained militarily imperative that the Russians join the war in the Pacific.

In Bohlen's opinion, the outcome of the United Nations discussions proved the "one solid and lasting decision reached at Yalta." Dumbarton Oaks had left the question of the veto and the representation of the Russian republics to be settled at the summit. Reluctant to trust Soviet security to an international organization, Stalin wanted guarantees that the permanent members of the Security Council would have an absolute veto. Roosevelt, in contrast, insisted that the Security Council had to assure the opportunity for the smaller nations to state their case, in his mind an essential factor to world peace. But characteristically pragmatic, he did not completely ignore the exigencies of power politics. He was willing to grant a Security Council veto for actions taken by the international body. He was certainly not naïvely prepared to trust America's fate to this body of nations and wanted to maintain great control after the war.

In the end, the American view prevailed. At the time, Bohlen was confident "that no great nation will be able to exercise the veto powers to block international action of disputes, but that international action requires the unity of the great powers."[7] He acknowledged that this was far from the best arrangement, but it was the best that could realistically be expected. As he pointed out to Churchill, it reminded him of a plantation owner who asked his slave how he liked the whisky he had been given for Christmas. "When the Negro replied that it was perfect, the master asked what he meant. The Negro answered that had the whisky been any better, the master would not have given it to him, and had it been any worse, he couldn't have drunk it."[8] With this realistic, but unenthusiastic evaluation, Bohlen was taking a wait-and-see attitude about the future of the United Nations.

In retrospect, he suspected that Stalin had deferred to Roosevelt on the veto partly because he expected his magnanimity to be reciprocated later and partly because the veto over substantive issues adequately guaranteed Soviet security.[9] Bohlen argued that this reciprocity did not include an arrangement to guarantee the Soviet Union three votes in the General Assembly. Bohlen knew that Roosevelt had been aware since Dumbarton Oaks that the Soviet Union would press for these additional votes. The president had opposed it at that time, declaring once that if Stalin persisted he would demand votes for all forty-eight states. The president persisted in his opposition even after Stalin reduced his demand to two or three republics—the Ukraine, White Russia, and perhaps Lithuania. But at Yalta, Bohlen watched as Roosevelt conceded, faced by the possibility of being outvoted. This was no surprise to Bohlen. Shortly after he and Hopkins had arrived at the conference, Churchill had approached them with a request that the British empire receive more than one vote, mentioning India in particular as a possibility. To accomplish his end, Churchill was willing to support Stalin's position.[10]

Bohlen maintained that in yielding Roosevelt had erred. Bohlen believed that the Stalin whom Roosevelt was dealing with at Yalta was more malleable and less intractable than the president may have believed. Bohlen doubted that Stalin would have insisted too strongly on this concession if Roosevelt had only remained adamant. The agreement, furthermore, bothered Bohlen because it gave a "fictitious cloak of independence" to these republics. Finally, Roosevelt seriously miscalculated in accepting Stalin's offer to include three votes for the United States. Roosevelt, Bohlen was certain, intended to go to the San Francisco Conference and relinquish these extra votes, hoping to compel Stalin to do the same.[11] But the ploy backfired. When the press got word of the secret arrangement, Bohlen lamented to Hopkins that "all hell [had] broken loose," the "chief yell" being that the United States was being duplicitous in seeking extra votes.[12]

The questions surrounding Germany were of even more concern, both immediate and long range. The United States, determined to prevent a recurrence of the economic problems which followed World War I, was reluctant to impose an exorbitant reparations burden on Germany. The Soviet Union, having suffered heavy losses and having endured the wrath of the German war machine, was less compassionate; reparations could provide economic compensation for Russia at the same time they could weaken Germany. The net result of the negotiations was another compromise. Rather than try to settle the final figure at Yalta, a commission composed of representatives from the Soviet Union, the United States, and Great Britain agreed to meet in Moscow to formulate an acceptable settlement. As a concession to Stalin, Roosevelt agreed to include in the final communiqué the state-

Bohlen and Harry Hopkins arrive at Yalta. (Courtesy Franklin D. Roosevelt Library.)

ment that twenty billion dollars would be a working figure, a decision with which Churchill refused to concur. Once again, Bohlen felt a determined stance might have produced Soviet concessions. He was disturbed that the president had British support in opposing Stalin's reparations demands, but had assented to the compromise after Hopkins had sent him a note describing how Stalin was beginning to feel that the president was siding with the British in their opposition to the Soviet Union.

Arrangements for Germany also were complicated by the French demand for a zone. The sometimes conflicting interests of the Big Three, according to Bohlen, now became crucial. Churchill adamantly supported the French. It was easy to reach an accord whereby France would be allowed a zone carved from the British and American zones. But it was more difficult to settle the question of French participation in the Allied Control Commission which, contrary to British requests, Roosevelt opposed. As Hopkins, Bohlen, and H. Freeman Matthews, the chief of the European Affairs Division, realized, however, the British position had merits, particularly since it would foster a unified western position. The three approached Roosevelt and argued that no plan to administer Germany could succeed without French participation. It was hard to overcome Roosevelt's disdain for Charles de Gaulle, but he ultimately gave in.[13]

If Germany was an immediate concern, the issue of Poland and Eastern Europe was potentially the most divisive. One aspect was Poland's postwar borders. Although Churchill and Roosevelt were willing to grant an eastern Polish border corresponding roughly to the Curzon line, they were likewise intent upon preserving some of Poland's urban areas, such as Lwow. Furthermore, the loss of territory in the east had to be compensated with territory for Poland to be carved out of Germany. At Yalta, there was no agreement on where that western Polish boundary would extend.[14]

The real problem, however, focused on the composition of the Polish government. The Russians persisted in their demand for recognition of the Lublin regime while the British, backed by the United States, reaffirmed their support for the exile government in London. Any interim government, they insisted, had to include a number of representatives from this exile group. Bohlen was painfully aware of the dichotomy between what could realistically be expected and what the Polish exiles wanted. After a meeting with Mikolajczyk on the way to Yalta, Bohlen knew that the Poles were aware of the dilemma as well.

Bohlen had conferred with Mikolajczyk during a stopover in London and had conveyed America's determination to negotiate with the exile government, not the Lublin Poles. Bohlen pessimistically admitted that this would be difficult. Mikolajczyk sympathized, but pleaded that under no circumstances should the West leave Poland at the mercy of the Soviet Union, even though Soviet occupation forces left the western allies with little leverage.

The Polish leader reiterated his pleas in a follow-up letter for Roosevelt which he forwarded to Bohlen in Paris on 27 January. Referring to the Communists as a "trifling group," Mikolajczyk set forth his belief that the territorial settlements were inextricably tied to the resolution of the governmental problem, so his major focus was finding a compromise which would prevent the domination of Poland by Lublin and insure the independence of the Polish state. After listing possible solutions—ranging from the return of the prewar president who would then appoint a new government (although Mikolajczyk acknowledged that this would be totally unsatisfactory to the Soviet Union) to the establishment of a provisional government composed of all interested parties—he emphasized that it was decisive "for the independence of Poland and for the freedom and the future of the nation—to establish without delay—a government based on all democratic political movements and to secure for this government the freedom of action, the assistance of the Allies and their confidence."[15]

The Polish matter did not arise at the summit until the third plenary session. Despite appeals both by Churchill and by Roosevelt, who offered a plan consistent with Mikolajczyk's letter, Stalin refused to budge. He restated his conviction that Poland was crucial to Soviet security and reaffirmed his recognition of the Lublin Poles. Frustrated after this session, Roosevelt turned to a new ploy, hoping to exploit his personal rapport with the Soviet dictator. He instructed Bohlen to prepare a note to Stalin incorporating many of the ideas from Mikolajczyk's letter. After making minor revisions to Bohlen's draft, he sent it to Stalin. In it, the president acknowledged the importance of Poland to the Russians, but declared that the United States still could not recognize the Lublin government. Arguing that he did not want a split in allied cooperation, he suggested that they call some representatives from Lublin to meet with a group of Poles from the outside. Then they could form a provisional government, bound to hold free elections in the near future. Roosevelt guaranteed that "the United States will never lend its support in any way to any provisional government in Poland that would be inimical to [Stalin's] interests."[16]

This letter helped break the impasse, even though its proposed solution was unacceptable to Stalin, who countered with a plan of his own— a provisional government based on the Lublin regime with émigrés added. This temporary government would endorse elections in the near future. The details of the final compromise along these lines was worked out by the foreign ministers. Bohlen, to his later dismay, helped draft this hastily prepared plan, filled with unclear and vague phrases, such as a call for free and unfettered elections. He doubted that the Russians had intentionally manipulated the document, but such phraseology, Bohlen later realized, provided loopholes they could exploit.[17]

Bohlen was far from pleased with the arrangement, but he conceded that little else could have been accomplished. Poland was a neighbor of strategic importance to the Soviet Union. The United States was "confronted with a condition and not a theory." Few believed that the Lublin government was truly representative of the Polish people. Yet opposition would have led either to a civil war, which would have hampered the Soviet army's advance against Germany, or the arrest and exile or imprisonment of all Polish pro-London groups by the Red Army, an action Stalin would not have hesitated to take since he was quite concerned with avoiding any disruption at his army's rear. Nevertheless, Bohlen stressed that the agreements reached, if "honestly" implemented, offered the best chance available for a "free, independent and prosperous Polish state." Had the United States and Great Britain insisted on the London government, it would have "led to a complete deprivation of the Polish people of the real hope contained in the solutions."[18]

As it was, the Polish agreement soon went the way of the Declararion on Liberated Europe, which called for consultation among the allied powers to guarantee democratic governments for the liberated countries.[19] But the difficulties would only appear later as a result of what Bohlen described as Soviet bad faith. Bohlen did not delude himself. The Yalta arrangements were based only on a fragile hope that they would succeed.

The Far Eastern accord was another controversial product of Yalta. Roosevelt's concessions on the United Nations, in Bohlen's judgment, had been the president's first big mistake. The second was this secret accord concluded behind the back of America's ally, China. Still, Bohlen could understand the reasoning that precipitated the blunder. Military concerns weighed heavily on the president. With predictions of massive American losses in an assault on the Japanese homeland projected for late 1945, time was of the essence. Prompted by this exigency, Roosevelt, accompanied only by Ambassador Harriman and Bohlen as his interpreter, raised the Far Eastern question during a private meeting with Stalin on 8 February.[20]

After this discussion, in which Stalin argued that he needed something to take to the Supreme Soviet to justify Soviet entry into the Pacific conflict, Harriman and Molotov in a series of meetings ironed out the details of an arrangement which Stalin and Roosevelt finalized on 10 February. Bohlen felt that Roosevelt signed reluctantly. The president was disturbed about not consulting with the Chinese, but wartime needs prevailed. By the terms of the arrangement, the Soviet Union agreed to enter the war within three months after Germany's defeat. In return, Outer Mongolia would remain independent of China, thus under Soviet influence; the port of Dairen would be internationalized; Port Arthur would be leased to the Soviet Union as a naval base; the Soviets would receive the southern half of Sakhalin Island as well as the Kurile Islands; and the Chinese-Eastern Railroad and the South Manchurian Railroad would be operated by a joint Soviet-Chinese company. Roosevelt further assented to work for Chinese concurrence in these plans.[21]

This arrangement and the others at Yalta began to establish the framework for the postwar world. Bohlen avoided exaggerating their importance, insisting that the map of Europe would have been the same had Yalta never taken place, since circumstances limited Roosevelt's options. He recognized the positive side of the agreements, such as paving the way for the United Nations and securing a seat for France on the Allied Control Commission for Germany.

Bohlen's evaluation of Yalta, however, was not completely positive. He admitted it was a failure in total, but he quickly added that "failure" did not necessarily mean that the accords were wrong. He was also uncomfortable about Roosevelt's hesitance to confront Stalin, as when he relented on the demand for votes for the Soviet republics. Roosevelt's lack of resolve would continue to bother Bohlen in the remaining months before the president's death. But on the positive side, Bohlen saw Yalta as an honest attempt to reach agreement, which enhanced America's status as a moral leader of the free world.[22]

Following the conference, Bohlen returned home with the ailing Harry Hopkins. Leaving the president's party at Algiers, they boarded the *Sacred Cow,* the presidential plane, making interim stops to help Hopkins regain his strength. Once back in Washington, developments reinforced Bohlen's misgivings about postwar cooperation. Harriman, working with the British and Russian representatives in Moscow, reported Soviet resistance to broadening the scope of the Polish provisional government. Soviet control over Rumania, Bulgaria, and other parts of Eastern Europe tightened in open defiance of the Declaration on Liberated Europe. Stalin also announced that Molotov would not attend the founding session of the United Nations in San Francisco, an indication that the Soviets placed little faith in that body.

Roosevelt was worried, but not ready to resort to an open break with the U.S.S.R. When Churchill wrote expressing his concern that the British and American views were diverging in the Moscow talks to establish a Polish government, Bohlen, along with Roosevelt's military aide, Adm. William Leahy, prepared a draft for Roosevelt's response on 15 March. It clearly and unequivocally stated that America's "chief purpose at the time was and remains without giving ground to get the negotiations moving again and tackle first of all the point on which they had come to a standstill [who would be invited to participate in the Polish provisional government]." Roosevelt expressed his resolve to implement the Yalta agreements. He refused to admit that the talks had broken down and stressed the need for Great Britain and the United States to agree on instructions to the ambassadors so the negotiations could continue. The prime minister had proposed that any Polish groups could be invited unless all three parties objected, a suggestion Roosevelt criticized because he could not see Stalin acceding to it. But he did agree with Churchill that the Poles invited should discuss the composition of the new government among themselves, with the commission serving only as an impartial arbiter.[23]

A month later, Bohlen was confronted with another suggestion by a member of British Foreign Secretary Anthony Eden's staff that five non-Lublin Poles from within Poland be invited to the discussions. Concerned with keeping the talks on track, Bohlen responded in the negative. These representatives combined with the Poles from the exile government would weight the composition of the Polish group eight to three against the Lublin Poles. This "would insure Stalin's refusal of the proposal and also expose us to the charge which he had made previously to President Roosevelt that we were attempting to interpret the Crimea decision in such a way as to eliminate the Lublin Government."[24] Bohlen, like others around Roosevelt, was struggling to preserve allied cooperation.

In the midst of these changing events, Roosevelt died on 12 April. Bohlen had reservations about Roosevelt's diplomatic abilities; in Bohlen's view, FDR treated diplomacy too much like domestic political issues, and Bohlen further wondered if the president really understood the Soviet weltanschauung. But he acknowledged the respect and prestige Roosevelt had fostered around the world, something the new president, Harry Truman, lacked. Bohlen also believed that in his final months Roosevelt was becoming frustrated with the direction Soviet-American relations were taking; Truman's policies, Bohlen concluded, were probably little different from what Roosevelt might have resorted to. But Bohlen felt that Roosevelt's manner and the respect other leaders had for him might have affected the tone and the thrust of future events.[25]

Roosevelt had been remiss in keeping his vice-president informed of international events. Thus the day after Roosevelt's death, Stettinius urged Truman to keep Bohlen as State Department liaison.[26] This, to Stettinius, was imperative. Truman had to become informed on the intricacies of American foreign policy in a very short time. Bohlen was one who could provide the needed insights. Events were moving rapidly. The Polish negotiations were still pressing, and the San Francisco Conference was scheduled for 25 April. Ambassador Harriman had appealed to Stalin's sympathies and convinced him to send Molotov to these meetings as a gesture of respect for Roosevelt. Harriman then hurried to Washington to brief Truman prior to Molotov's arrival.

At a meeting with the president, Secretary Stettinius, Undersecretary Grew, and Bohlen on 20 April, Harriman warned that the Soviet Union was following a dual policy: it was cooperating with the United States and Great Britain at the same time it was extending Soviet control over its neighbors. The Soviets had the false impression that the United States would let them get away with anything, especially since American business needed the Soviet Union for markets to maintain the health of postwar American industry.

The ambassador also cautioned that Truman should be ready to react to Molotov's stance on Poland when the Russian diplomat arrived in Washington en route to the San Francisco Conference. The Soviets, Harriman noted, had rejected American and British proposals for a settlement consonant with the Yalta accords. Truman agreed with Harriman that something would have to be done regarding Poland if the United Nations treaty was to have any chance of passing the Senate.

Harriman painted a dire picture. He advocated a firm policy, but he did not abandon the possibility of a negotiated settlement with the Soviet Union as Kennan, his subordinate, had apparently done. Harriman believed, however, that it would take a restructuring of American policy "and the abandonment of the illusion that for the immediate future the Soviet Government was going to act in accordance with the principles which the rest of the world held to in international affairs." As Bohlen watched Truman's reaction, he took heart that the president was ready to be firm and decisive in his dealings with the Russians, a firmness that Bohlen had viewed as lacking in America's stance at Yalta.[27]

After Harriman's meeting, Bohlen drew up a list to prepare Truman for topics he might raise during the Molotov visit. These included the future status of liberated areas of Rumania and Bulgaria, an improved American position on the allied control commission for the satellite states, the Soviet failure to implement the agreement regarding the exchange of liberated prisoners of war and civilians, and the upcoming meetings of the reparations committee in Moscow.[28] But it was upon the issue of Poland that the future of Soviet-American relations hinged. The United States could not accept the agreement reached between the Soviet Union and the Lublin government. But Bohlen advocated resolution and prudence. He joined with James Clement Dunn of the Western European desk in warning Truman that the results of the Polish negotiations could have a ripple effect. If the allies could not reach agreement on this issue, it would cast serious doubt on the "unity of purpose the allies had regarding postwar collaboration."[29] They wanted to avoid abandoning negotiation for confrontation.

Truman met Molotov on 22 April at Blair House with Harriman,

Stettinius, and Bohlen in attendance. Treating the initial visit as essentially a courtesy call, Truman turned the negotiating over to Stettinius, who would work with Eden and Molotov to reach a settlement. But Truman first made it clear to Molotov that, although territorial proximity made Poland important to the U.S.S.R., the American people were also concerned about the future of this Eastern European country.[30]

Before Molotov met with the president the following day, he was apprised of the fact that the negotiating session had failed to produce any progress. Bohlen, Dunn, Harriman, and Stettinius then joined the president for his second encounter with the foreign minister. When Molotov arrived, Truman quickly expressed his disappointment at the direction the talks had taken. He stressed his determination that the San Francisco meeting should continue as planned, but he affirmed his support for a 16 April proposal he and Churchill had made demanding that all democratic elements be represented in the Polish government. Molotov retorted that the Soviet Union was fulfilling the Yalta agreements and was cooperating. Ignoring this, Truman shot back that the only thing to do was to have Stalin carry out his word. When Molotov tried to compare the settlement in Yugoslavia with what might be expected in Poland, Truman would have none of this obfuscation, emphasizing that the agreement had already been made and should thus be implemented. Faced with Truman's determination and his assertion that friendly relations could not travel a one-way street, Molotov, Bohlen observed, turned "a little ashy" and replied that he had not been talked to like this before. Truman snapped that if he fulfilled his agreements, he would not get talked to like that and abruptly dismissed the foreign minister before he could continue the exchange.[31]

Truman took the more determined stand which Harriman had hurried from Moscow to urge upon him. The war was nearly over, and the tensions between the East and West could no longer be suppressed. Following the Molotov meeting, Bohlen accompanied Stettinius to the San Francisco Conference (25 April–26 June 1945) where Bohlen translated and contributed to the continuing dialogue between the Soviet Union, Great Britain, and the United States. Despite the Dumbarton Oaks preparations and the compromises at Yalta, Molotov once again raised the veto question. Old rifts persisted and new ones developed, including American support for Argentina's membership in the General Assembly despite its past collaboration with Germany, and the Soviet Union's insistence that the Lublin government was legitimate and should thus be seated.

Meanwhile, Germany surrendered on 8 May, freeing the United

States to concentrate on the Pacific theater and reinforcing the urgency of getting the Russians into this conflict. On 9 May, Harriman and Bohlen were discussing the bleak future prospects and the possible means to elicit Stalin's cooperation as they flew from San Francisco to Washington. Not wanting to infringe on Harriman's domain as ambassador, Bohlen reluctantly suggested that Truman might send Harry Hopkins on a special mission to plead the American case directly with Stalin. Stalin had been a friend of Hopkins since his 1941 mission to institute lend-lease aid. Bohlen argued that Hopkins would signal the continuity of American foreign policy under Truman as well as the president's commitment to cooperation. Far from being offended by the proposal, Harriman eagerly embraced it. The two, therefore, went to see Hopkins at his Georgetown residence soon after their arrival in Washington. Hopkins was seriously ill, but he agreed to make the trip. Harriman then went to propose the mission to Truman.[32]

Truman had earlier broached the possibility of such a mission to Hopkins on Roosevelt's funeral train, only to have Hopkins plead ill health and refuse; the president welcomed Harriman's proposal and Hopkins's acceptance now. Perhaps Hopkins accepted this second time because the state of Soviet-American relations had deteriorated and he now realized the need to emphasize the continuity of American policy in order to overcome the barriers to cooperation. A direct appeal to Stalin might accomplish this. There is no concrete evidence to support the contention of Gar Alperovitz that Truman was merely trying to delay confrontation until the atomic bomb could be tested.[33] Indeed, Bohlen's role in this affair reflects his continuing last-ditch effort to preserve cooperation.

Harriman returned to Moscow, with Hopkins following on 23 May, accompanied by Bohlen as his advisor and interpreter. Between 26 May and 6 June, Hopkins held a series of amicable talks with Stalin, striving to restore allied cooperation. Stalin agreed to invite Polish leaders from all segments of the political spectrum to meet the commission in Moscow. Then, as a concession to Stalin, Hopkins granted that the Lublin government would be recognized as having a predominant position in Poland. Stalin, furthermore, revealed his plans to meet with Chinese Foreign Minister T. V. Soong on 1 July to discuss the Far Eastern accords. He assured Hopkins that the meeting would be followed by Soviet actions against Japan in Manchuria as early as 8 August. Finally, at Stettinius's request, Hopkins asked Stalin to intervene to settle the veto dispute which threatened the San Francisco Conference. Stalin, acting as though he were not aware of the problem, ordered Molotov to withdraw the Soviet demands.[34]

In retrospect, Bohlen thought that this mission had failed. Hopkins lacked the standing with Truman he had had with Roosevelt, and the only real breakthrough was on the United Nations voting procedures.[35] Yet in 1945 Bohlen was more optimistic about Hopkins's accomplishments. Shortly after returning to Washington, he wrote to Harriman, encouraged by the feeling that cooperation still might succeed. "Harry's trip, and particularly since the announcement of the Polish invitations, has had a wonderful press and a very salutary effect here," he judged. "You will have seen the President's press conference this morning in which I think he struck just the right note of qualified optimism in regard to the Polish matter."[36]

In essence, the Hopkins mission was a stopgap measure, intended to pave the way for a more substantive meeting, another summit among the Big Three. Before the Hopkins trip, Truman had met with acting Secretary of State Joseph Grew, Harriman, and Bohlen on 15 May to discuss future negotiations with the Soviet Union. All supported a summit. Assuming that the situation would continue to deteriorate the longer the meeting was delayed, Harriman proposed that, although American troops should not be used for political bargaining, the meeting "would be more favorable and the chances of success increased" if it took place before America was out of Europe.

Truman concurred, but pleaded that pressing domestic issues hindered an early meeting. He then directed two queries to Bohlen. Truman asked if he was right in feeling that it was time for Stalin to meet with him on American soil, perhaps in Alaska. Then he wondered about the advisability of meeting with Churchill prior to the summit, since Stalin might perceive this as "ganging up" on the Soviet Union.

Bohlen replied that it would be better to meet Stalin near Moscow where the Soviet leader could keep in touch with the government, since much of the failure of the Yalta agreements could be attributed to the opposition Stalin encountered upon his return to the Kremlin. Bohlen later regretted this piece of advice, realizing that he had failed to convey accurately the total control Stalin had over Soviet decision making. Luckily, Bohlen's error made little difference in determining the meeting site. On the question of a preliminary meeting with Churchill, Bohlen speculated that it might have a salutary effect. The Russians, he suggested, considered close relations between the United States and Great Britain to be "in the logic of things" and might make Stalin "more reasonable."[37]

If nothing else, Truman was impressed with the urgency for such a meeting, but still it was delayed until 16 July at Potsdam, a suburb of Berlin within the Russian occupation zone. With the European war over and with expectations that the war in the Pacific would soon come to an end, Bohlen detected "a sense of relaxation, an absence of compulsion, and with this absence, a freer exchange of opinions" at these meetings. The personnel in the American delegation had changed from the previous conference. James Byrnes had replaced Stettinius as secretary of state on 3 July. Bohlen as a consequence now found himself more removed from the inner circle, being excluded, for example, from the private meetings between Byrnes and Truman. Byrnes had decided to act as his own White House liaison. But Bohlen still served as interpreter, advisor on Soviet affairs, and, along with Harriman, as a representative on the committee to draw up the final Polish agreement.[38]

On the trip to Potsdam aboard the *Augusta,* Bohlen had joined others in the State Department in briefing Truman and Byrnes daily. Still, as Bohlen would discover, Truman was not fully prepared for what he would encounter. The conference served as a learning experience for the president, even though its outcome was little more successful than Yalta. First, a Council of Foreign Ministers was established to work out peace treaties with the defeated countries. Second, Yalta had called for a joint occupation of Germany and had set up a commission to meet in Moscow to arrange reparations, but no reparations agreement had been concluded. Bohlen and others were alarmed that the Russians were taking advantage of this lack of an accord to strip "every area they are in of all movable goods under the pretext of war booty, while still demanding exorbitant reparations." So a formula was hammered out to coordinate the exchange of industrial and agricultural goods between the zones. Still, the reparations question persisted. Third, the appeal of a Polish delegation led by Mikolajczyk, which argued the case for Poland, resulted only in the Big Three allowing the Polish western border to stand as the Soviet Union wanted, pending final peace treaties.[39]

Aside from the European situation, the Pacific war particularly concerned Truman and was one of the first orders of business. Bohlen was present at the cordial first meeting between Stalin and Truman on 17 July when Stalin said that he had met with T. V. Soong and had agreed on the determination of Outer Mongolia. While obstacles remained on the status of Manchurian railroads and of Port Arthur and Dairen, Stalin expressed confidence that the Soviet Union would be prepared to enter the war by the middle of August.[40]

A new element in America's Pacific plans had been introduced the day before, however. Truman had received word that the atomic bomb had been successfully detonated in a test. The introduction of the bomb raised the possibility that not only could the Pacific war be ended

Bohlen, H. Freeman Matthews, James Byrnes, and Ben Cohen aboard the *Augusta* en route to Potsdam conference. (Courtesy Harry S Truman Library.)

quickly, but also that Soviet participation might not be essential. Suspicious of Soviet intentions, Truman nonetheless was determined to maintain allied cooperation, and after he received details of the test, he decided to inform Stalin. Following the plenary session on 24 July, he left Bohlen behind and casually walked around the table to speak with Stalin and Pavlov, his interpreter. Bohlen was impressed by the offhand expression on Stalin's face. He even wondered if Stalin understood clearly what Truman was telling him.[41]

This was certainly important news for the Russians. The potential shortening of the war compelled them to expedite negotiations with the Chinese. Bohlen doubted that the bomb was solely responsible for Soviet entry into the Pacific war, but it probably hastened the process.[42]

Truman also wrestled with the question of how to inform the Japanese of the new weapon, for the possibility existed that faced with the threat of the bomb's use the Japanese might be persuaded to surrender without further unnecessary destruction. State Department officials, particularly Joseph Grew, a recognized authority on Japan, argued that if Truman's declaration to Japan included a provision that the Japanese could retain their emperor, the Japanese government might be persuaded to surrender. Grew based his argument on the reverence the

Japanese held for the emperor. The draft ultimatum the State Department prepared reflected Grew's position, but this position went counter to the unconditional surrender doctrine that Roosevelt had promulgated as one of the basic tenets of the war effort. In arguing his case, Grew was dismayed that Bohlen spoke against including any such guarantee in Truman's letter. According to Grew, Bohlen opposed any provisions which might be construed as a desire on the part of the United States to end the war prior to Russian entry.[43] Bohlen also opposed guaranteeing the emperor's retention because, if the ultimatum failed to bring Japan's surrender and the fighting was prolonged, it would in Bohlen's estimation be "very bad propaganda" to have the United States committed to retaining the emperor.[44]

Truman weighed the advice he received, then with British collaboration issued an ultimatum to the Japanese on 26 July 1945. (The Russians were not a party to this declaration since they still had a nonaggression pact with the Japanese. Nevertheless, Truman kept Stalin apprised of what transpired.) Truman's message followed closely the State Department draft, but it excluded the provision for the retention of the emperor.[45] It is unclear how much influence Bohlen's advice had on Truman's ultimate decision. It is clear, however, that Grew's contention about Bohlen—that he opposed recognizing the emperor in order to avoid conveying the impression that the United States was intentionally trying to prevent Russian entry into the Pacific war—would provide ammunition for those who would later attack Bohlen when he was nominated as ambassador to the Soviet Union.[46]

Potsdam had attempted to sustain cooperation among the major powers. But this cooperation rapidly dissipated as the war drew quickly to an end. The atomic bombs were detonated at Hiroshima on 6 August and at Nagasaki on 9 August. The Soviet Union entered the Pacific conflict on 8 August. The Japanese surrendered on 2 September. The war was over, and all that now remained was to conclude the peace treaties.

Between the Yalta and Potsdam conferences, Bohlen had seen his role shift as Truman replaced Roosevelt. His skepticism about the future of Soviet-American relations was reinforced even as his hope was sorely tested. At the same time that Bohlen saw more clearly how national interest explained Soviet demands, the wide divergence between American and Soviet interests revealed how difficult compromise would be. After Japan's surrender, Bohlen would have to come to grips with the legacy of these wartime arrangements.

4.

THE FUTILITY OF DIPLOMACY

Efforts to structure a world based on cooperation proved an exercise in diplomatic futility when the war ended. National interest, the same force that drove the allies together to defeat Hitler, now split them apart. Contrasting viewpoints on various issues, including the appropriate treatment for Germany and the disposition of Eastern Europe, particularly Poland, reflected these growing differences. The United Nations, struggling for credibility, never succeeded in overcoming these nationalist impulses. Furthermore, although the atomic bomb created an aura of terror, it was a device too devastating to be successfully utilized as an effective weapon in the diplomatic arena.

Postwar negotiations served to clarify some of Bohlen's longstanding apprehensions. Still striving for diplomatic solutions, he would soon admit that the potential for diplomacy was limited. Since Roosevelt's death, Bohlen's influence in high places had declined as Hopkins and then Stettinius, both of whom had seen the value of a liaison between the White House and State Department, left the scene. Just before Potsdam, Stettinius had been replaced by James Byrnes, an independent-minded former senator from South Carolina who was his own man, choosing to carry on his own liaison and occasionally even deciding to negotiate without keeping the White House informed—a tendency which contributed to friction with the president and to Byrnes's resignation by 1947.

As Byrnes became involved in the deliberations of the Council of Foreign Ministers, however, he began to rely increasingly on State Department expertise. Bohlen was taken into his confidence.[1] While Bohlen was never as close to Byrnes as he had been to Hopkins or would later be to George Marshall, Bohlen's views were at least heard and considered, if not always clearly understood, as Byrnes tried to guide American foreign policy.

Byrnes's first major task after Potsdam was the foreign ministers meeting which convened in London on 11 September 1945. Intended to formulate peace treaties with the lesser members of the German coalition—Finland, Italy, Bulgaria, Rumania, and Hungary—before proceeding to what promised to be a monumental task, the German settlement, the conference quickly dissolved into controversy. Narrowly interpreting the Potsdam decision that countries which had signed armistices with the defeated countries would be signatories to the treaties,[2] the Soviet Union argued, contrary to the United States and Great Britain, that France and China should be excluded from the discussion of these treaties. Disputes erupted over the Italo-Yugoslav border, trusteeships for the Italian colonies, and the Japanese question. Finally, the United States refused to recognize the governments dominated by Communists in Bulgaria and Rumania.

This last point proved particularly vexing. Hoping to elicit a compromise, Byrnes had made a two-pronged proposal. He refused to negotiate a treaty covering Bulgaria and Rumania until governments broadly representative of all democratic elements had been established. At the same time, to soothe Soviet fears, he offered a twenty-five year four-power security treaty against German remilitarization to be linked with Soviet guarantees to withdraw from Eastern Europe. Bohlen, joined by John Foster Dulles, the Republican party representative on the delegation, opposed the first part of this scheme. The two correctly argued that the U.S. proposal would force the Soviet Union into a rigid stance in support of the Bulgarian and the Rumanian regimes, making an agreement with the Soviet Union nearly impossible.[3] But Dulles and Bohlen failed to sway Byrnes.

While Byrnes was rigid in his determination to oppose recognition of the governments in Bulgaria and Rumania, he took a different position on Hungary. Hungarian elections had produced a government with Communists in the minority. Byrnes viewed this as evidence of the elections' validity, so he was inclined to endorse American recognition. Once again, however, Bohlen and Dulles questioned Byrnes's position. Although they agreed with the assertion that Hungary had a legitimate and viable government, they were worried about the effect that singling Hungary out for special consideration might have on the negotiations, especially the use the Soviet delegation could make of it. The move could be a strong bargaining point and a valuable piece of propaganda for the Soviets.

Bohlen's and Dulles's admonitions were again ignored. Soon after the

London meeting, the United States extended recognition to Hungary. And as the two had predicted, Molotov on subsequent occasions would argue that the United States had chosen to recognize Hungary, but not Rumania and Bulgaria, because the elections held in the latter two countries had gone contrary to America's expectations.[4] However one evaluated the reasons for the American decision on recognition, Bohlen had realized that the American stance would convey just that impression and that the Soviet Union could derive considerable propaganda value from it, weakening the American position at the negotiating table.

This stand on recognition was clearly indicative of Bohlen's determination that all consequences of diplomatic decisions should be carefully considered. His understanding of the Soviet Union had tempered his optimism with a healthy caution during the Roosevelt years and constantly alerted him to possible areas of accommodation with the Soviet Union during the postwar period. The United States, he believed, should not act precipitously. A few days after the collapse of the first Council of Foreign Ministers session in London, for example, he counseled Byrnes that during this period every foreign policy decision would inevitably have a bearing on American relations with the Soviet Union. Using the question of the control machinery for Japan and a proposed loan to the U.S.S.R. as cases in point, Bohlen suggested that the United States do nothing "unconsciously" to make "the adjustment of our present differences" more difficult. The "Russian mentality" might misinterpret unconnected initiatives around the world "as evidence of a carefully thought out diplomatic offensive against Soviet interests reflecting a basic change in American policy."[5]

Careful consideration was essential. Bohlen comprehended the Soviet mind better than most in the State Department, yet with the shifts in day-to-day events, even he admitted a degree of uncertainty about the wisest direction for American policy. He, along with the rest of the department, was groping for some coherent policy.

As Bohlen assessed the situation, the Soviet Union was losing influence in Europe. The failure of what he called Soviet "stooge groups," a derogatory reference to Communist party members throughout Europe who blindly did the bidding of the Kremlin, the looting and removal of property, and the actions of the N.K.V.D. and native police were forcing the Russians, within the effective range of the Soviet army, to choose between more repressive measures or abandoning some control to groups considered hostile or dangerous. In areas beyond direct Soviet military control, Russian popularity seemed greater, but "stooge groups" seemed to have reached "the peak of their power and influence." The Soviets, therefore, had to recognize that their influence in

Western Europe would in the long run probably be weaker than that of the western democracies. And in Central and Eastern Europe, Soviet control would have to be based less on "friendly" political groupings and more on sheer military force, "less subtle and more direct." Bohlen concluded that they would be compelled to follow one of three courses: acquiesce and let the regimes become more representative; back up their "stooge groups" with the application of direct military force; or do nothing for the moment, hoping that the United States and its adversaries would make a mistake, at the same time using propaganda and pressure groups to confuse and discredit those challenging the Communist regimes in Central and Eastern Europe.

Bohlen ventured the guess that for the immediate future the Soviet Union would follow the third course, resorting only in extreme cases to the second. He warned, however, that the Kremlin, obsessed with maintaining internal control and national defense, recognized total domination of its immediate neighbors as the only certain way of insuring Soviet security.[6]

In light of this evaluation, Bohlen described America's major task as one "of integrating the policies of a dictatorship, directed virtually exclusively towards the furtherance of the national interest of the Soviet state, with the principles of world cooperation and international morality essential to the development of a peaceful and stable world." He noted that, while Soviet policy was not conducive to this, an evolutionary change could take place. But this evolution depended on the initiative and tactics of the United States.

Bohlen could see that Soviet policy left several options open for the United States. First, it could accept the Soviet thesis that future peace should be maintained by close cooperation among the three major powers, thus allowing for "the delimitation of the national interest of the three powers concerned and the division by agreement of the world into spheres of influence with a free hand for each of the three powers in their respective spheres of influence." He admitted that this step might be best for the immediate future, but it would turn the United Nations into a "facade," it would take a backward step from the principle of cooperation, which would not sit well with the American people, and it would only postpone the "eventual" clash with the Soviet Union under infinitely worse conditions.

A second option was to meet Soviet nationalism and expansionism with a "purely nationalist policy" based on the pursuit of American interests. This approach would include attaining strategic bases while attempting to limit Soviet expansion and acquisition. Such a course would not necessitate public repudiation of the United Nations, but would lead to a series of disputes with the Soviet Union on a purely nationalistic basis. Bohlen's particular fear was that this course would be adopted unconsciously. As it turned out, it was adopted consciously after 1947 as the containment policy was institutionalized.

Bohlen favored a third option, "full, vigorous support" for the principles of world cooperation. Only when American security interests were seriously impaired should the United States act on a purely nationalistic basis. World cooperation offered the best "platform" and "means" of dealing with Soviet policies. He referred, for example, to the case of the dispute at the London meetings over the Italian colonies when the United States sought to place them under United Nations mandate. Since the Soviet Union had subscribed to the principles of the Atlantic Charter and the United Nations, the U.S.S.R.'s withdrawal from the U.N. would be its own responsibility and would place the onus of furthering the cold war on Russia, elevating the United States to a position of moral leadership. Pursuing this third option would leave the Soviet Union the choice between "genuine cooperation" and a "self-imposed isolationism."[7] Bohlen opposed abandoning international cooperation precipitously and still supported the United Nations, but primarily as a vehicle for American foreign policy. Encouraging world cooperation would enhance American prestige and deflect much of world criticism to the Soviet Union.

Soviet influence in Eastern Europe was clearly the most pressing issue. Bohlen did not deny that the Soviets were heading in the direction of absolute control of the internal and external affairs of these countries. Furthermore, he conceded that Russian influence would ultimately lead to the abolition of world cooperation and the division of the world into spheres of influence. Still, he acknowledged the legitimate interests of the Soviet Union in Eastern Europe.[8]

Faced with this reality and already having tried to promote Soviet cooperation in the early Council of Foreign Ministers meeting, Bohlen began to see things differently from his views after the Yalta conference. Prior to that summit, Kennan had frankly suggested dividing the world into spheres of influence. Bohlen had responded negatively then because the impact of the Roosevelt approach was still a matter of conjecture. Soviet-American cooperation, however tenuous, had not broken down. Now Bohlen could see the need for and the legitimacy of spheres. This was no reversal in his thinking, but the culmination of a thought process which had been evolving since he had participated in the postwar planning committees during World War II.[9] With Soviet intentions much clearer, Bohlen wondered if the best course for the

United States might be to accept the situation as it existed and hope it would inspire Soviet goodwill in other diplomatic areas.

In an 18 October 1945 memorandum addressed to Secretary Byrnes, Bohlen warned of Soviet movement in Eastern Europe and distinguished between "exclusive spheres of influence," which entailed domination of all phases of the external and internal life of the Eastern European countries, and the "legitimate prerogative" of a great power over smaller countries which were geographically contiguous. He granted the Soviet Union its "legitimate influence" in the area, but carefully differentiated that from illegitimate domination and absolute control, citing as an example the relationship between the United States and Latin America.

Unlike Kennan's pre-Yalta suggestion, however, Bohlen's idea of spheres did not simply write off Eastern Europe. Bohlen emphasized that the United States had to make it clear to the Soviet Union that it "would not only not encourage but would actively discourage any attempts on the part of these states [Eastern Europe] to conclude political or military alliances or join combinations of political or military nature to which the Soviet Union was not a party." The American government, nevertheless, would oppose any illegitimate extension of Soviet influence. Bohlen's main concern was that the "Soviet mind" could not discern the difference between "legitimate and illegitimate influence," between "influence" and "domination," or between "friendly government" and a "puppet government." America, he warned, had to follow a "consistent," "patient," and "firm" policy, showing the Soviet Union that American cooperation could be insured only if it limited its influence to the legitimate sphere. This American posture would help strengthen factions in the Soviet government which favored modification in the domination of Eastern Europe and at the same time would give warning to those in favor of a more aggressive policy.[10]

Bohlen was not alone in advocating "open spheres." It was a pragmatic appraisal of the world situation, granting to the Soviet Union its legitimate interests while reinforcing the principles American foreign policy held so important. This was the type of advice Byrnes was receiving as he turned more to Bohlen in the aftermath of the frustrating London meetings.[11]

Much of Bohlen's effort to delineate a viable policy toward the Soviet Union was capsulized in a report entitled "The Capabilities and Intentions of the Soviet Union as Affected by American Policy," a document written by Bohlen and Geroid T. Robinson, a professor of Russian studies from Columbia University serving temporarily in the State Department. The first draft was completed in December with a revised version submitted in February 1946. This document was the end product of the deliberations of a committee set up in October of 1945 by Undersecretary of State Dean Acheson. Acheson charged the group with finding a focus within the department on the proper approach to Soviet-American relations. As submitted, the report constituted a realistic, cautious, and somewhat tentative assessment of Soviet intentions and how they would be affected by American policy. It took the middle road between the old Rooseveltian inclination to cooperate with the Soviet Union and the policy which was ultimately adopted by 1947, the containment of communism.

The report outlined conditions as they existed in 1945 and predicted how they would evolve. Acknowledging that the situation was a complex one, the authors looked at what might be called the military balance between the United States and the Soviet Union. Due in large part to the American monopoly of the atomic bomb, they judged the United States as definitely superior, predicting that it would take five to ten years for the Soviet Union to catch up, given the fact that that country faced immense postwar devastation both in terms of capital and population.

Looking toward the future, Bohlen and Robinson foresaw three possible periods in Soviet-American relations. "Period I" would be a time of American predominance, lasting until the Soviets developed the atomic bomb. "Period II" would be an era of uncertainty regarding the balance of capabilities when both possessed the bomb, the ability to produce it, a volume of production essentially equal, but no effective means of "neutralizing" it. "Period III" would come when one or both possessed the defensive means to neutralize the bomb. They described the task ahead as finding some acceptable policy during "Period I" which would ease the tension and uncertainty in the ensuing two periods.

Conceding that national interest played a dominant role in Soviet decisions, the report pointed to ideology as a complicating factor worthy of serious consideration. Russian foreign policy would always be that of the party leadership. This made the chief problem one of predicting, not necessarily the objective comparison of capabilities, but the "subjective conception" the Soviet leaders had of relations with the non-Soviet states. This latter was confused by the traditional suspicion among nation states, as well as Soviet communism, which was in a condition of flux. Marxism postulated inevitable conflict with the capitalist world, and at the same time contained "obscure" and "contradictory" ideas determining the strategy of compromise and confrontation.

Ideology, the authors emphasized, could always be modified when the Soviets needed allies. But it was wrong to assume that the Soviet leaders would not to a certain extent interpret the actions and motives of the West from a Marxian perspective. At the least, ideology would lead them to construe even friendly overtures by non-Soviet states as "sinister and to arm more and expand more for the sake of security."

The report maintained that the American monopoly over atomic weaponry and its industrial superiority placed the Soviet Union in an inferior position at the same time that Soviet strength was waning in Eastern Europe, Western Europe, and Germany. But it warned that this situation could change if something were not done to improve economic conditions in Europe.

Bearing this in mind, Bohlen and Robinson proposed three policy options the United States might pursue during "Period I" to insure favorable conditions later. The authors took into account both the immediate and long-range relationship between the two powers. "Policy A" tended toward accommodation rather than confrontation, an effort to stabilize Soviet-American relations in several specific ways: by sharing without condition the knowledge for the peaceful use of atomic energy; by avoiding unilateral statements of principle which would promote uneasiness and uncertainty; by using diplomatic means to solve problems promptly and clearly, in most cases settling for less than America's superior position might secure; and by promoting economic and political reform in Europe and Asia to prevent the rise of revolutionary situations.

At the opposite pole, "Policy B" tended toward what would later be called containment. It entailed withholding all knowledge of atomic energy and exerting all pressure short of war to build a balance of power to check the Soviet Union, regardless of what Soviet intentions might be. A third alternative, which the report really did not advocate, was to keep relations "indeterminate" and "fluid" by vacillating between the two preceding policies.

Bohlen and Robinson were inclined to support "Policy A," although they admitted that course would be fraught with risks. They were unsure what the Soviet response might be when faced with this approach. They were certain, however, that if the Soviet leaders were bent on expansion, a likelihood close analysis did not substantiate, "Policy B" would be justified. But that policy, they warned, would fix Soviet intentions, lead to Soviet aggressiveness, and appeal to revolutionary forces, creating a very dangerous situation.[12] Although the report was speculative and failed to reach definite conclusions, emphasizing the uncertainty of analyzing Soviet intentions and the risks and advantages of various American policy options, Bohlen and Robinson clearly favored a compromise, but one based on America maintaining and utilizing its strength in relation to the Soviet Union.

The draft report circulated in the department as Bohlen traveled with Byrnes to the Moscow foreign ministers conference and then to London for the first United Nations General Assembly meeting. By the time Bohlen submitted the final report in February 1946, Byrnes's ill-fated Moscow concessions had aroused adverse reactions within the government and among the American public, and support for continued cooperation with the Soviet Union was on the wane. But Bohlen did not succumb to this alarm. In his final report, he reaffirmed the analysis of the earlier draft. He did add, however, a realistic option which he felt might allow the United States to respond effectively to the growing Soviet challenge while not abandoning its commitment to the United Nations and to cooperation rather than conflict to solve world problems. The American government, he suggested, could support the non-Communist left, the "NCL." He argued that the Social Democrats, leftist labor unions, and other such groups in Europe were deserving of support if they showed themselves committed to the principles of civil and political liberties. Backing these groups might be one viable method of countering in-roads the Soviet Union was making in Europe.[13]

While this was a realistic approach, attempting to avoid confrontation, Bohlen failed to sway many of the policy makers, most of whom were moving toward an alternative compromise, more along the lines of "Policy B" than "Policy A," for several reasons. Not only was Bohlen's writing tentative and cautious, less persuasive and assertive than Kennan's alarmist "long telegram," which would appear shortly after Bohlen's final report was submitted, but also the adverse impact of Byrnes's concessions at Moscow was felt both in the department and in the White House.[14] Thus the department began to lean toward containment.

The pivotal Moscow conference, which evoked such a reaction in policy-making circles, was Byrnes's brainchild. Frustrated by the lack of progress at London, Byrnes was determined to find a way to break the stalemate. He was not prepared to admit failure. As he sat at his desk in the department on Thanksgiving Day trying to clear up a backlog of business, it occurred to him that the impasse might be surmounted if the foreign ministers of the three major powers were to meet in Moscow, where Stalin would be close by to be approached in case of difficulty. He immediately called Bohlen, who was visiting his family in South Carolina, and ordered him back to Washington to prepare for the trip.[15]

Byrnes's delegation left for Moscow in mid-December, the secretary eager to get the negotiations on track again. After stopovers in France and Germany, Bohlen was pressed into service translating between a Russian navigator and American pilot as the delegation's plane was caught in a blinding snowstorm en route to the Soviet capital. Bohlen endured a hectic period of translating instructions from Russian flight controllers before the plane finally broke through the clouds, to Bohlen's relief, and landed at an airstrip near Moscow.

Quickly recovered from the harrowing experience of the flight, Byrnes rushed into ten days of talks beginning on 16 December. His agenda was full, including preliminary discussion of plans for the possible control of atomic energy and several issues dealing with the postwar situation in the Far East. But of utmost importance to the future of treaty negotiations were two items which had plagued the London meeting—the role France and China would play in the treaty process and the U.S. recognition of the Bulgarian and Rumanian governments. As Byrnes had planned when he prepared for the Moscow trip, he resorted to direct appeals to Stalin to resolve both.

The first of these meetings took place on the night of 18 December. Byrnes took Harriman and Bohlen along as he tried to reason with the Soviet dictator. All the diplomatic language aside, Byrnes was so intent upon getting somewhere that he essentially capitulated to Soviet wishes. He proposed that France and China, neither of which had signed the armistices for all of the defeated countries in question, would be excluded from drafting the treaties; but the full Council of Foreign Ministers would call a larger peace conference, which would include France and China, to review and make recommendations on draft treaties drawn up by the Big Three. This advice would then be taken into consideration when the three powers met again to finalize the treaties. Stalin seemed unmoved that night, but to Bohlen's amazement, Molotov received a call from Stalin the next day during a formal negotiating session, and the Soviet delegation quickly decided to accept the American proposal.[16]

The status of the treaties with Bulgaria, Rumania, and Hungary was more difficult. At London, Bohlen had objected to Byrnes's refusal to discuss treaties with Rumania and Bulgaria until they had governments the United States deemed broadly representative. Bohlen was particularly worried that such rigidity would preclude diplomatic solutions. He recalled that a Soviet diplomat had asked him at London why

Byrnes did not live up to the American reputation of "horse trading," an obvious indication that the Soviets themselves were concerned about Byrnes's hard line.[17]

By the time of the Moscow meeting, Bohlen, as well as Harriman, had reached the conclusion that the United States could no longer gain anything by continuing to resist an extant situation, particularly since the Soviet army occupied Eastern Europe. Furthermore, the precedent of the Hungarian recognition weakened the American case. Both diplomats were, therefore, prepared to accept tacitly the governments of Bulgaria and Rumania without relinquishing American principles.

Swayed by such advice, Byrnes exceeded their counsel, executing a major shift from his rigid London stance. He became the horse trader he had not been at London. Once again, he took Harriman and Bohlen along on a nocturnal visit to Stalin on 23 December. After some preliminary discussion, Byrnes somewhat precipitously agreed to an arrangement whereby Stalin would advise Bulgaria to include a couple of non-Communist representatives in its government. In addition, a delegation representing the three powers would go to Rumania to discuss the situation with the elected government and try to reach some accommodation. Stalin then promised future free elections to assuage American principles. Byrnes had virtually conceded to the Soviet position. More discussion in the formal sessions ensued, but this basic agreement became the framework for the final settlement.

Harriman and Bohlen were far less elated with the solution than was Byrnes. The U.S. received only token concessions while Stalin tightened his hold on Eastern Europe. Not only had Byrnes exceeded what they had advised, but he had also, in their view, paid a high price for the settlement.[18] While the deadlock might have been broken, paving the way for another meeting of the full Council of Foreign Ministers in Paris during April 1946, the settlement angered Truman and evoked a negative response in the United States.

While Stalin apparently had the better of Byrnes in Moscow, such was not to be the case when the United Nations took up Iran's problems. As the treaty negotiations proceeded, Bohlen accompanied Byrnes to the first session of the United Nations General Assembly (10 January–14 February 1946). Intended essentially as an organizational meeting, it proved another forum for Soviet-American confrontation when the issue of Soviet troops in Iran was raised. At Teheran in 1943, Roosevelt, Churchill, and Stalin had agreed that the three nations would occupy Iran during the war to protect vital supply lines, but that they would withdraw within three months after the cessation of hostilities. When the war in Europe ended, however, the Soviet Union delayed its withdrawal. The Kremlin argued that the deadline was from the date of Japan's defeat, a contention Bohlen admitted was technically correct. [19] Meanwhile, the Soviets were supporting a revolt in the northern Iranian province of Azerbaijan, hoping that this province might ultimately be incorporated into the Soviet Union.

Bohlen was not surprised by the Iranian confrontation. As early as the fall of 1944, he had predicted an impending crisis after the Iranians had broken off negotiations for Soviet oil concessions. The Soviet press at that time had accused the Iranians of acting "contrary to public opinion in Iran." To Bohlen, this was a "disturbing indication" of the Soviet attitude. He was further concerned by an article in *Trud,* the publication of the Soviet trade unions, which made no mention of the oil concession question, but accused the Iranian government "of tolerating and encouraging acts of sabotage of the flow of supplies to the Soviet Union" by "pro-Fascist elements" in that country and "persecution" of officials who were carrying out their obligations to the allies. "This article," Bohlen wrote, had "all the customary elements of the build-up in order to justify extreme Soviet pressure if not action against the present Iranian Government." In view of these tactics, he suggested that the American government formulate a policy in advance of a crisis. [20]

The Iranian issue had fallen on deaf ears during the Moscow meeting in December 1945. So on 19 January 1946, with the support of the United States, Iran appealed to the Security Council which at the time deferred action since the Soviet Union and Iran were negotiating. When no settlement resulted, the Security Council took up the matter.

Throughout this episode, Bohlen had urged caution, especially when considering threats to move the Soviets. The American capacity to back up threats in the Middle East was limited, and the Soviets might call America's bluff. Bohlen felt it better to save the confrontation for Europe. But Byrnes chose to get tough, and he succeeded. [21]

In this first encounter in the United Nations, Iran emerged victorious with the help of the United States. After Iran formally protested Soviet activities on 5 March, the Soviet Union bowed to pressure. It withdrew its troops in May after receiving two apparent concessions: a joint Soviet-Iranian oil company (pending the approval of the Iranian Majlis) and a promise of autonomy for Azerbaijan. Following Soviet withdrawal the Majlis rejected the joint oil company, and Iran reestablished its control over Azerbaijan.

Russian actions toward Iran epitomized for Bohlen the absence of morality in Soviet foreign policy. He recalled that, during a dinner given by Byrnes at the end of the Security Council session, Molotov expressed puzzlement at American actions in support of Iran. Molotov asked Byrnes what overstaying a treaty agreement or a few thousand troops were among friends and allies. He suggested that, had the United States done the same in Mexico, the Soviet Union certainly would not have complained. Byrnes replied that both nations were signatories of the United Nations charter, a fact they could not ignore simply out of convenience.[22]

Bohlen's participation in the diplomatic exchanges during 1946 profoundly affected his outlook toward future relations with the Soviet Union. The precedents established by the U.S.-Soviet agreements offered little hope for closer cooperation. At different points during his career, and under different circumstances, he focused on various origins for the cold war, once even proposing that it began in 1917 when the Bolsheviks seized control of the Russian government. Whatever the starting point, cold war divisions were extant by 1946. As the negotiations were increasingly frustrated, leaders on both sides voiced their growing distrust of the other's actions. In February 1946, George Kennan sent his famous long telegram from Moscow, admonishing Washington to be wary of Soviet intentions, an admonition which served as the basis for his article on "The Sources of Soviet Conduct," published in the July 1947 issue of *Foreign Affairs*. In the spring of 1946, Winston Churchill traveled to Fulton, Missouri, accompanied by Harry Truman, to give a commencement address at Westminster College. Churchill warned of the iron curtain descending on Eastern Europe and exhorted the western nations to cooperate to oppose this growing Communist threat.

Yet Bohlen looked upon an "election speech" given by Stalin, which preceded both Kennan's and Churchill's remarks, as the true declaration of the cold war. Stalin reminded his people that, despite wartime cooperation, they were still committed to communism. To Bohlen, Stalin was bringing his people back to reality, turning away from what wartime required of the Soviet state to what the exigencies of the postwar world and the survival of the Stalinist system demanded. Stalin blamed the war on the uneven development of capitalism and postulated that no long-term permanent peace could exist until capitalism was destroyed, a traditional Marxist-Leninist viewpoint.[23]

Bohlen may have been a voice of moderation, attempting to influence Byrnes in order to avoid needless confrontation. But at the same time, he was acutely aware of how tenuous relations were with that totalitarian state. Thus when George Kennan sent his long telegram, Bohlen found much he could agree with, though he still had not reached Kennan's point of despair. In a memorandum of 13 March 1946, Bohlen acknowledged that Kennan had done an admirable job of analyzing the motives of the Soviet leadership. He agreed that Kennan's assertion that the United States faced an expanding totalitarian state acting on the premise that the world was irreconcilably divided into two hostile camps could be taken as an accepted principle. Unfortunately, the West worked on the contrary proposition that there was no reason the two sides could not peacefully coexist as long as neither attempted to expand its own area by forcible means. He delineated Soviet offensive moves into two categories: first, the threat to use or the use of military force, at the time confined to areas contiguous to the Soviet Union; second, the use of Communist parties and front organizations to exploit every weakness in the non-Soviet world through "political psychology," thus rendering the West incapable of resisting expansionist Soviet policy.

The two policies, according to Bohlen, had to be treated differently. To oppose the former, the United Nations was the best instrument, particularly while Russian military power concentrated on Eastern Europe. Once again Bohlen was presenting the United Nations more as an instrument of American policy than as a viable force with a life of its own. But even at that time he was growing pessimistic of the effectiveness and future potential of that organization, which, he hypothesized, would break down under the test of Soviet aggression. Nevertheless, initially using it would pave the way for the United States and like-minded nations to take appropriate actions. Beyond this point, especially in the event that Soviet power began to extend further west, the military establishment had to be brought to an adequate state of efficiency in order to preserve peace. The second part of the Communist threat could be met by countering Communist party activity with positive programs demonstrating that the non-Soviet system had more to offer than the "false promise of communism" did.[24]

The positive programs Bohlen endorsed included economic and political assistance for Western Europe. He also returned to a tactic he had first proposed in February, suggesting that one of the best ways to serve American interests was to support the "NCL," the non-Communist left in Europe—the Labor party in England and the Social Democrats on the continent. Although such a proposal was fraught with domestic political dangers, especially given the increasingly conservative atmosphere in the United States, the suggestion had merit. As one diplomat attracted to Bohlen's proposal put it in an unsigned memorandum,

> the reasoning is obvious. The non-Communist left . . . has a program calculated to accomplish the social objectives which the Communists claim as theirs. Only the NCL can oppose Soviet expansion without laying itself open to the charge of serving reactionary interests. Only the NCL can command

the broad basis of popular support that is necessary successfully to resist Soviet expansion.[25]

Byrnes, however, was not wholly convinced by Bohlen's argument; the secretary feared the repercussions of interfering in another country's internal affairs, but this pragmatic approach would be a part of the Marshall plan and other later American initiatives toward Europe.[26]

As Bohlen was striving to understand and reach a reasonable policy faced with the deterioration of Soviet-American relations, he continued his diplomatic travels with Byrnes. The concessions Byrnes had made at Moscow might have been maligned in the press, in the White House, and in Congress, but they did lead to another meeting of the full Council of Foreign Ministers in Paris beginning on 25 April 1946. The next six months Bohlen spent in Paris were busy ones. Since Byrnes had come to rely on Bohlen more and trusted his judgment, the secretary delegated Bohlen his press liaison. Bohlen now had the difficult task of explaining the negotiations to the press and through them to the American public.[27] As in the past, these discussions did not proceed smoothly, with the question of the Italo-Yugoslav border and the rightful claimant to the city of Trieste being at issue. After the border had been arranged and Trieste designated a free city under the auspices of the United Nations, a peace conference was convened (29 July–15 October 1946), attended by twenty-one nations.[28] Following their actions, the treaties were referred to the foreign ministers in New York from 4 November to 11 December.

But the Italo-Yugoslav issue cropped up once again, adding to Bohlen's growing frustration and pessimism and leading to an eventful meeting between Molotov and Byrnes, the result of which paved the way for the completion of the treaties. Bohlen's recollection of this encounter evidently reflected his growing feeling that the U.S. should stand up to the Soviet Union if any meaningful progress was going to be made, for his recollections—and those of Byrnes—differed in emphasis from the official account. As Bohlen recalled, Byrnes took him along to translate during a meeting in Molotov's hotel room on 25 November. There, Byrnes, a "smooth" operator, subtly threatened the Soviet foreign minister by declaring that, given the status of negotiations, the two powers should give up on trying to complete these treaties and go on to the German treaty. Bohlen, watching Molotov, who typically stuttered when excited, remembered that Molotov implored Byrnes not to be hasty and to wait until the afternoon session, at which time the two sides were able to set in motion discussions which led to the completion of the treaties.

The official record, however, differs somewhat. In response to Byrnes's call to terminate negotiations, Molotov was apparently concerned, but noted the Soviet need to do something to appease the Yugoslavs. Discussions followed in which the two haggled over the components of a settlement, culminating in a position at least acceptable to both sides.[29]

While the outcome of both accounts was the same, a series of less than totally satisfactory treaties with Germany's allies, Bohlen's impressions betray a diplomat who felt that a resolute tone was required to jar the Soviet Union into cooperation, a tone that was obviously lacking in Byrnes's Moscow concessions, but which had led to results when the Iranian crisis was brought before the United Nations. Perhaps Byrnes's approach was a sly diplomatic move, but it was accompanied by compromise, not capitulation by the Soviets.

As an advisor on Soviet matters, as an interpreter, and as Byrnes's press liaison, Bohlen had for fifteen months watched these discussions evolve. Cognizant of their shortcomings, he could not help but see these treaties as at least a start. Yet there was a long way to go. Bohlen agreed with Byrnes that the accords were not the most satisfactory settlements, but they were the best that the Council of Foreign Ministers could agree upon unanimously. "When they enter into effect, despite their imperfections, they will be the first real step forward toward a return to the normal peacetime conditions for these countries," he predicted.

> They will bring to an end armistice regimes giving to the occupying powers almost unlimited control over the national life of these countries, and they will, in some cases, mean the complete withdrawal of and, in others, major reduction in the occupying forces which, since the end of the war, have imposed such heavy burdens on their national economies.[30]

Bohlen's remarks reflect more resignation than satisfaction. Little more could be accomplished on these lesser treaties, so the best course was to accept the inevitable, even though it did not significantly improve the lot of some of the Eastern European countries, and hope that America's compliance would reflect on the important treaty negotiations concerning Germany. The dissension which had characterized the negotiations to this point boded ill for the foreign ministers meeting planned for March 1947, however. Delay had worked to the advantage of the Soviet Union in establishing its control over Eastern Europe. Delay also seemed to be part of Stalin's plan for Germany.

Nineteen forty-six was a momentous year. While Stalin and Churchill were rhetorically bringing down the iron curtain, and while steps were being taken to merge the western zones of Germany, efforts were still afoot to reach some satisfactory solution to the East-West confrontation. Certainly Kennan's long telegram helped convince many within the United States government that a firm stance was imperative. In Bohlen's case, he had seen the problems in American relations with the Soviet Union, and he recognized the value of Kennan's pessimistic assessment, but he continued to insist that some limited accommodation could be reached incorporating the legitimate interests and concerns of all sides. It seemed, however, that the more the confrontation between the two powers developed, the more limited the possibilities of accommodation became.

James Byrnes was his own man, a quality that contributed to his ultimate alienation from Truman. With little diplomatic experience, he began to rely on many in the State Department, particularly Bohlen, for advice. Although he listened to Bohlen's insights, he did not always comprehend Bohlen's nuances and accepted his advice selectively. Byrnes's compromise on the Eastern European governments was a case in point. Bohlen was not happy with Byrnes's rather impulsive concessions, but they nonetheless corresponded more closely to Bohlen's quest for conciliation than Kennan's pessimistic call to divide Europe once and for all and confront the Soviet Union.

Through it all, Bohlen maintained that the United States had to formulate a clear and coherent policy and negotiate from a position of strength if it wanted diplomatic discussions to succeed. This did not mean rigid positions or overly provocative strength. Relations with the Soviet Union would be difficult, but discussions were proceeding despite the frustrations of 1945 and 1946.

5.

FORGING A POLICY

Charles Bohlen was once asked for his evaluation of a particularly hard-line draft of a presidential speech. He remarked that it was all well and good to make a point and get it adopted over the opposite point of view, namely that of the Soviet Union. But "let's never forget that we're going to have to live with some of these things for a long time, and that you never want to take too hard a position, so that if things change you will have some leaway [*sic*] for negotiation."[1] This observation epitomized his approach to diplomacy. Cognizant of Soviet intentions and frustrated by past encounters, he was still reluctant to burn his bridges. Inflexible positions might become a burden later. Not one to be optimistic about future American relations with the Soviet Union, he still believed that diplomacy could be relatively effective since the Soviet Union was a nation with certain national interests which could be exploited. Russia was a threat, but one which could be dealt with if its motivations were understood and if the West approached the negotiating table in a strong and stable political, economic, and military position.

Between the promulgation of the Truman Doctrine in 1947 and the ratification of the North Atlantic Treaty in 1949, the U.S. containment policy was institutionalized. James Byrnes had resigned as secretary of state partly because of the reaction to his compromise on the Eastern European question. Bohlen himself had advocated "open spheres of influence" in 1946, but had had problems with Byrnes's method of implementation. Although Truman had taken issue with Byrnes's concessions, the United States had virtually conceded that area of Europe as the Soviet sphere and was intent upon shoring up Western Europe, its own area of interest, at the time the Council of Foreign Ministers met again in 1947.

The open spheres approach not only entailed accepting a degree of Soviet predominance in Eastern Europe, but also it presented some important ramifications for the West. The American perception of a satisfactory postwar European settlement had to change. For reasons of principle as well as politics, the Truman administration to this point had outwardly espoused a negotiating stance predicated on a united and integrated Europe—both East and West—and a reunited German nation. With open spheres, American principles, such as the belief in self-determination for all people, had to yield to reality. The American government had to refocus its attention on strengthening its own sphere, Western Europe, against potential Kremlin moves. The United States also had to acknowledge that, given Soviet aims, a permanently divided Germany, with West Germany participating as an active member of Western European revitalization, was the only viable option for world stability.

Bohlen believed that between 1947 and 1949 the Truman administration adopted these policies, a course he was confident could work to America's advantage. The United States was economically dominant. The Soviet Union was not a crusading, irrational ideological movement, but a cautious, paranoid power, a power dominated by a dictator who, although ruthless, was pragmatic enough to respond to a stronger force. Diplomacy, Bohlen argued, could exploit this Soviet pragmatism.

James Byrnes's exit from the State Department accompanied the entrance of George C. Marshall, a man who impressed Bohlen with his sense of direction and leadership. The relationship between the two became so close that one colleague likened it to that of a father and son. Marshall was stern and demanding, yet Bohlen was touched by the human side of the secretary. In 1948, for instance, Bohlen and his wife had been in Paris for several weeks while Bohlen attended United Nations meetings. When Marshall came to Paris, he brought them a picture of himself taken with the Bohlens' two-year-old-son, Charles. The general was concerned that they had been separated from their children for an extended period.[2]

During the Marshall era, Bohlen reached the pinnacle of his influence, both as advisor on Soviet affairs and, beginning in 1947, as department counselor.[3] Marshall deferred to Bohlen's expertise in Soviet matters. The two thought similarly, thus reinforcing each other's perceptions on cold war policies.

Faced with the upcoming meeting of the Council of Foreign Ministers in Moscow, Marshall held briefing sessions with Bohlen and others to boil American policy down to what he called the "ten commandments," a synopsis of goals and intentions. He wanted to insure a degree of continuity in America's stance toward the Soviet Union. As H. Freeman Matthews, another of the carry-overs from the Byrnes era, remarked, when the delegation arrived in Moscow "Molotov [would], to his dismay, see a number of old familiar faces."[4]

Bohlen's feeling of frustration clearly influenced his outlook toward the Moscow meetings. Holding little hope for significant progress at the conference, on 11 February he advised looking beyond the immediate points of discussion, and focusing on "the larger question of the problem of the policies and purposes of the Soviet Union"—its determination to maintain the "totalitarian idea" in the areas where it already existed and to spread it to new ones. The whole Soviet intent was to create the "most favorable conditions" to spread this totalitarianism.

Bohlen exonerated the United States from blame for postwar conflicts while implicitly criticizing it for its naïvete, a naïvete he had accepted during the Roosevelt administration. He described the United States as trying "to do away with the divisions in Europe and to break down the so-called 'iron curtain' through the medium of agreement." America to this point had "on the whole avoided the adoption of measures which would further accentuate the present division of Europe as a permanent state of affairs." He argued that America's ends had not been achieved. Agreements like those made at Yalta and Potsdam had not hindered the Soviet Union, but had only slowed consolidation of Western Europe. Byrnes had decided to merge the British and American zones in Germany only after he realized that cooperative efforts to save the economic situation were not going to work.

The only hope for courting a favorable Soviet response, Bohlen said, was for the United States to take the initiative rather than merely react. Implementation of practicable measures by the western allies without reliance on the Soviet Union might improve the chances for agreement along the lines the United States desired.

He warned against going to Moscow seeking agreement for its own sake. Any arrangement had to be abundantly clear, "so as to leave no room for indirect violation through real or alleged differences of interpretation." A German accord should involve neither American concessions nor restrictions on American "liberty of action" without adequate safeguards. Only an Austrian treaty which called for the removal of all occupying forces would be acceptable.[5]

Bohlen's experience at the negotiating table had driven him to this skepticism. It was little wonder to him that, when the conference began, the major issues of German reparations and the ultimate reunification of that country could not be settled. Faced with this impasse, Marshall took what Bohlen saw as a crucial step in the delineation of American policy. On the night of 15 April, he summoned Bohlen and carried the United States' case directly to Stalin. The secretary came away from the meeting deeply affected by "Stalin's seeming indifference to the matters at hand." As Bohlen watched, Stalin criticized Marshall's pessimism and sense of urgency. To the Soviet leader, these were "only the first skirmishes and brushes of reconnaisance forces" on the German question. Bohlen noted that Stalin seemed unconcerned, feeling that compromise would come after people had "exhausted themselves in dispute."[6]

Stalin's casual approach was more than Marshall could take. He interpreted Stalin's call for patience as one more stall for time; given the deteriorating economic situation, Europe would collapse "in his lap" if the Soviet leader just waited long enough. Marshall could not get this off of his mind. He talked about it with Bohlen all the way back to the embassy and on the return trip to Washington. The more he talked, the more determined he became to stem what he saw as the tide of Soviet domination.[7]

Marshall's Moscow experience reinforced his support for the administration's decision to take action already set in motion before his arrival in the Soviet capital. The Middle East situation became critical during Marshall's absence, prompting Truman to issue his Truman Doctrine speech, a draft of which reached Marshall's delegation during a stopover in Paris. Marshall showed it to Bohlen. Although the two agreed that the administration had to assume Britain's responsibility in Greece and Turkey, they were disturbed by the "flamboyant anti-Communism" in the speech and conveyed these concerns to Washington. Nevertheless, the White House saw fit to proceed with the speech as drafted, countering Marshall's and Bohlen's concerns by arguing that the language was necessary to persuade Congress to appropriate the necessary funds. Once again politics took precedence over diplomacy. But the stage was set for an innovative policy.[8]

Marshall acted quickly to save the deteriorating situation. After consultation with Bohlen and others, he called George Kennan from the National War College, where Kennan had recently been assigned, and made him head of the newly formed Policy Planning Staff within the State Department. As its first charge, Marshall commanded this body to develop proposals to revitalize Europe. His only specific instructions to Kennan were to prepare a response in short order and "to avoid trivia."[9]

By 23 May, Kennan was circulating a report advocating a program for short-term measures to lift Europe's spirits and a long-range plan based on European cooperation, a necessity if economic revival was to be firmly based. He urged that a clear distinction be made between a European plan for revitalization and a program of American support for it. An interim program was insufficient. Kennan's report coincided with the analysis of Undersecretary of State for Economic Affairs William Clayton, who had just returned from Europe with dire warnings that the United States had seriously underestimated Europe's economic plight. He, too, proposed a broad program of economic aid.[10]

The reports were circulated and a meeting convened on 29 May attended by the heads of the various offices in the department, including Bohlen. Clayton set the tone with his prediction that a depression would engulf the West if the United States did not act before the end of 1948. The United States had to move to take over the Ruhr coal fields, appropriate six to seven billion dollars annually over the next three years to rehabilitate Europe, help secure annual loans from the World Bank and International Monetary Fund, and encourage a system of closer economic cooperation to break down existing trade barriers.

This program of economic aid sparked extended discussions. Participants wondered if such aid should include the Soviet Union and Eastern Europe. Clayton postulated that Eastern Europe needed Western Europe more than vice versa. An economic federation, therefore, could be structured without Eastern European participation. Most of those at the meeting, including Bohlen, agreed that only if Eastern Europe abandoned its strictly Soviet orientation should it be invited to participate.

Granting the desirability of such an economic program and accepting the qualifications to be imposed on Eastern European participation, Bohlen believed that it should be a European program, but one conforming to American parameters. The initiative had to come from Europe, yet the United States had to play an active role in assuring the program's viability. Balancing the alternatives of appearing to force the American way on Europe against the danger of possible failure if the major responsibility was left to Europe, he proposed that the United States

> place strong pressure on the European nations to plan by underscoring their situation and making clear that the only politically feasible basis on which the U.S. would be willing to make the aid available is substantial evidence of a developing overall plan for economic cooperation by the Europeans themselves, perhaps an economic federation to be worked out over 3 or 4 years.

Europe was the focus of planning and had to take the initiative, but the American influence was crucial.[11]

Discussion of the timing and the machinery proved less conclusive. Clayton opposed using the already existing Economic Commission for Europe, a United Nations agency established to stimulate economic revival along European rather than national lines, because the Communists who were participating could paralyze any progress. Dean Rusk countered that abandoning the Commission precipitously would appear to the public abandoning the United Nations. Bohlen backed Clayton's position, remarking that if jurisdiction were given to the European Commission, that jurisdiction would be hard to withdraw if progress were blocked. Rusk seemed swayed by Clayton's and Bohlen's insights, so the meeting adjourned with agreement that Britain, France, Italy, and the Benelux countries should be encouraged to meet to initiate a cooperative program.[12]

Intent upon maintaining the European focus of any such program, Marshall pondered the best means of proffering the assistance. Rejecting the advice of Acheson and others, he chose to announce his offer at a low-key forum, a college commencement, so that the initiative would be left to the Europeans themselves. He had recently been asked to speak at Harvard's graduation ceremonies and now decided to accept. Marshall delegated Bohlen to draft the speech since Bohlen probably knew better than anyone what the secretary wanted to convey, having witnessed Marshall's eye-opening encounter with Stalin in Moscow and having been apprised of department assessments of the European situation.

As the basis for the speech, Bohlen combined the Clayton and Kennan memoranda with ideas gleaned from department meetings held during May. The plan he described was a cooperative effort at European recovery with economic support from the United States. Marshall did not want to leave the impression that the proposed program was directed against the Soviet Union, so Bohlen's draft portrayed the plan as a fight against hunger and poverty wherever they existed. His draft was accepted with few modifications.[13]

Marshall's sensitivity to the need to justify the program in terms other than the emerging confrontation with the Soviet Union, however, was only a tactical maneuver. Covertly the Marshall Plan was a key element in the struggle to prevent the spread of communism. The possibility of a role for the Soviet bloc had been raised at the 29 May meeting, and Marshall once again expressed his concern to Bohlen and Kennan as he prepared for a press conference the day after his 5 June Harvard speech. Clearly, Eastern Europe would not be needed to implement economic revival, but if the United States excluded the Soviet Union and its satellites from participation, world opinion might accuse it of making permanent the split between East and West. If the Soviets were invited to participate and accepted, however, it would be well nigh impossible to secure necessary congressional consent for the program, given Congress's prevailing attitude toward the Soviets.

Bohlen and Kennan confidently assured Marshall that the Soviets and their satellites would not accept such a proposal because of its cooperative nature and the need for close monitoring of the aid's use. America could make an open-ended offer with the confidence that the Soviets would not accept.[14]

This plan, in Bohlen's view, was a sly piece of propaganda that attacked the cause of particular problems rather than treating the symptoms. The Soviets preyed upon weakness and discontent. Economic revival alleviated this weakness at the same time it contained the spread of communism. Here was an initiative which potentially could strengthen the West while weakening and dividing the eastern bloc, declared Bohlen. It painted the United States as Europe's savior and identified communism and more particularly the Soviet Union with "misery, hunger, chaos," and other evils.[15]

The Marshall Plan even held the potential of driving a wedge between the Soviet Union and its eastern neighbors, for the Soviet economy, Bohlen believed, was incapable of replacing the western role in the economic life of countries like Czechoslovakia. Such nations would in the long run move closer to the West, where they could get the "maximum benefit." It would then become clear that the plan was "not directed toward perpetuating the split in Europe," but was "directed toward eliminating it."[16] Although the Soviet Union was determined to maintain its control over Eastern Europe, Bohlen foresaw at least a long-term possibility that the economic strength of the West might serve as a magnet to attract these Soviet bloc nations and thus weaken the hold of the U.S.S.R.

Ernest Bevin and Georges Bidault, the foreign ministers of Britain and France, swiftly seized the initiative once Marshall offered aid. Working closely with the State Department, they convened a European meeting on 27 June where, as Bohlen and Kennan had predicted, the eastern bloc quickly withdrew. This was followed by formal discussions beginning on 15 July. Despite volatile issues like Germany's participation, the Organization of European Economic Cooperation took shape, with the participation of the United States and Canada. A four-year American aid package originally estimated at between $16.4 and $22.4 billion was to accompany reduced tariffs, monetary convertibility, and other trade agreements aimed at reviving Western Europe. Bohlen reflected the department's prevailing feeling about these developments when he commented that the multilateral pledges of the sixteen countries meeting in Paris were not conditions for American aid. Rather, they were voluntary commitments of a reciprocal nature which were essential if the whole effort were to succeed.[17]

The Marshall Plan proved a rousing success, especially in light of Europe's needs and the political situation in the United States. Congress, often a barrier to such diplomatic initiatives in the past—either because of the isolationist propensities of some of its members or the partisan politics which often confounded diplomatic efforts—ultimately proved receptive to this program, as Bohlen discovered firsthand. When Robert Lovett replaced Dean Acheson as undersecretary, Bohlen, as department counselor, assumed the added task of liaison with Congress. The worry about Communist participation took care of itself when the eastern bloc withdrew; now congressional critics attacked the plan as another example of American "charity." Given the structure of the program, however, Bohlen could confidently respond that it was not charity, but a cooperative endeavor. Europe on its own initiative was moving from despair to a more independent position, which would benefit the United States by increasing the possibility of peace and security. Furthermore, he could reply to those who saw the Marshall Plan as an example of American imperialism by pointing out that its thrust was to create an independent Europe, not one dependent on the United States. Only as a result of such positive measures could Soviet designs be checked.[18]

Hope for a better world had run high at the end of World War II, but by 1947 Bohlen readily admitted that there were now "two worlds." Spheres of influence were firmly established, not because the United States wanted them, but because of postwar developments. America and its western allies had to realize that the Soviet Union was consolidating its position in Eastern Europe based on this "two world" thesis. The West had to respond by consolidating its position through political, economic, and, "in the last analysis," military means. Little could be done to alter the status of Eastern Europe, so Bohlen advised that planners focus more resolutely on Western Europe. In the short range, perhaps in a matter of months, he foresaw a showdown between the Soviet and non-Soviet world.[19]

Nothing happened in ensuing months to change Bohlen's outlook. The session of the Council of Foreign Ministers (25 November–16 December 1947) that Bohlen attended in London did nothing but exacerbate the differences over Germany. A Communist coup in Czechoslovakia shocked the West during February of 1948. In the same month, the Kremlin was pressuring Finland to sign a mutual defense pact, an ominous sign to many western observers.

But by April 1948, Bohlen was heartened a bit as some of America's efforts began to bear fruit.[20] Following the London foreign ministers meetings, America encouraged England, France, and the Benelux countries to work toward a cooperative defense alliance. Washington indicated that it would respond favorably and support such a European initiative. On 17 March 1948, these countries signed the Brussels Pact, leading to America's ultimate adherence to the 1949 North Atlantic Treaty. Truman signed the Marshall Plan into law on 1 April 1948, and aid began to flow to revive Europe's economy. Influenced in part by this American aid, the Italian elections produced a non-Communist victory; many observers had predicted a Communist sweep.

By April 1948, Bohlen was becoming more confident about his contention that America's foreign policy could best be served by concentrating on Western Europe and thus insuring against Soviet expansion of its influence. Bohlen had not abandoned hope for an open sphere in Eastern Europe, but he believed it would materialize only after the West had established the fact that it was determined and strong enough to stand up to the Soviet Union. Only then might the Soviets moderate their position.

His proposals regarding the Soviets fit his conceptions of America's foreign policy objectives. In Bohlen's view, America historically had first aimed to protect its national existence from external aggression. Sounding like a Wilsonian idealist, Bohlen observed that, second, the United States wanted to offer to other countries the same benefits it enjoyed, especially by promoting conditions in which each country's development could proceed "in accordance with its national traditions and by the free choice of its people and not as a result of external threats." This, to him, was not total altruism. There was a reciprocal relationship between American well-being and that of its allies. The United States was intent upon promoting conditions in which it could enjoy the maximum of fruitful intercourse with the world, both economically and culturally, and "in which each nation with its distinctive culture will be able to make its contribution to the sum total of human knowledge and advancement." Achieving these ends involved keeping the "signals" clear to the Soviet Union and rejecting recourse to war. America had to maintain what Bohlen called the Marshall Plan perspective, a perspective he contrasted with prewar isolationism. Protecting Western Europe and other areas engaged in recovery meant protecting American civilization.[21]

Clearly Bohlen now recognized the value of the containment policy, but he worried that the Soviet Union with its ideological bias might misconstrue western actions, might get the wrong "signals." Not only were some of the West's moves potentially provocative, but he and Kennan also worried that election year politics in 1948 might add to Soviet confusion. No matter how far presidential candidate Henry Wallace's statements diverged from official American policy, the Kremlin might view Wallace's conciliatory rhetoric as representative of American public opinion. After an April meeting with the Soviet ambassador to the United States, Bohlen was even more worried that the confusion might cause the Soviet Union to overreact. He joined Kennan in proposing a direct overture to Stalin to discuss outstanding matters and to clarify America's stance. The two Soviet experts tried to convince Marshall of the benefits that might accrue from such a meeting:

> The reason for our conclusion is that the passage of ERP, the results of the Italian elections and the combined effect of these events on the situation in Europe ushered in a period where the Kremlin will be forced to make a very basic decision in regard to its future action. We feel that it is important to have on the record evidence that the Government has not neglected any opportunity of dispelling any misconception which the Soviet Government might have as to our policy as a result of which they might be tempted to action which would set off an armed clash.[22]

Bohlen suggested a private unpublicized meeting between U.S. Ambassador Walter Bedell Smith and Molotov and Stalin. Smith could stress that any Soviet expansion beyond its limits would be perceived as "an act of Soviet aggression directly inimical to the vital interests of the United States." At the same time, Smith could reassure the Soviets that the United States had no imperialist expansionist intentions of its own and contemplated no military aggression against Eastern Europe or the Soviet Union.[23]

Marshall accepted this advice and instructed Smith to approach Molotov in May. He also sent an outline Bohlen and Kennan had prepared for these proposed discussions. Smith's instructions were forceful but at the same time intended to defuse any future misunderstandings. They blamed world tensions on the Soviet Union and emphasized that the great majority of the American people supported their government's policy. Nevertheless, the instructions continued, the United States had no aggressive intentions against the Soviet Union.[24]

Smith followed Marshall's directive, but the plan backfired. Not only did the Soviets respond by shifting blame for world tensions to the

United States, but the Kremlin also leaked details of this meeting, describing it as an effort by the United States for high-level talks. Since the approach had been made without allied consultation, the Soviet revelation sparked suspicion of American intentions among its allies and set off a spate of criticism in the press both at home and abroad.[25]

It was left to Bohlen to justify to the press Smith's meeting with Soviet leaders. Bohlen argued that at that time it was important that the Soviet Union clearly understand America's position. He said that the U.S. was not seeking negotiations, and he doubted that the Soviets were, either. He was uncertain why the Soviets released the information, but speculated that it was for propaganda purposes—to try to show the Russian and Eastern European peoples that the United States, not the Soviet Union, was the obstacle to peaceful negotiation. One aspect of the affair, however, heartened Bohlen. He doubted that the Kremlin would have taken the action had it plans for expansion at the time.[26]

This incident was symptomatic of the state of Soviet-American relations. Mutual suspicion and distrust abounded. In this tense atmosphere, two significant and parallel developments evolved, one the Berlin blockade and subsequent airlift, which heightened the urgency of implementing the second, the North Atlantic Treaty.

The Berlin blockade followed the breakdown of discussions between East and West over the status of Germany. After the failure of the Council of Foreign Ministers in December of 1947, the western powers instituted plans for the creation of a West German state during February 1948 meetings in London. The Soviet Union responded by withdrawing from the Allied Control Council in Berlin on 20 March. When the western powers announced the creation of the German state in their zones and implemented currency reform, the Soviet Union clamped a total blockade on all land traffic into the western zones of Berlin.

Gen. Lucius Clay, commander of American forces in Germany, and his political advisor, Robert Murphy, quickly proposed that an airlift to supply the city be followed by the dispatch of an armed convoy through East Germany to break the blockade. Like a great majority in the State Department, Bohlen rejected this course of action. He contended that America's diplomatic posture should be firm, opposing any Soviet intimidation, while its military response should be restrained. Under no circumstances, Bohlen emphasized, should the United States agree to negotiate until the Soviets had consented "to lift the blockade (as opposed to relaxing it in fact)." He opposed taking the issue to the United Nations, but in the event that it was, he urged against succumbing to "blackmail."[27] He was confident that the diplomatic approach would work because he was certain the Soviet Union was not ready to carry the issue to the point of war.[28]

Bohlen's position coincided with and reinforced that of the Truman administration. He was encouraged when Truman initially opted for an airlift and sent B-29s capable of carrying nuclear weapons to Europe as a sign of determination, but eschewed ordering a directly provocative military response.[29] Nevertheless, it was clear that, if the airlift and diplomatic effort were going to succeed, the West would have to form a united front. To this end, Marshall sent Bohlen to Berlin at the end of July to brief Ambassadors Smith from Moscow and Lewis Douglas from London. The three then flew to London to meet with allied leaders for the purpose of coordinating a uniform response and bolstering their spirits. This meeting was none too soon, for Bohlen found Bevin in a "highly volatile and explosive mood." So perturbed was Bevin that he suggested to Bohlen in a "semijocular fashion" that America obviously wanted war. Bohlen tried hard to disabuse him of these impressions.[30]

Leaving London, Bohlen returned to Washington to head the "Berlin group," an ad hoc departmental committee to monitor the developing situation. Smith headed for Moscow to join other western ambassadors in a direct approach to Stalin. Bohlen was personally skeptical that this would produce any results. But he conceded that certain factors— including the decline in Soviet prestige stemming from the blockade and the deteriorating relationship between the U.S.S.R. and Yugoslavia—weakened the Soviet bargaining position. These elements, combined with a genuine Soviet desire to avoid war, apparently made Stalin at least amenable to talk with the ambassadors on 2 August.

Stalin's willingness to talk did not, however, convince Bohlen that he was prepared to retreat. Bohlen cautioned that it was "of the utmost importance to note" that during the meeting Stalin stressed that the suspension of the West German government remained his objective. In fact, according to Stalin, if the London decisions regarding the West German state and currency reform were not suspended, there was nothing to discuss and the Soviets were prepared to proceed to their second option of establishing a rival government in the eastern sector, rendering the western position even more untenable. Bohlen admitted that there would be pressure at home and abroad, particularly in France, to suspend the London agreements pending the outcome of negotiations. Yet "to halt these measures because of Soviet insistence," Bohlen suggested, "would have a very serious effect on Germany, would certainly be opposed by General Clay and Ambassador Murphy, and might make their resumption in the event of a breakdown of the four-power talks difficult if not impossible."[31] In Bohlen's mind, it would be a grave error to make concessions at this time, for he worried that the Soviets might construe them as evidence of a lack of resolve on the West's part.

A week later, Bohlen was more adamant that the U.S. should not bow to Soviet pressure. He described the Russians as acting as if four-power occupation and control of Germany were at an end. He warned that United States acceptance of the Soviet terms would mean in effect that "the U.S. was a vassal staying in Berlin by sufferance rather than by right."[32] Negotiations were at an impasse. When the western ambassadors referred the issues back to the military governors in Berlin after a second futile meeting with Stalin on 23 August, Bohlen held virtually no hope for real progress.[33]

Only after this effort to solve the crisis directly with Stalin and after the airlift and western counter blockade against the East had proven effective did Bohlen rather unenthusiastically acquiesce in the administration's decision to take its case to the United Nations. He accompanied Marshall to this U.N. session and joined with U.N. Ambassador Philip Jessup in coordinating America's appeal to the Security Council.

Bohlen lacked confidence in this course because he believed it created a whole new set of problems. The United States, he exhorted, had to monitor Soviet tactics closely and counter them every step of the way. Even the U.S. legal justification, Chapter Seven of the U.N. charter, which sanctioned actions in situations creating a threat to world peace, Bohlen predicted, could be countered by the Soviets, who could argue that Germany was an issue to be settled among the wartime allies. Russia might also place the blame on the western powers by accusing them of making separate arrangements for Berlin and violating wartime four-power agreements. In that light, Bohlen could see how the Soviets could portray the blockade as a defensive measure.[34]

Undoubtedly the U.N. provided the Soviets with a diplomatic gold mine. Thus Bohlen told Marshall that the United States should counter these maneuvers, for "to begin with conciliation is to invite inflexibility on their part."[35] To complicate matters further, France and the neutral members of the Security Council were more intent upon conciliation than on presentation of a strong front against aggression. Bohlen enjoined the members of his delegation to resist this pressure as well because the future of world peace hinged upon the outcome of these negotiations.[36] As he anticipated, appealing to the U.N. produced no solution.

The rationale for his advocacy of an inflexible American position emerged more clearly in an exchange of views he had with George Kennan in October. Kennan and the Policy Planning Staff had been analyzing the Berlin predicament, and he sent a summary of the staff's proposal for Bohlen's perusal. In it, Kennan contended that it was to America's interest to avoid war at this time since its military strength and the well-being of its allies would be greatly improved in a year or two, given the movement toward a North Atlantic Pact. Kennan suggested that at the moment the positions of both the antagonists were quite tenuous. The U.S., on the one hand, was trapped in Berlin with little hope that the blockade could succeed in the long run, especially in consideration of the psychological impact of the sacrifices the Berlin population had to endure. On the other hand, as the Germans saw the cost and suffering inflicted by the Soviet blockade, the Soviet Union was bound to lose steadily much of its political support in Germany. A protracted crisis, therefore, threatened the United States with the loss of Berlin, but the Soviet Union with the loss of Germany.

Kennan's reading of the Soviet position revealed signs of weakening. The Kremlin, he noted, had initiated the blockade to prevent the establishment of a West German state, but by the fall of 1948 the Soviet Union seemed to have lowered its expectations simply to driving the West out of Berlin. Thus Kennan thought there might be merit in confronting the overall issue of Germany in order to end the blockade, in his words "losing" Berlin in an overall German settlement. The U.S., he admitted, could not discuss this directly with the Soviets under duress, but it could let it be known that a compromise solution under the auspices of the United Nations might be acceptable. In return for opening discussions on Germany, the United States could accept a temporary lifting of the blockade. Among the options for a comprehensive German settlement, Kennan proposed a mutual withdrawal from Berlin under U.N. supervision; establishment of a neutral unoccupied area where German authority would by mutual agreement assume rights, combined with western forces withdrawing from Berlin and the removal of a number of the German population to the new capital; establishment of a neutral zone embracing the Brandenburg Province under German control with Berlin as its capital; or a general termination of military government with occupying forces of both the East and West withdrawing to garrisoned areas.

Kennan was pessimistic that these discussions would succeed, but he maintained that "we must consider ourselves well out of it if we can find any solution which gets us out of Berlin without serious detriment to western prestige and does not at the same time deliver up Germany as a whole to communist control." Besides, even if the negotiations failed, they would gain time, would provide some temporary relief for the people of Berlin, and would demonstrate to the besieged city and to all of Germany America's determination to proceed with a broad and constructive solution to the problem. If the Russians failed to agree on America's minimum terms, then the deadlock would give America a propaganda advantage and would provide it with a strong moral position in further attempts to resolve the conflict.[37]

Bohlen agreed that a satisfactory solution to the Berlin dilemma was intimately tied to the total German picture, but to "lose" the immediate problem of Berlin at this time was "to beg the problem" of the blockade. Facing this Soviet challenge, Bohlen persisted that America had to avoid being too conciliatory. Furthermore, he ventured that if the airlift continued successfully through the winter, the Soviets might become even more malleable and accept an agreement more consistent with America's terms.

Bohlen also questioned Kennan's proposed tactics. First of all, he perceived the United Nations as a poor intermediary, particularly since neutrals on the Security Council would be hesitant to act forcefully and would eschew discussing Germany, feeling it was an issue better settled by the Council of Foreign Ministers. Second, Kennan's suggestion to let the Germans form their own government without outside interference was in Bohlen's estimation unrealistic. Economic and political integration of the eastern and western zone was no longer "a reasonable political objective." Given the degree of sovietization in the East, unity could only be accomplished by the compulsion of occupying forces. Bohlen believed, furthermore, that withdrawal of British and American forces would have an adverse effect on the morale of western countries, particularly on France, with its "neurosis on security."[38] Bohlen had all but abandoned any hope for a reunited Germany.

Still the long-term solution to the Berlin crisis was inextricably tied to an all-German settlement, even if the settlement conceded the division of Germany. For the moment, however, Bohlen believed the United States had no alternative but to remain firm. The Soviet Union's veto of Security Council action made him even more certain that the only price America "could afford to pay for lifting the blockade could be an agreement to hold a meeting of the Council of Foreign Ministers with an agenda which would be agreed on by the four powers subsequent to the lifting of the blockade."[39]

The standoff continued into the winter of 1948–49. On 31 January, Bohlen, ever on the alert for signals from the Kremlin, detected a potential Soviet shift. Stalin responded to a reporter's question about Berlin without referring to the currency issue, still the expressed excuse for the blockade. Bohlen brought the omission to the attention of Dean Acheson, who had just succeeded Marshall as secretary of state.

Acheson quickly summoned U.N. Ambassador Philip Jessup for consultation. Taking Bohlen's advice, Acheson instructed Jessup to feel out Soviet U.N. Ambassador Yakov Malik informally. When Jessup approached Malik on 15 February, Malik had no answer as to the significance of Stalin's omission. But he came back to Jessup a month later with word that it was no mistake. Bohlen encouraged Acheson to follow up on the possible shift, but to do it through secret diplomacy. Russians, Bohlen had learned, negotiated quietly when they were serious about accomplishing something, so Jessup and Malik continued to serve as diplomatic facilitators.

Ultimately, private discussions between the two left only one major obstacle to Soviet acquiescence in lifting the blockade prior to a Council of Foreign Ministers meeting. Malik asked that the West delay the formation of a West German government until after the foreign ministers had met. Eager to conciliate now that the Soviets were coming to terms, Bohlen submitted that the western allies could not alter the program for West Germany, but that the process could be slowed. So Jessup told Malik that preparations were already set in motion, but establishing an early meeting date would almost certainly insure that this would predate the establishment of the West German state.[40] As Bohlen had predicted, America's persistent support for the airlift through the winter took its toll on the Soviets and led them to come to terms. The blockade was lifted on 12 May and the Council of Foreign Ministers scheduled to convene in Paris on 23 May.

As the Berlin crisis widened the East-West split, it also provided impetus for a formal alliance between the United States and its allies. Just as the Berlin crisis was portended by the failure of the 1947 London foreign ministers meeting, so at that same meeting had British Foreign Secretary Ernest Bevin broached the possibility of a military alliance. The State Department was favorably disposed toward Bevin's efforts and encouraged the Western Europeans to consider establishing a regional military alliance patterned after the Rio Pact, a 1947 U.S.-Latin American alliance. The Brussels Pact of March 1948 resulted, and the Europeans followed up by turning back to the United States for a commitment on its part.[41]

Deliberations leading ultimately to the North Atlantic Treaty began at a time when important developments were pressing both abroad and domestically. As the Berlin airlift attracted world attention, the 1948 American presidential election campaign inclined Truman to proceed cautiously. Still, among State Department officials concerned with Western European affairs, there was a feeling of urgency and an undercurrent of support for such an alliance.[42] This group, which influenced

Undersecretary of State Robert Lovett, who was initially in charge of the negotiations, pressed for the early commencement of discussions. As a consequence, British-Canadian-U.S. talks during March and April of 1948 led to lengthy exploratory talks on western security beginning in July. A draft treaty was completed in March 1949.

Bohlen's normal duties in the department and the additional pressures resulting from the Berlin blockade prevented him from focusing on these deliberations, but he did contribute, albeit tangentially, to the discussions leading to the North Atlantic Treaty. When consulted for his opinion on the Soviet reaction to western moves, he more often than not was at odds with those who heartily endorsed the pact. He was especially concerned that the Senate might refuse to approve such an entangling alliance. His disquiet was eased rather early in the deliberations, however, when the Senate approved the Vandenberg Resolution in June 1948, which declared that Congress was willing to support American participation in an arrangement for European security.[43]

But Bohlen had misgivings about the very nature, intent, and structure of the treaty as well. Of particular note were prevailing assumptions about the Soviet threat, which related directly to the need for and dimensions of a military response by the West. The question of western military involvement in turn raised the question of the consequent Soviet reaction.[44]

Bohlen's attitude was grounded in developing world events as he saw them in 1948. To him, disturbing events—such as the coup in Czechoslovakia and the growing rift over Germany—were balanced by hopeful signs—such as the failure of the Communist party in the Italian elections. He, along with Kennan, felt that American policy had to be tailored to a realistic appraisal of Soviet intent. The two advisors advocated proceeding slowly, being sure that circumstances dictated the response being considered.

In that vein, Kennan penned a memorandum to Lovett at the end of April 1948. In it, he tried to convey both his and Bohlen's concerns during the early phases of the negotiating process. He wrote that the British and French in particular were not concerned whether the United States would be on their side in the event of a Russian attack, but they worried that "we do not have any agreed concept between ourselves and themselves as to what we would do in the event of a Russian attack." This uncertainty stemmed from reported defeatist attitudes "prevailing among some in the military establishment and predictions by segments of the American press that it would be futile to try to stop Russian advances in Western Europe." The two Soviet experts did not reject the treaty idea, but, as Kennan wrote, the time for such action had "not come yet." To proceed without a thorough consideration of the military realities might not only fail to give the Europeans a sense of security, but it also might open rifts among them. More talks were needed to coordinate military reactions in the event of Russian attack, soundings had to be taken on the political level to discover the views of all possible European participants, and the American military had to assure the Western Europeans that the United States had not resigned itself to defeatism.[45]

Not only did Bohlen and Kennan see that there needed to be clear coordination with the Europeans, but decisions had to be based on the situation as it actually existed in Europe, more precisely on a clear understanding of Soviet intent and how it really threatened European security. Bohlen raised these issues during several sessions of the working groups in July. He called for consideration of Soviet intentions, of the nature of the Soviet threat, and of the impact collective arrangements would have on Soviet policy. He granted that the latter was a very speculative matter since concrete evidence was scarce. But he admonished the participants to analyze and understand the general situation the war had brought to Europe, especially the Soviet attitude toward "this abnormal situation."[46] Only then should the conference participants consider other essential questions, such as the necessity and proper place for a military commitment and the relationship between this pact and the United Nations.

Bohlen did not minimize the Soviet threat, but joined with Kennan in judiciously portraying the real danger for Europe. The Soviets were unlikely to start a war by a deliberate program of aggression; but war would result if situations developed from which the Soviet Union would find it difficult to withdraw. Here Bohlen and Kennan rejected the thesis so predominant in the government that the Soviet Union was a Communist state bent on domination.[47] At one point, Bohlen ventured that the West's position vis-à-vis the U.S.S.R. was better at that time than at any time since the end of the war. He doubted Russia's intention to dominate the world since "Stalin, unlike Lenin and Trotsky, would seek to achieve only the maximum, feasible extension of the power of the Kremlin."[48] Signs certainly indicated at this point that Stalin was not maneuvering from a particularly secure position.

The two Soviet experts did not deny the Soviet threat. But they wanted to put it in perspective. They wanted to proceed only after careful consideration of all the factors, one of the more significant of which was the military one. Kennan avidly opposed stressing the military aspect of the treaty. As he had declared earlier in the year, any military union should "flow from the political, economic, and spiritual union—not vice versa."[49] Bohlen was less averse to the military component. He only wanted to determine whether the Soviet threat to Western Europe "was primarily military or of some other nature, for if it were concluded that a military threat principally menaced our security our response will be of one kind, whereas if it is primarily economic or political we would react, presumably, in another manner."[50]

Still, he doubted in July of 1948 that circumstances called for a military union with Europe. War had left Europe in a dangerous state of imbalance. But the most dangerous years, according to Bohlen, had been 1945 to 1947 when the American military was disintegrating and when the American public was not adequately alerted to the Soviet challenge. Yet, significantly, the Soviet army had not moved during that time. Even in 1948, the U.S.S.R. had not transgressed the line commonly called the "iron curtain." Bohlen believed that America's "goal should be to create a Europe that is viable economically, strong militarily, and unified and politically stable to a degree that Soviet expansion could be opposed or held." America, he warned, had to "be careful not to adopt measures here which would be weakly provocative," and "care should be taken to provide the substance on which can be built in Europe a total sense of confidence." This confidence, Bohlen proposed, would result from psychological security that was not necessarily tied to a direct military arrangement. He stressed that Russia's leaders were unprepared to fight a long war, especially since they were "dubious of the attitudes and affections of their own people."[51]

Bohlen had been a proponent of a firm response by the United States in the Berlin crisis. But he was constantly wary of crossing the line between a determined stance and outright provocation. Even as the Berlin blockade suggested that a more drastic military response was in order for deterrence of Soviet expansion, Bohlen still avoided overreaction. His concern about the course of the alliance negotiations paralleled his overall estimation of the world situation and the role of the military. At the end of October 1948, for instance, Secretary of Defense James Forrestal had asked Marshall for an assessment of how the world situation had changed since the spring of that year and whether augmented military expenditures would be required if it worsened. Before replying, Marshall consulted Bohlen, Kennan, and Robert Lovett. Bohlen concurred with Lovett and Kennan in their conclusions that the situation had remained relatively static since the spring, with the Berlin blockade being the only new element.[52]

Then Bohlen went further and speculated on the relationship of America's military establishment to its responsibilities in foreign policy.

He argued that the United States had "to be in such a state of continuous readiness as to cause the Soviet Union to fear immediate retaliation on our part" if Russia engaged in aggressive activities. This state of preparedness entailed a ready strike force, especially involving air power. But Bohlen emphasized that in the last analysis it was the productive potential of the United States which constituted the real restraining factor. "It would be unwise for the United States to devote such a proportion of our national production to the maintenance of an existing military establishment so as to impair the potential productivity of our national economy."[53]

Bolstered by such advice, Marshall replied to Forrestal much in the same vein, arguing that the world situation was neither better nor worse, acknowledging America's responsibility for restraining Soviet aggression until the Western Europeans were capable of doing it themselves, and advising that America should not expand its military expenditures to build up ground forces with the purpose primarily of deploying them in Europe.[54] Bohlen's advice reinforced those of others and influenced Marshall's outlook. As in past analyses Bohlen conceded the need for military strength, but measured it against what world circumstances realistically demanded. He also tried to place it in the context of the key factor encouraging Soviet restraint, America's economic productive capacity.

Military strength was essential to the conduct of foreign policy. Indeed, Bohlen had argued that in 1948 and 1949 the United States and Soviet Union were in their military phase. But speaking of American policy during a State Department meeting in 1949, he questioned the feasibility of locking the United States into an inflexible stance. He conceded the beneifts of long-range planning, but he wanted some sort of a "flexible blueprint or method." Looking to the future, he predicted that in 1953, if the Russian war wounds were healed, its industry and military reestablished, the American planners might look back and ask what they might have done in 1949.[55]

Now, however, Bohlen's perceptions were shaped by the relationship between Soviet actions and Western European events. There were mixed signals. The Kremlin was certainly still active; a Communist coup had rocked Czechoslovakia in 1948. The Berlin crisis had shown Soviet determination, yet Russia had suffered setbacks as well. The Berlin airlift was clearly a victory for the United States, for example, and in Italy the Communists, after a concerted effort, had failed to win the elections. And most notable of all, Tito's defection had revealed the serious overextension of the Soviet Union. As Bohlen remarked, "as many people as she [the Soviet Union] has, that is just too much. She is overextended far beyond her capacity, really to make it [control of the iron curtain countries] work on a permanent basis." Tito, from Bohlen's standpoint, was "very much a symbol of that." He was a Yugoslav who did not see why his country "should be completely subordinated to the Soviet Union."[56]

Bohlen's was a speculative and balanced analysis combined with a receptiveness for any feasible approach that fit the needs and did not unduly provoke the Soviet Union. Not wildly receptive to a military alliance in the beginning, he came to see its necessity by the end of 1948. He had initially believed that the United States could stand apart and reassure its European allies without resorting to an entangling alliance. He soon realized, however, that, while some had exaggerated the Soviet threat, the Europeans had come to associate this alliance with their perception of security. His doubts about the necessity of the alliance had dissipated by the time he was discussing membership in the organization with a delegation from Norway in early 1949. The pact promised more than mere deterrence of Soviet military expansion. It would stabilize America's insecure allies. Whether there was an immediate threat or not, the Europeans believed there was one. As Bohlen told the Norwegian diplomats, two thoughts underlay the proposed treaty: "(1) An aggressor should not be left in doubt about what he would run into if he started something, and (2) we wanted European countries to have a sense of security which would be vital in regaining normal economic and political existence."[57] The North Atlantic Pact was as much the product of the perceived needs of the Western Europeans as it was a cog in America's containment policy. In fact, the former was more of a positive determinant for Bohlen.[58]

A military alliance was not the primary vehicle for combating communism in Europe, but Bohlen conceded that it played a prominent role. Once the countries involved had reached agreement on the treaty, he looked back on what had occurred during the past year and more. Even if, as he had adamantly argued during the discussions, there were no real immediate threat, a dictatorship like the Soviet Union was unpredictable and, therefore, understandably left the Europeans with feelings of insecurity. Stressing the military, he admitted, could lead to a rearmament program in Europe which could interfere with the all-important economic welfare of these countries. But this welfare was already being impeded by the absence of a sense of security. So the alliance combined with balanced rearmament was invaluable. The short-range goal of reassuring Europe could lead to long-range benefits such as Europeans being more willing to cooperate in integrating Europe, and perhaps even could lead in the distant future to a European federation.[59]

There was, in Bohlen's opinion, an intimate relationship between economic recovery, political stability, and a sense of security against aggression. The scale was now tilted against the Soviet Union. But he did not believe that the Soviet Union would be provoked to war by Western European rearmament. The Soviet Union built the area it controlled militarily while using "fear of its reaction as a weapon to prevent a similar consolidation on the western side of the line." He concluded that "there [were] always risks when nations [began] to draw together in the face of the threat of aggression, but the alternative [was] to yield to the fear of a Russian reaction, which [was] more of a threat than a reality, and do nothing. In other words, commit suicide for fear of death."[60]

Resigned to reality, Bohlen worked with Acheson to persuade Senate leaders Tom Connally and Arthur Vandenberg of the wisdom of the North Atlantic arrangement. Article Five of the treaty, which portrayed an attack upon one as an attack on all, particularly bothered the senators. They had to be convinced that it did not unequivocally commit the United States to a military response.[61]

This concern was accompanied by a public perception that the North Atlantic Pact was a repudiation of the United Nations, an organization which the United States had so staunchly supported in the past. In public forums, Bohlen denied that perception. On the contrary, the treaty helped promote the U.N.'s ends. American foreign policy had to be realistic and idealistic at the same time: realistic in that it had to deal with the world as it was rather than how America felt it should be; idealistic in that it always strove for the goals and aspirations of the American people and of all mankind. This reasoning underlay the policy the U.S. pursued toward Europe, Bohlen explained.[62]

However, even in his defense of the United Nations, Bohlen at least indirectly admitted its failure. The United Nations never lived up to expectations. It had been established as a means to an end, "the progressive development of a peaceful and stable world order where law rather than force and anarchy will govern the conduct of nations in foreign relations." Bohlen observed that the charges of undermining this body always came when the American policy ran counter to the designs of the Kremlin. But it was the Soviet Union through its use of the veto which had weakened and prevented the United Nations from accomplishing its stated ends. Since Article 51 of the charter permitted collective defense establishments, and since the goal and purpose of the North Atlantic Treaty sought the same ends as the United Nations, the treaty was in accordance with and reinforced, rather than undermined, the United Nations. Furthermore, the provisions of the treaty provided that actions of the North Atlantic Alliance terminated when the Security Council took effective action and that all steps taken under the auspices of the treaty had to be consonant with the United Nations charter.[63] Bohlen was tacitly admitting that the ineffectiveness of the United Nations had made the North Atlantic Pact necessary for the peace and security of Europe.

Amid this show of western unity and determination, preparations were underway for the Council of Foreign Ministers session to discuss the German situation. Acheson was adamant that western unity be maintained to oppose Soviet demands successfully. To this end, he dispatched Bohlen to Paris to reassure America's allies and to coordinate plans.[64]

Bohlen was rather jaded when it came to this foreign ministers meeting. He anticipated no improvement in the situation, the conference being a means for the Soviets to extricate themselves from a bad situation. In the prelude to this encounter, therefore, he was inclined to look with suspicion on possible Soviet concessions. Their strategy, he suggested, would take one of two forms. The most likely would be a general program with few guarantees along the lines of previous Soviet proposals—a program for a "democratic, unified, nonmilitarized" Germany. Such a plan would emphasize creation of an all-German government, the rapid conclusion of a peace treaty, and the evacuation of all occupying forces within a year of the treaty's promulgation. This program, Bohlen cynically observed, would allow the Soviets to extract propaganda value, avoiding the complicated questions such a general proposal would entail. Thus, in his opinion, the American delegation had to be prepared to expose the lack of serious Soviet intent by pinning the Soviet delegation down to specific questions regarding German unity.

A less likely Soviet approach, Bohlen guessed, would be a proposal for a more fundamental change in their policy, "a willingness to make far-reaching concessions including an abandonment of the Soviet system in the Eastern zone" in return for a unified Germany. Bohlen advised caution in the unlikely event that the Soviets made such a proposal. The delegation had to keep an eye on making the agreement work further down the road. Any such arrangement had to be "as self operating as possible," needing "the minimum of Soviet collaboration to be effective." The United States had to be prepared to present clearly and precisely its demands and have all safeguards prepared to keep the Soviets in line in the future.[65]

When the conference convened (23 May–20 June 1949), his predictions were confirmed, and he encouraged the U.S. delegation to concentrate on safeguards to prevent the reimposition of the blockade. In addition, the proceedings had to be viewed for their propaganda value. As Bohlen saw it, more important than the Soviet reaction to the American proposals was the impact of these negotiations on the European allies and on American public opinion.[66] The conference failed to loosen Soviet control of East Germany or East Berlin, but Bohlen agreed that "the changed circumstances in Germany . . . have forced [the Soviets] to emphasize in less attractive form what has been consistently their main intention in Germany: to hold on to what they have."[67]

So fruitless were the Paris discussions that, at one point, a member of the Russian delegation, General Vasili I. Chuikov, chief of the Soviet military administration in Germany, approached Bohlen and asked why the two sides could not get along like "the good old days" during the war. He went on to lament that the American position would "let these Germans loose," possibly to destroy the Russians.[68] This brief exchange brought home pretty clearly to Bohlen that little hope existed for solving the German dilemma. The Soviets were still intent upon insuring a weak and nonthreatening Germany. The lack of progress not only epitomized the foreign ministers meetings—which adjourned, as Bohlen had feared, with no major advances—but it also characterized the whole of Soviet-American relations.

In this, his most influential period, Bohlen had participated in constructing America's postwar policy, a policy which would remain intact for more than two decades. In one sense he assumed a hard-line posture toward the Soviet Union, but in another he never despaired that, if Russia were approached properly and from a position of strength, some diplomatic gains could be made. To do so, the U.S. had to seize the initiative. More often than not a cautious diplomat, Bohlen's advice was sometimes heeded, at other times ignored. What lay ahead was a period when the effects of America's new initiatives would begin to be realized.

6.

GROWING
CONFRONTATION

The North Atlantic Pact not only marked a national turning point, with the United States once and for all abandoning the nonentanglement policy it had espoused since 1800, but also signaled a change in the direction of Charles Bohlen's career. He had been in Washington for seven years, four years longer than the normal tour for a professional Foreign Service officer, and his relationship with Acheson was not as close as it had been with Marshall. His desire to get a new perspective on international affairs reinforced his decision to seek a transfer. He declined Acheson's offer of a minor ambassadorship, opting instead for the post of minister in the embassy in Paris, a city he had had a special fondness for since childhood. Furthermore, this post eased his fear of advancing too quickly through the professional ranks and placed him in a country critical to American policy.[1]

Transferred in June of 1949, his duties expanded when Congress passed the Mutual Defense Assistance Act, aimed at aiding America's allies in rearming. As Bohlen coordinated French aid, he began to understand more fully the continental attitude toward the postwar situation.[2] He became acutely aware of a divergence between American visions for Europe and European concerns. Washington had been encouraging integration of the economic, political, and military aspects of European redevelopment; such an approach included an expanded British commitment to the continent and a greater role for the West German state. Not only was Western Europe still apprehensive about a remilitarized Germany, however, but a degree of jealousy and competition also persisted between Great Britain and its continental neighbors—especially France—which threatened to disrupt progress toward a strong and cooperating Europe.

Despite the Soviet threat, the western alliance was far from cohesive. Thus when a series of newspaper articles appeared, purportedly based on discussions George Kennan had had with British officials regarding America's evolving relationship with Great Britain, Bohlen became alarmed and penned an urgent letter to his old friend, describing the European reaction to Kennan's remarks. The Europeans, Bohlen pointed out, worried that the continental members of the Organization for European Economic Cooperation would end up as "junior partners" in the relationship between the U.S. and England. The French, he suggested, feared that they would be left to face the Germans alone. The European response so far was "calm," but Bohlen predicted this suspicion would have a long-range detrimental impact. To alleviate this concern, Bohlen contended that the United States had to keep intact a conception of the Atlantic community based on political and military ties; that it had to minimize the existence of a special relationship with Great Britain and Canada; and that it had to continue to pursue every possible measure to link Great Britain to the continent.[3]

Bohlen's continental orientation contrasted with Kennan's perspective, which unabashedly acknowledged the special relationship between the United States and Great Britain as a given. In his reply to Bohlen, Kennan described the talks which were the source of the newspaper stories as having been aimed only at solving the pound-dollar crisis affecting international economics, not at separating England from the continent. Kennan reminded Bohlen that Britain was an essential part of both American and continental well-being, and that the problem of British reserves was a problem potentially affecting the whole western world. Turning to the broader issue of French anxiety, Kennan somewhat caustically asked what else the United States—after the Marshall Plan, the North Atlantic Pact, and other initiatives—had to do to reassure the French. The French were neurotic in their fears of U.S.-British ties as well as the possibility that Germany might become an "American pet." Kennan worried that such neuroses might hamper German integration and might intensify what he viewed as the troublesome tendency for Europeans to see all their problems from a military light.

He acknowledged that Bohlen's emphasis on France's importance in Europe was well-placed. He further anticipated that Bohlen might argue that American reassurance was essential to keep the French center in power, since as France went, so went Europe. But Kennan wondered what else could be done. If France in particular did not face up to reality soon, Russia might be "breathing down the European neck" with a Europe no closer to unity than before. France and the rest of Europe had to quit worrying so much about England and face up to their own responsibilities.[4]

If Bohlen had expressed a sense of urgency in his first letter to Kennan, his concern was heightened after attending a Paris meeting of U.S. European ambassadors, who saw the dangers to integration in much the way he did. Writing once again to Kennan, he argued that, despite Kennan's disclaimers, his outlook betrayed a change in the U.S. position regarding integration. Intentions aside, to follow Kennan's course would lead to a "desolidarization" of the United Kingdom from the continent. The European ambassadors who had just met, according to Bohlen, agreed that Germany could only be integrated by some sort of European union. The continental nations were not "sufficiently preponderant" to prevent Germany from dominating such a union. Thus to Bohlen it seemed unrealistic to expect France to take the lead. Unless England went as far as it could economically and all the way militarily, there was no chance that the continental powers could progress very far. England, he remarked, had been "backsliding" since 1948, refusing to face the fact that it was no longer a world power, but only a European power. The United States had coddled its ally too long.[5]

Clearly, if the problem of English-continental cooperation could not be surmounted, there was little possibility that Germany could successfully be integrated into the European system. This was still a major topic of discussion in the spring of 1950 when the U.S. ambassadors once again met, this time in Rome. Taking part in these talks, Bohlen underlined the need for Germany's participation, especially in the defense plans for Europe. Reflecting on the first year of the North Atlantic Treaty, he noted that Article Five's provision that an attack upon one member would be construed as an attack upon all had proven an effective deterrent to the Soviet Union, but it had not brought instant security by creating a sufficient number of well-equipped military divisions in the field. He saw a discrepancy between the results the treaty had attained and the hopes it had engendered. It had warned the Soviet Union and psychologically bolstered the spirits of the Europeans, but it had not led to a Europe really capable of defending itself. Before this military discrepancy could be remedied, one had to turn to the treaty's political scope, which included a solution to the German problem.[6]

Later during the same conference Bohlen expanded upon this point, contending that the Europeans' "past experiences with Germany [were] still too fresh to permit them to act wholeheartedly upon policies which rationally they [recognized were] necessary." Their attitudes, however, were undergoing a steady metamorphosis which the United

States had to encourage in an understanding manner. The interplay of two contradictory currents of thought dominated this evolution. The traditional fear and distrust of Germany remained and was now updated to believing that, unless controlled, German nationalism would re-emerge—pitting East against West. Opposed to this, a more positive and realistic concern was finding currency. Without Germany, the community of Western Europe had little political, economic, or military substance. The Europeans, according to Bohlen, were deadlocked on the degree of independence and the speed of integration of the German state.[7]

Bohlen was not alone in his emphasis on integrating Germany into Europe's defense structure. Washington was also stressing that necessity. Following the outbreak of the Korean War, the United States as well as its European allies were even more edgy about potential Soviet aggression. In response the Truman administration expressed its intention to increase America's commitment of troops to Europe, but at the same time emphasized that the troops were to be part of a balanced allied force, which was to include German troops.

In reaction, French Premier René Pleven announced a plan for a European Defense Community in October 1950. Pleven's plan called for a continental army with West German troops participating. Bohlen saw some merit in this approach, especially since it committed France to a policy of German participation and at the same time would probably be acceptable to the Germans, calling as it did for their integration into a continental force under the auspices of the North Atlantic Pact. But Bohlen could not quell his suspicion of French intent. The plan might have been a delaying tactic rather than a genuine French concession. Furthermore, in Pleven's program the European nations would bear sole responsibility for integrating Germany, making it difficult for the United States to intervene if the talks bogged down.[8] These initial steps were clearly influenced by past European prejudices, but Bohlen still perceived Europe's stance as shifting gradually. The Soviet threat was becoming more serious to the Europeans than the German one. Although the Pleven plan was never implemented, it represented at least some movement toward acceptance of a German contribution to Europe's defense.

In addition to Germany's role, underlying any efforts at European self-defense was the role to be played by a militarily strong and actively participating United States. America's military establishment, however, had not kept pace with its commitments. When Tracy Voorhees, undersecretary of the army, formed a Department of Defense group to study this problem, he invited Bohlen to attend and discuss the situation with his committee during one of Bohlen's trips home in early 1950. Bohlen laid the basis for his assessment of America's military strength by contrasting the American and European viewpoints. The words "security" or "successful defense," he emphasized, had different meanings depending on who was doing the defining. To the United States, "security" meant the capacity to win a war, a capability which it clearly possessed. But to the Western Europeans, "security" meant to prevent war and, if a war did occur, to deter Soviet penetration of European territory. They feared being "mashed up" while the United States gained time to win an armed conflict.

The state of the European economies prevented matching the Russians tank for tank and led to heavy reliance on American technology, thus reinforcing Europe's concern. The "psychology of 1940," Bohlen insisted, was prevalent. Not only did the Europeans suspect American intentions, but in Paris Bohlen had become painfully aware that they also distrusted Great Britain. The Europeans thought that the continent's defense was secondary in England's planning, just as it had been at the outset of World War II.

America's technological advantage stood out in Bohlen's mind as the most effective means to combat these fears and bolster the western allies. The French, Bohlen speculated, would certainly have the will to fight if they had the means to protect their country. Contending that the United States had to stress the preventive nature of the North Atlantic Pact, he concluded that stockpiling nuclear weapons had no real impact on Soviet policy. Rather, America's productive capacity, linked to its technological strength, held the key to deterrence. Stalin had developed a healthy respect for American productivity during World War II.

A first step toward European security had been taken with the Mutual Defense Assistance Act, but its weakness was all too obvious to Bohlen. Western defense arrangements were scattered "all over the lot." If the North Atlantic Pact were going to be a truly successful arrangement, there had to be better coordination and the relationship between Western Europe and the rest of the Atlantic community had to be clarified, including finding the proper place for Germany.[9]

Bohlen's testimony before the Voorhees committee was no new twist in his thinking, for he had always believed that economic and political stability were critical but that they went hand-in-hand with a strong military posture. In the latter part of 1948, in the midst of the Berlin crisis, Bohlen had cautioned against reducing American military forces since the U.S.S.R. persisted in its hostility toward the West. The United States had a responsibility to the struggling Western Europe; it had to remain prepared and marshal its much-vaunted productive capacity to "cause the Soviet Union to fear immediate retaliation on our part" in the face of any aggression. He warned, however, that success entailed finding the proper balance between the maintenance of the existing military establishment and the overall healthy productive capacity of the national economy.[10] Just as military preparedness in Europe was hampered by weak economies, so, according to Bohlen, military preparedness in the United States had its base in a healthy and sound economy.

His apprehension increased after the Russians successfully tested an atomic bomb. The bomb may have done little to alter the immediate political and diplomatic situation, but that did not preclude its use if the situation were to change in the future. Even more consequential to Bohlen was the growing Soviet advantage in conventional weapons. If necessary measures were not taken, he predicted that the gap between East and West might widen to the point of "real critical danger in the future."[11]

To Bohlen, it was essential that military preparedness be grounded in a clear understanding of Soviet intentions. He believed that the Soviet Union wanted to avoid war as much as the United States did. The U.S.S.R. was a threat, but a manageable and pragmatic one. In this attitude, he differed with other government planners. While at home in 1950, he was asked his comments on a draft report prepared by a joint state-defense committee under the chairmanship of the new head of the Policy Planning Staff, Paul Nitze. Prompted by the Soviet detonation of an atomic weapon, Truman had ordered this committee to analyze the state of American military preparedness. This study became NSC-68.

The draft document Bohlen read advocated a major increase in expenditures for the military to counter a Soviet Union driven by a "fanatic faith" bent on world domination.[12] Bohlen had mixed feelings about the study. Although he saw a study of this nature focusing and setting clearer directions for policy decisions, he also worried that its adoption might impose too much rigidity, something that to him was inappropriate, especially in relations with the U.S.S.R. While he may have been pessimistic about what could be gained through diplomacy, he insisted that the effort at discussion and compromise should not be abandoned. Bolstered by a strong military, America could apply the old principles of realpolitik and make some limited headway in negotiations.[13] As he remarked while trying to organize a foreign ministers meeting in June, "We should never get in a position of being terrified to talk to the Russians. We should not get in a position of expecting to lose."[14]

Bohlen agreed with the study's advocacy of military preparedness, but in his judgment the rationale was faulty. It portrayed the Soviet Union as an ideological force bent on world domination. In contrast, he contended that the Soviet Union was motivated more by national interest than by a desire to dominate. Soviet goals were primarily to consolidate the internal regime and only secondarily to spread externally as far as possible without threatening the stability of the internal situation. The U.S.S.R. was a prudent state. If it thought it could achieve world domination, Bohlen admitted that it would seize the opportunity. But other priorities were more influential on its planning. To stress world domination, Bohlen remarked, "tends to oversimplify the problem and . . . leads inevitably to the conclusion that war is inevitable."[15]

Acheson, an advocate of the approach in this study, was not convinced by this part of Bohlen's argument, even though George Kennan had similar criticisms. To Acheson, the Soviets' intentions were less important than their capacity for aggression. Unfortunately, Bohlen neglected to press his concern in his criticism and tacitly conceded Acheson's point by admitting that he did not wish "to belabor this point since it is obviously better to over-simplify in the direction of greater urgency and danger than it is to over-simplify the side of complacency when dealing with Soviet intentions."[16] Acknowledging the Soviet threat, Bohlen tended to follow the assumption that the end justified the means in this instance. His reservations, therefore, had little impact on official policy.

Proceeding from Soviet intentions to NSC-68's discussion of American military weaknesses, Bohlen suggested that the paper should emphasize the growing military gap between the Soviet Union and the United States and its allies. He was disturbed that the paper placed too much emphasis on America's limited capacity of defense "in the territorial sense." If it were America's intention to defend the areas of the world not under Soviet domination, and if these areas were perceived as of direct interest to the U.S., this defense would entail "full-time war mobilization both in the United States and in the Atlantic Pact countries." Bohlen cautioned against such overexpansion and universalization of the containment policy. America's military had to be strengthened, but in an unprovocative manner. The gap between the Soviet and western military had to be closed, but planners had to recognize that the short-range impact of closing it might have a detrimental effect. The public, both in Europe and the United States, had to understand that, while the process of militarization was taking place, the cold war might be intensified.

Finally, Bohlen believed it essential to clarify the term "deterrence." The American atomic monopoly had had little real influence on Soviet diplomacy. Bohlen therefore warned that the paper should detail what was necessary in the political and economic, as well as the military, realms to insure that the United States had a sound position in relation to the Soviet Union. The U.S. had to set an intelligent direction, drawing upon its technological and scientific superiority—an American advantage he had stressed before the Voorhees committee—to develop new weapons at less cost. The psychological and political advantage for America's European Allies would then be evident. He advocated a primarily defensive direction of military development, mitigating Soviet progaganda charges of provocation. Such a development would allow for a smaller and more professional standing army and, of overriding importance, would reduce the strain on the European economies.[17]

Bohlen opted for a realistic, restrained, but strong role for the American military, taking into consideration Soviet intentions as well as the impact of the buildup on America's allies. But Bohlen's attitude was inconsistent with Acheson's and Nitze's, and consequently had little influence in the final form and rationale of NSC-68. Furthermore, his prudent portrayal of Soviet foreign policy soon also seemed inconsistent with the real situation in the world, given the North Korean invasion of the South in June of 1950.

Word of the invasion reached Bohlen while he and his wife were vacationing outside of Paris. Bohlen rushed back to Paris to consult with Ambassador David Bruce and Averell Harriman, who was then in charge of coordinating Marshall Plan aid. All three were particularly worried about the invasion's effect on the European allies and thus were heartened when word reached them that Truman had decided to intervene with naval and air forces. Encouraged by Truman's reaction, Bohlen accompanied Bruce in a visit to French Foreign Minister Robert Schuman to reassure him that the U.S. was intent upon resisting aggression.[18]

The Korean crisis obviously involved Soviet-American relations, so Bohlen and Kennan, as the recognized authorities on the Soviet Union, were consulted as the administration charted its course of action. Bohlen joined with Kennan in prompting a resolute response by the United States. Both supported taking the issue to the United Nations, which the U.S. did on 27 June. Bohlen and Kennan ventured that the cumbersome Soviet bureaucracy, which had been boycotting the Security Council over that body's refusal to seat Communist China, would be unable to send a delegate to the council in time to block any resolutions the United States might present. Bohlen opposed an alternative proposal to approach the Kremlin directly. Although he postulated that the Kremlin had "set in motion" and was directing the

Korean operation, it had not accepted responsibility publicly. To approach the Soviet Union would, therefore, afford it the opportunity to confuse or delay, whereas, if the Kremlin was confronted with "strong, determined countermeasures," it might judge the risks as too great and might intervene to restrain North Korea. The United States had to show "maximum firmness" to convince the Kremlin that the U.S. meant business, taking care not to force the Soviets "publicly into a position from which there could be no retreat."[19]

Bohlen, recalled to Washington for a month to advise on American strategy, clearly delineated the rationale of his position.[20] He rejected the notion that Acheson's January 1950 "defense perimeter speech" before the National Press Club, in which the secretary failed to include South Korea in the area of America's primary concern, precipitated the invasion. Rather, Bohlen put events in the context of Soviet cold war machinations. Stalin had come to realize that there was little chance that he could repeat in Japan what he had done in Germany, so he decided to round out his hold on Korea. Like a good Communist, Stalin was deluded by Marxist ideology, expecting the invasion to trigger an internal uprising by the Korean poor, the workers, and the peasants, bringing quick victory. It was obvious to Bohlen that, not only had ideology clouded Stalin's judgment, but he had also seriously underestimated the American will to resist. While blaming Stalin for this crisis, Bohlen did not see the invasion as legitimizing the assumptions behind NSC-68. Stalin was playing realpolitik, exploiting a perceived weakness. This was not the work of a dictator rashly moving to overthrow capitalism.

Many policy makers, most notably Acheson, were convinced that Korea was the prelude to Soviet moves elsewhere. Bohlen disagreed. The invasion showed him nothing new. The Soviets were probing for "weak spots." Consequently the United States had to remain steadfast, but cautious, avoiding provocation. He doubted that the Soviet Union would intervene directly unless America engaged in activities near areas strategically important to the Soviets, such as Vladivostok.[21]

By early July, Bohlen's reading of the Soviet press reinforced his certainty that a resolute American stand would bring results. He believed that Stalin was showing signs of wanting a way out of his dilemma. In Bohlen's estimation, Stalin feared that American strength would shortly turn the tide. U.N. forces would soon cross the 38th parallel, presenting the dictator with choices he did not wish to make— either do nothing and let these forces move "next door to Vladivostok" and other strategically important areas or occupy North Korea with Soviet troops.

What happened in Korea would have ramifications in other parts of the world, so Bohlen suggested that the United States remain diplomatically and militarily prepared. Diplomatically, Bohlen anticipated that Stalin might propose a settlement along the lines of the status quo ante with the withdrawal of North Korean troops above the 38th parallel and the removal of U.S. troops from the south. This latter condition was unacceptable in Bohlen's mind. But if the United States did not prepare a careful justification for the retention of these forces, Stalin could derive great propaganda value from American "aggression."

Militarily, if America did not show that it could mount the strength to turn around its reverses and bring pressure "to bear on the spot," there might be a hardening of the Soviet position, even to the point of refusing to terminate hostilities in the south. If the defense establishment, therefore, was not up to the challenge, Bohlen felt it imperative that the government "adopt some measure which would indicate a mobilization of our power to correct this situation."[22]

Bohlen's concern was particularly focused on the impact of the crisis on America's overall foreign policy, especially in Europe. Relations with the North Atlantic allies were already strained over German integration. Now Korea was leading them to question their political and military association with the U.S., creating a soft spot for the Kremlin to exploit. Bohlen urged drastic measures, including federalization of the national guard and increased Mutual Defense Assistance aid to reinforce European military production, and an escalated schedule for producing new defensive weapons to instill confidence among the Europeans.[23] He held little hope of further diplomatic progress in Europe if these measures were not taken.

When Bohlen offered this advice to Acheson, it meshed with the views of others in encouraging the Truman administration's forceful response. After the U.N. command was created under the leadership of Gen. Douglas MacArthur in early July, Truman called for partial mobilization and increased expenditure for American rearmament. Thus when Bohlen returned to Paris after his month in Washington, he was in a better position to present America's case to its allies and call upon them for their own self-interest to place more emphasis on rearmament in order to deter the Soviet Union.

Joining Ambassador Bruce to brief America's British and French allies, Bohlen confidently encouraged them to be on their guard. In June he had pressed Washington to develop a justification for its stance in Europe as a response to the Soviets. Now in August, he was articulating this rationale to receptive allies. The United States, according to Bohlen, was engaged in a political move in Korea to show that aggression could not be tolerated. He conceded that that course was full of risks, but he once again described Stalin as a prudent leader who would respond to pressure. Bohlen postulated that as long as things went well for the U.S.S.R., which was in his opinion waging a war of proxy in Korea, Russia would not be conciliatory. In fact, only by rearming could the West deter the Soviets from taking steps of an "equally grave nature," not just in Korea, but elsewhere. Thus he promoted a European role in rearmament, assuring them that $3.5 billion of Truman's $10-billion rearmament request would be for Europe.[24]

Bohlen watched as his scenario for a successful American policy came to pass—MacArthur landing at Inchon on 15 September followed by a counteroffensive. But from Paris he became increasingly alarmed as U.N. forces moved further and further above the 38th parallel. Bohlen realized that direct Chinese participation was just as possible as direct Soviet participation, if China felt its security threatened. He became quite uneasy as MacArthur moved closer to the Chinese border and especially when Chinese forces began a counteroffensive of their own in late November. At this crucial juncture, Bohlen was apprehensive that there was no one of any real stature in Washington to advise Acheson on Soviet intentions and the course to pursue.

Prompted by these developments, he called Kennan, who was on leave at the Princeton Institute for Advanced Studies, and entreated him to go to Washington. He wanted Kennan to impress upon the administration that, as Bohlen had been saying all along, the possibility for Chinese intervention existed. He implored Kennan to warn against both overreaction and defeatism. Negotiating with the Soviets during an American retreat would be disastrous; Russia would interpret any such efforts as signs of American weakness. Thus the United States should resist the Chinese in order to stabilize the situation, but not allow events to escalate into a global conflict. Bohlen was relieved when Acheson heeded Kennan's plea and responded accordingly.[25]

The United States did not succumb to defeatism and ultimately led the United Nations forces in a counteroffensive at the end of January 1951. On 1 February the General Assembly passed a resolution condemning the Chinese Communists as aggressors. By March, the U.N. forces had returned to the 38th parallel, and the battle line stabilized.

As the conflict unfolded, Bohlen discreetly joined other diplomats in seeking private contacts with the Soviets in quest of a settlement. One such opportunity came when Bohlen met with Yuri Zhukov at a dinner given by C. L. Sulzberger of the *New York Times* on 2 January 1951. Zhukov, a correspondent for *Pravda* with known links to the Kremlin, took Bohlen aside and in a long private discussion affirmed his government's interest in negotiations. But Bohlen reiterated that America would agree to nothing until the U.S.S.R. secured a ceasefire. Zhukov apparently reported this to his superiors, setting in motion meetings with other diplomats, ultimately contributing to a ceasefire and armistice.[26]

Truce talks began in earnest during the summer of 1951, more than a year after the conflict began. Bohlen's contacts with Soviet diplomats in Paris proved to him that even in 1951 the Soviets still believed a Chinese and North Korean victory possible, thus leading them to delay serious negotiations.[27] This realization reinforced his opinion that a determined stand suited America's interests, for the Soviets had to be disabused of any belief that a Communist victory was possible.

In the midst of these developments, Bohlen received word at the end of 1950 of his reassignment to Washington. His transfer was delayed by a futile series of meetings from March to June of 1951 as he attempted to arrange a Council of Foreign Ministers session. These talks concluded, Bohlen, carrying his infant daughter Celestine in a basket, boarded a train and headed for southern France, where he rendezvoused with his wife and other children for the trip back to the U.S. Once back in Washington, he replaced Kennan as department counselor in July.[28] In this capacity, his duties more directly involved Korean developments, and his response to the crisis, rather than changing, was further substantiated. During the fall, he joined Gen. Omar N. Bradley in a fact-finding trip to Japan and Korea. Visiting the front lines in Korea, he was impressed with the favorable military position of United Nations troops. He became more certain than ever of the wisdom of America's firm stance.[29]

But his new responsibilities did not focus exclusively on Korea, even though that war could not be ignored as a backdrop to Soviet-American relations. He also served as advisor to John Foster Dulles at the Japanese peace conference in San Francisco and joined a committee established to assess the growing problems in former European colonies.[30] Bohlen was also the department's senior representative to the National Security Council, where he continued his crusade to fashion a realistic assessment of Soviet activities. Now in a more influential position than 1950, he reiterated his reservations about NSC-68's emphasis when President Truman charged the Council with evaluating past programs spawned by NSC-68 and recommending revisions in preparation for his fiscal 1953 budget proposals.[31]

Bohlen eagerly joined the discussion, restating essentially what he had argued previously. Despite his support for increased military preparedness, he still maintained that there was no evidence that the

Kremlin was bent on world domination. The Soviets were not such "mechanical chess players," he stressed. The same leaders who controlled the Kremlin dominated the international Communist movement. And, as a result of their doctrine, they were "implacably, unrelentlessly, and unappeasably" hostile to the United States and other nations not under their control. As a consequence, the Soviet Union was in a constant state of preparation for war. He emphasized, however, that that doctrine was the "servant," not the "master," of the Soviet state.

Nothing that had transpired since 1950 had changed Bohlen's mind about Soviet motives. Korea was not a new phase in Russian foreign policy, but rather was a Soviet miscalculation. The Soviet decision to begin talks to defuse the crisis, perceived by some as a sign of Soviet "softness" and by others as a ploy to "lull the world to sleep" in order to disrupt western rearmament, was interpreted by Bohlen as an indication of a Soviet desire to avoid war and ease global hostilities. He worried about the American propensity to believe that, should this "soft" approach fail to disrupt rearmament, the Soviets might resort to a preventive war to disrupt the situation. The thought of a preventive war was dangerous "as it might tend to condition us to an unwise response to a Soviet 'peace offensive' in order to avert the alleged danger of Soviet preventive action." All of this was not simply "metaphysical speculation." Bohlen believed that the greatest danger of conflict lay in Soviet misjudgment of what the U.S. would or would not do in a given local situation. Thus he was intent upon delineating a clear and consistent basis for American policy.[32]

Bohlen's eloquent and persuasive arguments failed. Paul Nitze spoke for the Council in rejecting most of Bohlen's reasoning. Nitze doubted that Bohlen could substantiate his contentions and judged that Bohlen saw "certain unspecified limitations" on Soviet hostilities, something Nitze could not see. Besides, Nitze noted that at one point Bohlen had argued that the rate of rearmament should be based on what the economies of the free world could support without retrogression, rather than a time-table based on probable Soviet intentions and capabilities. Nitze, however, pragmatically insisted that the U.S. had to convince the free world of the need for sacrifice. It would consequently be dangerous to understate the Soviet threat, which might lead to complacency.[33] Bohlen's insights, therefore, had relatively little impact on what became NSC-114. It was difficult to produce hard data to substantiate such speculative matters as Soviet intentions. Despite Bohlen's acknowledged expertise in observing the Soviet Union, his evaluation, so different from the prevailing opinion, could do little to alter the assumptions underlying American policy.[34]

Bohlen failed to alter the direction of policy, but he nevertheless had reason to feel optimistic in these waning years of the Truman administration. American efforts were beginning to pay off. The armistice talks in Korea were stalemated, but the United Nations' stand encouraged those who hoped that collective security could work. The western powers had followed the American lead and had voiced firm opposition to the North Korean aggression. Europe's increased military preparedness, furthermore, had diminished its fear of Russian military activity.[35]

This seeming increase in European security prompted his feeling that negotiations might lead toward accomplishing American ends, an opinion he expressed to Kennan when Kennan was preparing to leave for his new post as ambassador to the Soviet Union. At the behest of Acheson, Bohlen had gone to Princeton during the summer of 1952 to help persuade Kennan, who had retired from the Foreign Service, to accept the ambassadorship.[36] Bohlen had done so not just because the secretary had asked him, but because Bohlen respected Kennan's expertise in Soviet affairs and felt this was an opportune time to have such an expert in Moscow, for Bohlen saw potential opportunities for improving relations with the Soviet Union. With this in mind, he advised Kennan that this might be the time to approach Stalin. The dictator might be in a more open mood, and many pressing issues might be solved. Bohlen suggested to Kennan that the world was "in a period where the Soviet Government [was] endeavoring to ascertain whether or not negotiations are still possible on any subject and particularly Germany."[37]

His advice to Kennan flowed from his reading of the current world situation. The American position had improved since 1951. Geographically the Soviet Union had failed to make any gains; in fact, no land had been lost to the Soviets in Europe since the end of the war. Soviet-American relations, which influenced all aspects of world affairs, were pivoting in the West's favor. As Bohlen saw it, the Communists had threatened in Korea, but had been pushed back, forcing the Soviet Union into a "more quiet phase." These positive developments did not lead Bohlen to conclude that the West could let its guard down. Western defense capability, he warned, had to be maintained. The Western European allies still had to solve the problem of reconciling the need for military spending with the ability of their economies to sustain this buildup while paying adequate attention to domestic social needs.

Such were the potential weak spots that the Soviet Union could exploit, for Bohlen still worried about that dictatorship living on "fear and suspicion." But he recognized that the U.S.S.R. had lost some of its confidence, creating a "defensive, worried character" in comparison with the more confident and assertive character of other periods.

Bohlen cautioned that a frightened dictatorship was apt to react precipitously to minor provocations. Still, he felt that the West could cope with Russian sensitivity.

Bohlen was also starting to recognize the third world's role in this global struggle. His tenure on a committee to examine the problems of colonial territories exposed him to what he described as the "absolute unreasoning nationalism" in Iran, Egypt, and other Middle Eastern countries. This area, so vulnerable to Soviet exploitation, demanded a clear and rational policy approach.

His concern naturally extended also to the Far East. Korea had stabilized, but Indochina was potentially threatening, directly affecting America's European policies. The French, he judged, were in a rather good position by 1952. Yet he worried that, if large numbers of French troops were committed to Indochina, there would be insufficient forces to balance out German units in Europe, thus impeding the integration of West Germany into the European community; a military imbalance surely would encourage anti-German sentiment in France. In addition, Bohlen wondered if even the large numbers of French forces in Indochina were sufficient to withstand possible Chinese intervention.[38]

In acknowledging the relevance of the third world, Bohlen was wrestling with a problem which would later assume major proportions for American policy. But he viewed it from a primarily European perspective. He worried more about Moscow seizing the advantage than about the underlying cause of the problems. He had during the late 1940s seen clearly what was needed for Europe to resist aggression. He did not see things quite so clearly in the third world at this point. One of the prime causes of third-world disruptions he discounted merely as "absolute, unreasoning nationalism," indicating his apparent lack of real sympathy for the goals and ambitions of these movements. Their impact on the European situation and the potential for Soviet exploitation of these conditions biased his perception of these growing forces as factors to be reckoned with in and of themselves.

Still cautious in his assessment of the Soviet Union, and committed to the ultimate effectiveness of diplomacy, from the time of the conclusion of the North Atlantic Treaty Bohlen had become more convinced of the essential validity of a strong military as a bulwark to effective diplomacy, not to bully the Soviet Union, but to balance Soviet power. He stressed the need to approach any negotiations from a position of strength, never betraying weakness or lack of determination. Bohlen's view coincided with the perspective of many hard-liners in the Truman administration. Unlike these men, however, he opposed overemphasizing the Soviet threat and saw military preparedness only as a means of eliminating potential weak spots which the Soviet Union could exploit.

With the coming of a new Republican administration, Bohlen succeeded to the post of ambassador to the Soviet Union, his highest diplomatic position. But this accomplishment was accompanied by a decline in his influence within the government, and it thrust him into the domestic political limelight at a time when McCarthyism gripped the United States.

7.

A DEFEAT FOR McCARTHY

On 23 January 1953, President Dwight Eisenhower's newly appointed secretary of state, John Foster Dulles, offered Charles Bohlen the ambassadorship to the Soviet Union. Bohlen accepted, but not without misgivings. Given the political climate of the time, Bohlen was especially worried about how the Senate would react to his nomination and consequently the effect the nomination would have on Eisenhower's political standing. Conservative and isolationist sentiment, fanned by the activities of Sen. Joseph McCarthy and others, was running strong throughout the country. Eisenhower had been elected in part with the support of these conservatives, who used his campaign to voice their opposition to the Roosevelt-Truman-Acheson foreign policy of the Democrats, to whom they attributed the United States' purportedly poor position in relations with the Soviet Union. The particular target of their wrath was the Yalta Conference.

During the January meeting, therefore, Bohlen felt obligated to list some of the drawbacks to his nomination, as if Dulles was not already cognizant of them. First, Bohlen pointed out that he had been a part of the Roosevelt and Truman administrations, holding posts that involved him in the formulation and implementation of policy toward the Soviet Union. Second, he had been with Roosevelt at Teheran and Yalta, with Truman at Potsdam, and at the Council of Foreign Ministers meetings after the war. He had publicly voiced his evaluations of these exchanges in the past and had disagreed with criticisms leveled against them, particularly by conservative Republicans. Bohlen emphasized to Dulles that by raising these considerations, he was in no way placing any conditions on his accepting the ambassadorial post; Bohlen merely wanted the secretary to be aware of what in his background might constitute an embarrassment to the administration. Uneasy with Bohlen's assertions, Dulles suggested that as a professional Foreign Service officer Bohlen might decline to discuss the policies of previous administrations. But Bohlen replied that, while he strongly believed that Foreign Service officers were similar to army officers in that they should loyally carry out the policies of their superiors, the nature of America's concern about the Soviet Union and the positions he had held in the previous administrations placed him "in a somewhat different category." Bohlen told Dulles that if asked his opinion before a Senate committee, he would have to be forthright and honest. Bohlen recommended, therefore, that Dulles take preliminary soundings in the Senate before submitting the nomination and that the announcement be made as routinely as possible to avoid excessive publicity.[1]

Bohlen's relationship with both Eisenhower and Dulles went back a number of years. Bohlen had first met the future president, who was then commanding the Allied forces in Europe, in 1945. Bohlen, en route to the Yalta Conference, had stopped in Paris for some diplomatic discussions and was housed for a few days in Eisenhower's villa. Later Bohlen was serving in the Paris embassy at the same time Eisenhower was NATO commander. Both had a passion for golf and they played the game together quite regularly. As Bohlen got to know Eisenhower, he developed a respect for him as a person and a leader. He felt the general possessed an incisiveness and directness which did not come across in press conferences and other public encounters. Bohlen granted that the new president was no intellectual in the academic sense, but he had natural leadership abilities and a strong power of command. The respect was reciprocal. Eisenhower appreciated Bohlen's competence and chose him for the ambassadorship for that reason. He judged Bohlen a "tough," "firm," but "fair" diplomat.[2]

Bohlen's regard for Dulles was more subdued. He had worked with Dulles intermittently in the years after the war when Dulles was the Republican party representative to the Council of Foreign Ministers and other diplomatic delegations. During Dewey's 1948 presidential campaign, it was a foregone conclusion that Dulles would be the next secretary of state. At the time, the London and Moscow meetings of the Council of Foreign Ministers were in session. Bohlen disdained Dulles's constant worries about press reaction to his activities there. Bohlen also served with him later on the delegation that finalized the peace treaty with Japan in 1951.

Bohlen conceded that as secretary of state Dulles was hard working. But he relied on only a small group of associates, leading Bohlen to surmise scathingly that Dulles wanted no one around him who knew more than he did. Like many in the ranks of the State Department, Bohlen became disillusioned, especially after Dulles appointed Scott McLeod, a McCarthy ally, as department security chief, and then made an address calling for "positive loyalty" within the ranks. It was clear to Bohlen that Dulles, having coveted the secretaryship for so long, was bowing to pressure from McCarthy and others.[3]

But the two disagreed even more on the direction of American foreign policy. Dulles had a tendency to portray affairs in terms of black and white, while Bohlen, the consummate diplomat, saw things in shades of gray. During the 1953 campaign, Dulles had talked of "liberation" and the "roll back" of communism in order to gain the support of conservative Republicans. When Dulles became secretary, Bohlen was shocked to see that he seemed intent on carrying through with these policies.[4]

While Bohlen did not speak out publicly against the Dulles program, there was no doubt that he disagreed with it. Addressing a group of Defense Department officials in the fall of 1952, he granted that the term "liberation" sounded positive and dynamic, a declaration that Americans would not allow people to be enslaved by communism. But in a totalitarian state like the Soviet Union, the means to provoke and sustain a revolt were limited, unless one intended to lead a war of liberation, which he was sure Dulles did not intend. Thus one could not liberate Poland or Czechoslovakia by propaganda or subversive action. Bohlen did not think Dulles was being realistic, for, as he explained to the Defense Department group, "you can say what you would like to see; you can say what you would hope to see reasonably; and then, unfortunately, you say what is probably going to happen." From his experience, there was "a vast difference in what you would like to see and what you would commit your country to bring about, because a country that is as powerful as the United States cannot make idle promises. We cannot say to these people we will liberate you, that is our policy, and then fail to deliver on it."[5]

The statement is indicative of Bohlen's disagreement with Dulles on specific policies. When Dulles, speaking before the National Security Council shortly after the election, had suggested unleashing Chiang Kai-shek for an all-out assault on mainland China, Bohlen took issue. How could a small nation hope to conquer the mainland? Such talk itself was provocative and failed to reflect a realistic policy.[6] On another occasion, Bohlen in his capacity as department counselor had approved a speech George Kennan gave before the Pennsylvania Bar Association on 16 Jaunary 1953 in which Kennan tried to identify the source of America's conflict with the Soviet Union. Kennan criticized those who would make it the purpose of the United States government actively to promote the internal disintegration of Soviet power, a remark which the press interpreted as a critique of Dulles's liberation policy. Upon hearing of this address, Dulles was enraged. Bohlen, however, had called the speech "very good stuff" which successfully dealt with the problem of the menace of communism in American society.[7]

Nevertheless, it was Eisenhower, not Dulles, who chose Bohlen for the Moscow post. The president, despite misgivings about Bohlen's role at Yalta, supported him because he respected his abilities. Eisenhower further anticipated using Bohlen to defy the McCarthyites and establish his own administration's leadership in the foreign policy field. Dulles acceded to Eisenhower's choice because he wanted to remove Bohlen from the circle of policy makers in Washington. With Bohlen safely ensconced in Moscow, Dulles could tap his expertise when necessary without having to involve him in the actual formulation of policy. Making him ambassador, furthermore, would avoid problems that would have resulted with the Foreign Service professionals had Dulles appointed Bohlen to a lesser position in Washington. Dulles also tangentially hoped that the nomination might prompt Democrats at some future date to support legislation the administration might need.[8]

Dulles ignored Bohlen's initial suggestion to take soundings in the Senate before presenting the nomination. The secretary did not want to run the risk of leaks of information on the administration's nominations, leaks which were all too prevalent in that august chamber. But Dulles did try to avoid fanfare by making the nomination as routine as possible. It was sent to the Senate on 26 February, along with several others. The effort to obscure it failed.[9]

A storm of criticism erupted even before Bohlen was called to appear before the Foreign Relations Committee. Nonetheless, in preparing for his testimony, Bohlen underestimated the antagonism he would face even though he had been the one to warn Dulles of his own political liabilities. Bohlen was confident that he could handle the situation and prepared for his testimony in a superficial fashion. He met with Dulles only once during his preparation and restated his determination to speak out forthrightly even in the face of Dulles's desire to avoid any disruption which would discredit the Eisenhower administration's foreign policy.[10]

The Senate at this time was divided into three factions. The Democrats, now the minority party, had been linked to the Roosevelt-Truman foreign policy, as had Bohlen. With the exception of Pat McCarran of Nevada and Edwin Johnson of Colorado, this group supported Bohlen's nomination and relished the ensuing brouhaha, which pitted Republicans against Republicans.

On the other extreme was a group of Republicans who vehemently opposed Bohlen's nomination. Joseph McCarthy and others were determined to rid the country of previously established foreign policy, which, in their estimation, had lost China and Poland to the Communists, had prolonged the Korean War, and had ushered all the Communist subversives into Washington. A vociferous minority, they laid the blame for these ills on the Democrats and the Ivy League elite who constituted the infrastructure of the State Department, and they saw Bohlen as a member of that elite.

Finally, in the middle ground regarding the nomination was a group of Republicans who were determined to preserve party unity and who wanted to give the new president a chance. Sen. Robert Taft of Ohio, the respected party leader, alarmed at the McCarthyite attacks and intent on maintaining party unity, reluctantly assumed a leading role in support of Bohlen's nomination. He did not see the squabble over Bohlen as one "sufficiently important" to destroy party unity. Ultimately, thirty-four of the forty-five Republicans in the Senate voted in favor of the Bohlen nomination, but the battle was not without its casualties, and after the fight ended, Taft quickly warned Eisenhower that he should put forward "no more Bohlens."[11]

When on 2 March Bohlen appeared for the first time before the Foreign Relations Committee, all three groups were ready to voice their support or misgivings. Bohlen's most adamant opponent during the hearings was the caustic Homer Ferguson of Michigan, a Republican from an area with a large percentage of Polish voters. Hubert Humphrey, the liberal Democratic senator from Minnesota, emerged as Bohlen's strongest advocate. The questioning, which extended well into the evening, tended to focus more on Bohlen's interpretations of diplomatic decisions and his place in the Democratic foreign policy establishment, particularly at the time of Yalta, than it did on Bohlen's personal qualifications for the ambassadorship.

In the political arena of the early 1950s, to be associated with Yalta was a definite liability. Alger Hiss, a member of the Ivy League elite who had been convicted of perjury in 1950 for apparently lying about his communist activities before World War II and who was then serving a prison term, had been an authority on international organizations at that summit; any association with or references to Hiss were a definite liability. Yalta was also where Roosevelt had allegedly conceded Poland to the Soviet Union and finalized the Far Eastern agreement, thus opening the door to Soviet influence in the Pacific.

Bohlen, confronted with these issues, responded as he had warned Dulles he would and defended Roosevelt's decisions. Criticism of Yalta was an exercise in "hindmyopia," he declared. To understand and judge the decisions properly, one had to put himself in the position of the times. Bohlen admitted that there were valid critiques of Roosevelt's actions—the fact that ultimately there was no need for Russian troops in the Far East; that the Far Eastern agreement had been made behind Chiang Kai-shek's back; and the stubborn adherence to the principle of unconditional surrender—but overall the major reason for the agreement's failure was the Soviet Union's disregard for its terms. Had the United States not made the effort at Yalta to cooperate, however, he believed that its position of moral leadership in the world would have been eroded.

Not surprisingly, the question of Alger Hiss's role at the conference arose. Bohlen responded that, based on his observations during the meetings, Hiss, an advisor to the secretary of state, was never in a position to influence the president. The connections between Hiss and the Yalta agreements, he stressed, were erroneous.

When asked about Poland, Bohlen lamented some of the agreement's phraseology and conceded that even in 1945 it was a long shot to expect the Soviet Union to cooperate, but the fact of the matter was that the Soviet Union was already occupying virtually all of Poland at the time Yalta took place. Roosevelt was facing a *fait accompli*. For the Soviet Union to agree to elections and to accept limits on its control over Poland was a victory for the United States. Even Mikolajczyk, Bohlen reminded the senators, recognized this and accepted the Yalta terms as the best that could be expected. The agreements aside, Bohlen maintained that the map of Europe would not have been much different in 1953 had the conference never taken place.

The Far Eastern accord received the greatest attention. Acknowledging that the United States might have erred in dealing with the Soviet Union without Chiang Kai-shek's participation, Bohlen asserted that, at the time, the decision was considered a victory for Chiang. *Life* magazine, he pointed out, the avid supporter of Nationalist China, had interpreted the Yalta agreement as such. Roosevelt was dealing with a war, and the decisions he made, according to Bohlen, were strictly military. Estimates of possible American losses in the event of an invasion of Japan ran high. It was imperative to get the Soviet Union into the war in the Pacific. Russia received only what was necessary to secure its aid, most of which was territory it had lost during the Russo-Japanese War. Furthermore, the decision that the Soviets should seek Chiang's concurrence implied a recognition of his government by the Soviet Union.

Senator Ferguson was not entirely satisfied with Bohlen's assessment. He countered that this secret understanding had violated the

Atlantic Charter, the arrangement with Chiang at the Cairo Conference, and the Nine Power Agreement of 1922, which protected the territorial integrity of China. Bohlen retorted that such violation was made necessary by the military situation. China, he reemphasized, had not lost its sovereignty, but had gained recognition.

Finally, the committee was interested in Bohlen's evaluation of the postwar containment policy. Bohlen argued rather circumspectly that the term "containment" only represented a part of American policy and suggested a negative and somewhat passive approach. To him, the term described only the military side of international policy, aimed at stopping communism where it was. He preferred to stress the constructive aspect of American policy, for instance its efforts to help revive the economic life of Europe.

When queried about how he could support containment and yet adhere to the new program of liberation, Bohlen applied his own interpretation of "liberation," thus disguising his misgivings. Liberation suggested a more dynamic approach to foreign policy, he said, but it did not require the use of military power to free countries behind the iron curtain. Therefore, he did not envision that he would have trouble representing that policy in Moscow. Besides, reflecting what he had told Dulles earlier, he conceived his ambassadorial role within the confines of a loyal Foreign Service officer—to report on events and offer suggestions. Should he so violently disagree with a certain policy that he could no longer work with the administration, it was his prerogative to resign. However, he did not anticipate that as being necessary. Under no circumstances could he foresee an ambassador publicly criticizing the administration he represented.[12]

Bohlen's defense of the past foreign policy combined with his admission that an ambassador's role primarily entailed observing and reporting apparently took some of the senators by surprise. Six other nominations that had been sent by the administration along with Bohlen's were approved by the committee and sent to the full Senate. Bohlen's was held back for further consideration.

In the interim between Bohlen's first and second appearances before the committee, Stalin died on 5 March, making it imperative that someone be in Moscow to be close to the situation in the Kremlin and in the country. George Kennan, the previous ambassador, had been declared *persona non grata* in the fall of 1952 because of derogatory remarks he had made comparing the Soviet Union to Nazi Germany. Since that time, the post had remained vacant.

Although Stalin's passing militated in favor of a speedy confirmation, other events put the nomination's success in serious jeopardy. Rumors spread through Washington suggesting Bohlen was a homosexual, had a drinking problem, and had committed other immoral acts. A controversy involving Scott McLeod also surfaced. McLeod, a cohort of McCarthy's, had been appointed State Department security officer by Dulles, an appointment which had aroused the ire of most of the professional diplomats.

Supposedly, McLeod had seen Bohlen's FBI file, which had been compiled during a hurried investigation after Bohlen's nomination had been announced, and found questionable material in it. Dulles, purportedly presented with this material, had nevertheless overruled his subordinate and sent the nomination to the Senate. When McCarthy entered the battle, these rumors assumed added significance. While the Foreign Relations Committee had concentrated on Bohlen's part in and defense of Yalta and the Democratic foreign policy, the new allegations raised suspicions of Bohlen as a security risk.

Misinformation also leaked regarding Bohlen's confidential testimony before the committee. To combat the problem, Bohlen agreed to the publication of his testimony after he had the opportunity to edit it. But when news reached Washington of Stalin's death, Bohlen joined with Dulles in urging that the situation was too sensitive to risk releasing the material at that time. Thus the committee withheld publication until 22 March.[13]

The growing reaction to Bohlen's nomination caused Dulles to have serious doubts about his approval of the appointment. He was inundated with messages from congressmen and senators opposing Bohlen. One of the few prominent figures coming to Bohlen's defense was James Byrnes. He told Dulles that the late Sen. Arthur Vandenberg, an influential Republican and former chairman of the Foreign Relations Committee, would have endorsed Bohlen. Despite the vociferous opposition, Sen. Alexander Wiley, chairman of the Foreign Relations Committee, who had been counting heads, told Dulles that there were sufficient votes to get Bohlen's nomination out of committee.[14] But this did not totally satisfy the secretary. To assure the prestige and strength of the new Eisenhower administration, the appointment not only had to win approval; it also had to be an overwhelming vote of confidence—not so much in Bohlen, but in the ability of Eisenhower as a leader.

The FBI investigation particularly vexed the administration. Dulles was so irate at the leaks that he contemplated firing McLeod, the obvious source of the rumors. But he realized that it would not be politically expedient to remove an appointee so soon after his appointment. So he contented himself with passing a message on to McLeod reminding him that he was part of the State Department and was not working for any other person or individual.[15]

Political expediency dictated Dulles's stance toward Bohlen at this point. As James Byrnes had warned him, if the Bohlen nomination failed, Eisenhower would have trouble getting other nominations approved in the future. Therefore, when Bohlen himself became so frustrated that he offered to withdraw on 16 March, Dulles argued that he could not "quit in the middle." He assured Bohlen of the president's commitment and cautioned him against doing anything which might embarrass the administration.[16] Bohlen regained his composure and waited for his second appearance before the committee.

That appearance was delayed for two days when Bohlen contracted the measles; the delay gave the rumor mills additional time to work.[17] When the hearings did reconvene on 18 March, the senators first heard from Dulles. Hesitant to give Bohlen his total approval, he did, however, give him his complete and formal endorsement. He admitted that he disagreed with some of Bohlen's views, but he saw no reason to doubt Bohlen's loyalty or to categorize him as a security risk. Dulles pointed out that the Moscow post was not a policy-making position anyway.

When the question of the FBI report was raised, Dulles conceded that he had seen only the summary, not the complete file. He stated that the summary contained a long list of prominent figures who had endorsed Bohlen and he granted that McLeod had not cleared Bohlen, largely because of certain derogatory information. In cases like this, Dulles posited that it was customary for the secretary of state to assume final responsibility.[18]

When Bohlen was recalled, he was more subdued and cautious than before, but he reiterated his defense of Yalta. Clearly trying to avoid more detailed discussion of the Far Eastern agreement, he pleaded that he was not a Far Eastern expert. He also tried to deflect some questions by arguing that he had been primarily a translator at Yalta, although he could not completely negate his advising role.

Senator Ferguson, still trying to weaken Bohlen's testimony, asked about an address Bohlen had made in 1947 entitled "U.S. Relations with the Curtain States." In it, he purported that Bohlen had called Yalta "our most glorious diplomatic triumph," somewhat stronger support for the accords than Bohlen had voiced before the committee. But Bohlen categorically denied that he had ever made such a statement. "That is not the kind of expression I would use," he declared. The testimony concluded, the committee voted unanimously to send Bohlen's nomination to the full Senate.[19]

Throughout the whole affair, Bohlen suspected Dulles's sincerity in supporting his nomination, especially after the secretary, worried about his own public reputation if Bohlen's nomination should be defeated, took pains to avoid being photographed with him. Based upon Bohlen's

personal relationship with Eisenhower and the president's firm support
at two news conferences on 19 and 26 March—two crucial times during
the senatorial debate—Bohlen never doubted the president's resolve,[20]
despite the fact that these news conferences took place after the nomination had cleared committee and when Eisenhower was all but certain
that the votes were there for confirmation. Politics necessarily influenced Dulles as well as the thinking of all concerned, including
Eisenhower. Bohlen was a pawn in the game. On 17 March, the day
before Bohlen's second hearing, Eisenhower was informed of the FBI
report and J. Edgar Hoover's declaration that he would not give Bohlen
a complete security clearance. The worried president was ready to let
Bohlen withdraw, suggesting to Dulles that it would seem too political if
Bohlen withdrew because of the suspicions which had been raised, but
that Bohlen might do so for health reasons, even though Eisenhower
granted that this would look almost as bad. Only after the committee
had voted Bohlen's nomination out, and after Dulles had reassured him
concerning the contents of the FBI file, did Eisenhower publicly affirm
his support for his nominee.[21]

When Bohlen's nomination reached the floor of the Senate, Senator
McCarthy was prepared to enter the conflict. The senator had already
been briefed by McLeod and had attempted to get the security officer to
testify before his subcommittee of the Government Operations Committee. When Eisenhower and Dulles discovered this, they put McLeod
"on ice" in New Hampshire where he could not be served a subpoena.[22]

McCarthy needed McLeod's testimony because he had no concrete
evidence against Bohlen. Prior to the Senate debate, McCarthy had
visited the farm of Whittaker Chambers, the notorious *Time* magazine
editor and reformed Communist who had brought Alger Hiss down.
When their conversation turned to the Bohlen nomination, McCarthy
confided to Chambers that he had little chance of stopping the nomination and that he had little concrete material to use against the nominee
other than that Bohlen had "consorted with leftists and morning glo-
ries." Although McCarthy hinted that there was much more he was not
telling Chambers, Chambers concluded that "there wasn't more."
When McCarthy said he was going to ask Bohlen to take a lie detector
test, Chambers reminded him of the stigma attached to an ambassador's
effectiveness if he submitted to this. He then asked why McCarthy and
others, such as Pat McCarran, did not use their opposition—since the
battle was lost—as an opportunity to explain why they opposed the
nomination, elevating the conflict from politics to statesmanship. Mc-

Carthy countered that "sometimes you had to be a politician to be where you could manage some statesmanship." After McCarthy left, Chambers realized that he had been part of McCarthy's plans. The visit left the implication that Chambers had some damning evidence against Bohlen. Not wanting to be an accomplice, Chambers issued a statement denying he could link Bohlen to communism, admitting only that he considered Bohlen a poor choice as ambassador.[23]

McCarthy did not have a case, so characteristically he resorted to slander and innuendo in its place when the nomination was debated on 23 March. To the glee of the Democrats, who relished seeing the Republicans fighting among themselves, McCarthy went on the attack following Senator Wiley's committee report. Along with other opponents, he questioned some of the material Wiley presented in Bohlen's defense. Wiley had mentioned, for example, that Undersecretary of State Walter Bedell Smith endorsed Bohlen when he appeared before the Foreign Relations Committee on 5 March. Smith's challenged testimony was produced, confirming that he had indeed supported the nominee.[24]

McCarthy was forced to base most of his attack on the mysterious FBI report. He insisted that the question of derogatory information could be laid to rest by calling McLeod to testify—he now conceded that he could not call him before his investigative committee, but that the Foreign Relations Committee could do so—and by having Dulles testify under oath and Bohlen submit to a polygraph test. McCarthy charged that many Republicans were "holding their noses" in voting in favor of Bohlen simply because they wanted to give the president a chance.

Taft and others defended Bohlen. Taft denied the reliability of polygraph exams, noting that even J. Edgar Hoover lacked faith in them, and upheld the administration's prerogative to make the nomination. He was especially bothered that Dulles's credibility was being impugned by McCarthy's suggestion that the secretary testify under oath. Taft further argued that FBI operations could be seriously compromised if Bohlen's file were released. In an effort to break the roadblock, Taft agreed that two senators might be chosen to look at the file and return to report to the Senate.[25]

Taft had already spoken to Dulles about this tactic. By this time, the secretary was so worried about the political ramifications of the appointment struggle that he was quite willing to invite representatives to review the summary file. But such a solution was not that easy. The implication was that one of the reviewing senators would be a Democrat, leading Attorney General Brownell to oppose the review. Furthermore, the White House feared that opening the file to even two senators might constitute a dangerous precedent. The issue, however, had reached such proportions that the president overrode Brownell's objections and the invitation was tendered with the specific assertion that "the Executive Branch of the Government would not consider that this constitutes a precedent so far as it is concerned, but is due in this instance to a desire to recognize, so far as seems practical, the bipartisan approach to foreign policy matters."[26]

On 24 March, the Foreign Relations Committee chose Sen. John Sparkman, the 1952 Democratic vice-presidential nominee, to accompany Taft to the State Department to study the file.[27] The senators did so that afternoon and reported to the committee the next day.

The summary they examined contained a hodgepodge of material, curtly reporting the derogatory information. At the end, there was a list of other people interviewed who had nothing critical to say of the nominee. The derogatory evidence fell into two categories: questions about Bohlen's character and morals; and disagreements with the foreign policy viewpoint he espoused, on a few occasions questioning his loyalty to the country.

The former included allegations that Bohlen at one time had had a drinking problem, prompting his recall from Moscow in 1935. The report, however, stated that he got "drunk much less frequently" since his marriage. There were scurrilous references to possible homosexual tendencies. One woman noticed a "definite shading in his conversation and in his manner of speech which indicates effeminacy." She described him as sounding "quite girlish," except when he spoke the French language. Guilt by association furthered this charge. Some known homosexuals had visited him both in Paris and Washington. Finally, there was a reference to an illicit relationship between him and his brother-in-law, Charles Thayer. Because of his relation to Bohlen, Thayer himself, who was then consul-general in Munich, became the subject of an investigation regarding an alleged affair with a Russian woman and unsubstantiated charges of homosexuality. All of these allegations were typical of the charges leveled against many others under investigation during this time, and none of them had been substantiated.

The second category of criticisms touched on Bohlen's personal ambition and his policy views. One informant stated that Bohlen was "definitely more interested in his own career than in his own country." Bohlen, to one, had no character, but was an opportunist. The only substantial comments came from those who opposed his stance toward the Soviet Union. They associated Bohlen with the "Hopkins line" and with the "appeasement" of the Soviet Union. Consistent with prevailing political concerns, the fact that he was at Yalta and that he was a "Harvardian," like Alger Hiss, provoked suspicions. But no one could concretely substantiate any disloyalty in Bohlen.[28]

Taft and Sparkman examined the summary, then pressed to see the raw data. Hoover refused, however, assuring them that the summary accurately reflected the full file. Pressing the issue would politically do more harm than good, so the two senators contented themselves with the summary. Taft was satisfied, noting the allegations of immorality, but concluding that most of the material consisted of "differences of view on foreign policy" and that Bohlen's loyalty was "100%."[29]

On 25 March, backed by Sparkman, Taft presented his conclusions to the committee. Their examination of the summary file along with a letter Taft had received from McLeod stating that he, too, had seen no more than the summary, had convinced the two senators that the allegations were unfounded. They assured the committee that the bulk of substantive material involved differing viewpoints. They discounted the charges of homosexuality and concluded that there was nothing to suggest Bohlen was a security risk. The committee responded by authorizing Taft to give an abbreviated report to the full Senate.[30]

When Taft appeared before that body in the afternoon, he hoped to end the matter and call for a vote. But Sen. Pat McCarran persisted in his determination to have McLeod testify in order to ascertain whether he indeed disagreed with Dulles. McCarthy also spoke up again, reviving charges of Bohlen's connections with Yalta and the Truman foreign policy. Then to obfuscate the issue further, McCarthy presented a statement by a former Soviet foreign office official, Igor Bogolepov, who had defected to the West and become a professional witness for the anticommunist forces. Bogolepov described most of the diplomats in the prewar Moscow embassy as "friendly" to the Soviet Union. This group included Bohlen.

Styles Bridges, another hostile senator, also challenged Dulles's credibility. A committee composed of three professional diplomats—Joseph Grew, Norman Armour, and Hugh Gibson—had been established to evaluate the Eisenhower administration's diplomatic appointments. Dulles, he noted, had stated in his testimony before the Foreign Relations Committee that Bohlen's nomination had been cleared by the tripartite committee. But Bridges had spoken to Gibson's lawyer (Gibson himself was bedridden at the Mayflower Hotel following a heart attack) and had been advised that Gibson had not approved the Bohlen nomination. Sen. Everett Dirksen, another opponent, apparently clarified the matter further when he spoke with Gibson personally and discovered that Bohlen's name had been mentioned only casually. Although Gibson could not speak for the other two members of his group, Gibson asserted that he had not passed on the Bohlen case.

To defuse this latest attack, Sen. William Knowland, an administration supporter, produced a classified document given him by Dulles. It was signed by all three members of the committee and had attached to it a list of administration nominees, Bohlen included. Knowland would not allow inspection of the document since it contained names of other nominees which had not yet been made public, and McCarthy and others challenged its veracity. This new development postponed a vote until 27 March.[31]

On that day, the apparent inconsistency was quickly rectified. New Jersey Sen. H. Alexander Smith introduced letters from Joseph Grew and Hugh Gibson. Grew's letter, which also expressed the opinion of Norman Armour, the third member of the screening committee, described the process used in approving the nomination and assured the Senate that both men supported Bohlen. Gibson's letter acknowledged that Bohlen's name had come up. But since he knew little about Bohlen and had only met him casually on three occasions, he had deferred to his colleagues and voted neither way on the nomination. Rhetoric continued to flow after these letters were presented, but in essence the final obstacle had been surmounted. When the vote was called, Bohlen received seventy-four votes with only thirteen in opposition. Eleven of the opposition votes were Republican.[32] Bohlen had his ambassadorship, and Dulles had his political victory.

Senator McCarthy and his supporters were soundly defeated by Eisenhower. Their strength was sapped, and their decline had begun. Athan Theoharis, commenting on this episode, remarked that "in the future McCarthyites would need strong evidence; when they failed to produce it, the failure was costly."[33]

Throughout the episode, Bohlen had stood on the sideline as his future was determined in the political arena. Dulles's maneuverings increased Bohlen's disdain for him. Not only was Bohlen angered at Dulles's half-hearted support, as evidenced by his conspicuous refusal to be photographed with Bohlen, but Bohlen was further upset that McLeod's investigation of him had uncovered some allegations of immorality on the part of his brother-in-law Charles Thayer, leading to Thayer's decision to resign from the State Department rather than face a subpoena from McCarthy's committee, and that once again Dulles failed to intervene on behalf of a diplomat under attack.[34]

Besides being of personal concern to Bohlen, Thayer's fate was just one example of the tribulations faced by those in the State Department, which Bohlen believed was unfairly under attack by the McCarthy forces. Bohlen blamed Dulles for failing to defend the department, and he raised his concerns about department morale as a result of this state of affairs in Dulles's presence when the two went to the White House for Bohlen's farewell visit with the president. Dulles offered to leave the room when Bohlen broached the subject, but Bohlen responded that there was nothing he had to say to the president he would not say in Dulles's presence. The president responded to Bohlen's concerns by acknowledging that the appointment of McLeod was an obvious mistake, but that it would be poor politics to remove him at that point. Although Bohlen had failed to sway the president, he at least made his feelings known.[35]

Bohlen and Dulles had differed professionally, and their professional differences were enhanced by personal animosities. Even in Bohlen's departure for Moscow, these differences surfaced. Dulles discovered that Bohlen planned to leave for the Soviet Union alone and meet Avis

John Foster Dulles, Dwight D. Eisenhower, and Bohlen at the farewell visit before Bohlen's departure for Moscow in 1953. (Courtesy Dwight D. Eisenhower Library.)

later, after she had completed some last-minute arrangements. Dulles suggested to Bohlen that he revise these plans and travel along with Avis. When Bohlen asked why, Dulles reminded him that there had been allegations of his immoral behavior and it would look better if he left for Moscow in the company of his wife. As it happened, Bohlen did revise his travel plans, but not because of the tactless suggestions of Dulles, which was just one more aggravation.[36] The chasm between Dulles and Bohlen precluded much future influence on Bohlen's part in shaping American foreign policy as long as Dulles ran the State Department. Yet on a more optimistic note, Bohlen believed that his stand against McCarthy had given him added stature in the eyes of the Soviet leaders he would be dealing with for the next four years.[37]

8.

RETURN TO MOSCOW

Joseph Stalin had so dominated the Soviet Union that with his death on 5 March 1953, many observers, both inside and outside of government, expected drastic changes, possibly major breakthroughs in cold war tensions. Aware of this possibility, Bohlen arrived in Moscow in April 1953, alert to any diplomatic opportunity which might arise. As one observer remarked, "if the Russians wanted to talk turkey, Bohlen was the man who would listen."[1] But to Bohlen's dismay, his tenure in Moscow proved essentially a "sterile period," devoid of significant advances in Soviet-American relations, with many issues still unresolved when he left for his new post in the Philippines in 1957.[2]

Bohlen's duties in the Soviet Union were challenging, but frustrating, particularly because of his deteriorating relationship with Dulles. Bohlen's responses during the nomination controversy had not endeared him to the secretary, and as Bohlen's reports from Moscow repeatedly conflicted with Dulles's own impressions, the two moved further apart.[3]

Bohlen was at a watershed in his career. Thrust before the public during the squabble over his nomination, as ambassador he remained before the public eye. But the period of his greatest influence on American policy had passed with the end of the Truman administration. In his new post, he exuded confidence. Still youthfully handsome, six feet tall, and slender, Bohlen surprised his subordinates with his lack of formal diplomatic decorum. He shunned the traditional diplomatic attire of striped pants and cane and was often seen with his feet propped up on his desk, smoking a pipe as tobacco fell on the carpet. Yet beneath his informal demeanor, he was an experienced diplomat who had studied the Soviet Union closely for twenty-five years. Contrary to the practice of many other ambassadors, Bohlen directly contributed to the preparation of analyses and reports sent to Washington. His subordinates, his diplomatic colleagues in the other embassies, and the Soviet leadership all respected his competence.[4]

Nevertheless, Bohlen was left to observe and report with little influence on policy decisions. Still, there was much to observe. Soviet internal affairs were in a state of flux now that Stalin was gone. These shifts directly affected Soviet foreign policy, both toward Eastern Europe and in the all-important relationship with the United States.

Since Stalin had left no heir-apparent, three men in the Kremlin hierarchy collectively replaced the once all-powerful dictator—Georgy Malenkov, who held the post of premier; Lavrenti Beria, the minister of the interior, who controlled the secret police; and Vyacheslav Molotov, the foreign minister. Nikita Khrushchev, whom Bohlen initially overlooked as a contender for power, even though Khrushchev assumed the powerful post of party secretary relinquished by Malenkov, lurked in the background. The old dictatorship from what Bohlen could see adapted well to this new leadership. Obviously the government would maintain a monopoly on power, but the new leaders were eager to remedy some of Stalin's legacy by improving the peoples' standard of living, curbing arbitrary police power, and to a degree respecting the rights of national minorities.[5]

Although the framework for this new regime was a collective leadership, Bohlen fully expected that one of the group ultimately would dominate. Malenkov, a Stalin cohort who had impressed Bohlen long before the dictator's death, was Bohlen's choice. "Warren G. Malenkov," Bohlen sarcastically remarked, was an urbane and well-educated technocrat who was guiding the Soviet Union in a "back-to-normalcy" movement. Nonetheless, Bohlen viewed Malenkov's ascendancy with trepidation. Stalin had had "a great sense of prudence, caution, and unwillingness to take risks." As a "pure product of the Stalinist regime" who had never traveled abroad, Malenkov might be tempted, Bohlen feared, to more rash and impetuous actions than his predecessor.[6]

Bohlen saw in the new regime's policies a conscious plan to decentralize the "smothering bureaucracy" which had stifled a Soviet economy so preoccupied with heavy industry and to engineer reforms that might bring flexibility and efficiency to that industry. He worried that Americans misperceived the Kremlin as populated by "a bunch of Keystone cops shooting each other up in the halls."

The June 1953 arrest of Lavrenti Beria and his subsequent execution fed this impression. But Bohlen interpreted even this extreme action as a move away from, not toward, more use of terror. Beria had controlled the secret police. His demise, in Bohlen's judgment, suggested that the government was now trying to deemphasize the secret police and terror as an instrument of policy.[7] In analyzing the events surrounding Beria's arrest, as so often was the case in Soviet society, Bohlen had to rely heavily on indirect evidence. One of the earliest indications of Beria's decline was the omission of his name when *Pravda* printed a list of guests expected at a Moscow opera. At that point, Bohlen saw little of significance since Beria might simply have been outside the country. So Bohlen and his wife decided not to postpone a planned vacation in France. Even when the Kremlin announced that Beria had been arrested, Bohlen was not overly concerned and only grudgingly complied with Undersecretary of State Walter Bedell Smith's request to cut short his vacation and return to Washington for consultation.[8]

Upon his arrival, Bohlen found Dulles excited that Beria's purge would lead to a bloody struggle and the overthrow of the regime. To disabuse him of this misconception, Bohlen speculated that Beria apparently had resisted the collective leadership's effort to rein in the secret police. Dulles had the further misimpression that Beria represented a "soft" policy, leading to the conclusion that his purge meant a tougher dictatorship and more cold war. To the contrary, Bohlen countered that Beria was being held personally responsible for the policy of increased repression in East Germany which had led to protest and trouble soon after Stalin's death. Bohlen believed that the so-called "soft" policy which had begun would continue.[9]

As Bohlen was trying to unravel the internal changes, he was also serving as a conduit to facilitate foreign policy initiatives emanating from Washington. Eisenhower anticipated the possibility of a shift in cold war relationships following Stalin's death and did not want to miss the chance to ease tensions.

During March 1953, Bohlen, who personally doubted that there would be drastic changes in Soviet policy, had tried to temper Eisenhower's enthusiasm with a realistic and cautious portrayal of the situation. At the time, the president was considering an address that opened the door to dialogue and proposed a meeting of the Council of Foreign Ministers. Bohlen advised waiting until the situation was clearer. He warned that if the speech were simply a gesture and contained no substantial proposals, its impact might be counterproductive and hinder rather than further the foreign policy possibilities stemming from Stalin's death. Not only did Bohlen urge that substantive proposals be judiciously conceived, but also he suggested that they be coordinated beforehand with the British and the French, which, he reminded the administration, could not be done precipitously "without causing great difficulties with those two Governments and evidences of disunity which would be most damaging at the present time." A European defense community integrating West German forces into the military defenses of Western Europe was uppermost in the mind of America's allies at the time. A foreign ministers meeting, Bohlen predicted, might slow the process toward this community.[10]

Although Eisenhower followed Bohlen's advice and did not act at that moment, he was unwilling to wait too long. Soon after Bohlen arrived in Moscow, he received a draft of a proposed presidential address. Seeing much that was good in it, Bohlen nevertheless was still skeptical. It was "highly probable" that the Soviet response would be much the same as would have been the case under Stalin. The address would "set off a new round of the propaganda battle in which . . . we would have the best of it but any serious business would be lost in the welter of charges and counter charges." Bohlen therefore continued to advocate postponement.[11]

Eisenhower decided to follow his own inclinations, however, and delivered his speech before the American Society of Newspaper Editors on 16 April 1953. He criticized the Soviets for disrupting the international situation, yet posited that tensions could be eased. He deplored the military expansion taking place on both sides of the iron curtain and expressed hope that Stalin's death might be a turning point in U.S.-Soviet relations.[12]

The speech was received favorably by the Moscow diplomatic corps, but Bohlen had to wait a week for the full Soviet reaction. When it appeared in *Pravda* on 25 April, he was somewhat surprised that it was not just propaganda, as he had expected, but a response that evidenced much thought and apparent compromise among the leadership, who clearly tried to avoid "throwing cold water" on the prospects for peace, while endeavoring to shift responsibility for the world's problems back to the United States. Bohlen's reading of the Soviet response indicated a definite preference for pursuing negotiations through diplomatic channels rather than through the United Nations. Since there was no concrete indication of the Soviet position, however, Bohlen still hesitated to jump to conclusions. The advantage now lay with the United States, he argued, so Washington should carefully structure its reply to avoid letting this important exchange deteriorate into a propaganda war.[13]

Eisenhower's address was merely an overture. Later developments would be a mixture of cooperation and confrontation. One thing was certain, however; any Soviet-American rapprochement would be severely hampered until something was done to bring about a solution to the Korean War. At the time of Eisenhower's inauguration, the repatriation of Chinese and North Korean prisoners remained the major obstacle to the conclusion of an agreement. The Truman administration had insisted on the right of all prisoners to decide whether they wanted to be repatriated. Although Eisenhower did not dispute Truman's stance, he was intent upon finding a settlement. Bohlen, consulted on the feasibility of enlisting Molotov's assistance in getting the North Koreans to come to terms, proposed that the United States might offer to delay the release of prisoners as a concession to break the deadlock. But along with this concession, he felt Washington had to make it clear that it had reached the limit of compromise and would yield no further.[14]

On 25 May, the U.S. delegation at the Panmunjon armistice talks presented a final offer quite in line with Bohlen's advice. It appeased Communist demands by providing that prisoners who declared before a neutral repatriation commission that they did not want to return home would be freed and demobilized only after a 120-day waiting period, in order to give them adequate time to change their minds. But also consistent with Bohlen's warning to be resolute, the document did not budge on the forced repatriation question and insisted that the U.S. would bend no further.

To enlist Soviet help in this endeavor, Dulles dispatched Bohlen to plead America's case with Molotov. Dulles concurred with Bohlen's recommendation that an unofficial approach with America's terms typed on plain sheets of paper would be best; for, as Bohlen argued, an official meeting might force the Soviets into a position of formally backing its allies.[15]

Bohlen met with Molotov on 28 May. To underline U.S. seriousness, he suggested that the rejection of this offer might lead to the termination of armistice talks and the resultant escalation of the war. Molotov listened intently, but gave no indication of a response at the time. But he summoned Bohlen to his office on 3 June and delivered a carefully worded statement implying that the Soviet Union had persuaded North Korea and China to accept American terms. By 27 June an armistice was signed. Unbeknownst to Bohlen, his efforts played only a partial role in prompting the Russians to intervene. At the same time he was approaching Molotov, Dulles was suggesting through Indian diplomats that the United States was contemplating the use of nuclear weapons in Korea, reinforcing the seriousness of Bohlen's message.[16]

The Korean impediment removed, the American government was ready to exploit the favorable reaction to Eisenhower's call for a dialogue. Perhaps the United States and Soviet Union could turn to other problems threatening world peace, including the arms race, now made more dangerous by the vast proliferation of nuclear weapons. Bohlen fostered some hope that such efforts might bear fruit, for he perceived a willingness on the Kremlin's part to pursue disarmament.

A step in this direction was the president's address before the United Nations in December 1953, promoting his "atoms for peace" plan. The United States, the Soviet Union, and other nations possessing fissionable materials would contribute fissionable material to a United Nations-sponsored international atomic energy agency, which would use that material to fulfill peaceful needs of the world. Prior to this speech, Dulles cabled Bohlen from Bermuda where he and the president were meeting with British and French leaders. He ordered Bohlen, when alerted by a prearranged signal, to go to Molotov to encourage him to study Eisenhower's address carefully. Although Bohlen was not informed of the speech's content beforehand, he was told that the president was serious about what he was going to propose. After Eisenhower gave the address, Bohlen went to the Kremlin to deliver a copy of it to Molotov to stress the president's determination.

When the General Assembly of the United Nations reconvened in September of 1954, the Russians expressed some interest in pursuing Eisenhower's proposals. But Bohlen, serving as a go-between, watched the talks deteriorate through Soviet insistence that discussion of control of atomic energy be broadened to include the whole issue of disarmament. Lacking needed support from the Soviet Union, it took until 1957 for the International Atomic Energy Agency to become a reality.[17]

Apparent Soviet intransigence did not mean, however, that the Russians eschewed disarmament. This contradiction was brought home to Bohlen in a discussion with Marshal Zhukov during a British reception in June of 1955, a month before the Geneva summit meeting. Zhukov so emphasized the need for arms control that Bohlen concluded disarmament was the real "concern of the Soviet government at present juncture." Zhukov told him that the arms race was senseless, dangerous, and potentially disastrous should a new war erupt. Bohlen was amazed at how Zhukov's remarks contrasted with the traditional Soviet viewpoint, how they were "not at all in accordance with the party line that atomic war would mean only the destruction of capitalism." Zhukov indicated to Bohlen that he thought the time was ripe for a "bold move" in arms control.[18]

Although the potential for disarmament agreements existed, discussions were only in the preliminary stages during Bohlen's tenure in Moscow. Real progress would not come until the 1960s. If the arms race seemed far from solved at this time, the East-West conflict over Germany was equally frustrating. The United States, intent upon shoring up Western European defenses, pressed for a European Defense Community incorporating West German troops into the NATO military structure. America's allies, particularly France, were nearly as uneasy about the implications of a possible German resurgence as was the Soviet Union.

In 1954, the Council of Foreign Ministers met in Berlin (25 January–18 February), seeking a solution to the German dilemma. Bohlen attended in his capacity as ambassador, but was excluded from Dulles's circle of advisors and thus contented himself with observing. As he saw Soviet tactics here, the Russian goal was neither to reach agreement on a German or Austrian treaty, nor to plan for general European security. Rather, the Soviets hoped to use these meetings, he suspected, to hamper movement toward a defense community. It was obvious to Bohlen that Molotov was trying to break down American-European cooperation, thus isolating the United States. Once again, therefore, Bohlen was not surprised that nothing was accomplished.[19]

Both sides left Berlin determined to pursue their goals. The western allies finally settled their differences over Germany's future; at meetings in London and Paris during October of 1954, the Western European Union was created, bringing West Germany into the alliance system and allowing it to rearm with certain restrictions. On 5 May 1955, the United States, Britain, and France ended their occupation of Germany. Not surprisingly, the Soviets took this initiative quite seriously, and Bohlen warned Dulles to expect a reaction, although, as the western plan evolved, he was struck by how "restrained" the Kremlin's action ultimately was. Based on this restraint, Bohlen told the department that he did not foresee direct Soviet military action; still, he did not rule out a radical shift in policy, especially since Soviet prestige was at stake. He anticipated that the Soviet Union's reply would probably take the form of continued steadfast support for East Germany, further consolidation of the Eastern European military system, and increased expenditures in the eastern bloc. He exhorted Dulles to expect such developments and not to overreact.[20]

At the same time that the western alliance was coalescing, the leadership in Moscow was undergoing more change. Nikita Khrushchev now was responsible for guiding the Soviet reaction to the Western European Union. Bohlen for a long time had underestimated Khrushchev, even though the Soviet leader had held the key post of party secretary since 1953. Bohlen had disdained him as a crude politician, a "baby kisser," a conservative Stalinist, and doubted that he would prevail over the managerial group led by Malenkov.

But beginning in 1954, signs of growing rifts in the collective leadership began emanating from the Kremlin. Malenkov, for example, remarked publicly that nuclear war might mark the end of civilization. When others in the leadership reiterated the traditional line that nuclear war would lead to the collapse of the capitalist system, Malenkov publicly recanted his "error." Other signals of Malenkov's decline came to Bohlen's attention until Malenkov "requested" in February 1955 to be removed from the premiership.

Once again Dulles expected a ruinous power struggle. And again Bohlen saw the transfer of power in a different context. The change involved issues, not personalities, he insisted. Malenkov had pushed for consumer goods at the expense of heavy industry and had injected more private enterprise into the agricultural system. Unfortunately for Malenkov, his reforms were timed poorly, given West Germany's incorporation into NATO. Bohlen suspected that others in the Kremlin favored reorientation back to heavy industry to reinforce military preparedness. With Malenkov's passing, Khrushchev seized the reins of power, but, as Bohlen was quick to interject, again only as first among equals.[21]

Bohlen perceived a certain pattern in Khrushchev's reactions to the establishment of the Western European Union. As Bohlen had predicted, the Kremlin increased its military preparedness and tightened its hold on Eastern Europe, announcing the Warsaw Pact in 1955. Furthermore, in a surprise move in April, the Soviet leader invited representatives of the Austrian government to visit Moscow; a treaty was concluded, with the Soviets agreeing in return for Austrian neutrality, to end occupation and abandon their demand to reintroduce troops.

Dulles was worried about how quickly this treaty was concluded, fearing it might be a move to block German rearmament by holding out neutrality as a possible alternative. Bohlen, however, doubted this assumption. Because the Soviets had occupied the poorer area of Austria, they realized that a neutral Austria would be preferable to an Austria incorporated into NATO. According to Bohlen, the Soviet Union had accepted as inevitable both the status of Austria and the division of Germany. Consequently he advised the State Department that any attempts to impede the Austrian treaty might be interpreted as obstructionism and would thus be counterproductive.[22]

In a move parallel with the conclusion of the Warsaw Pact and the Austrian treaty, Khrushchev began to improve relations with Eastern Europe. As Bohlen would note in 1957, Eastern Europe had been a "projection" of the internal Stalinist regime. Thus in certain respects the problems confronting the Soviets in Eastern Europe were more serious and less manageable than those inside Russia proper, "if only for the reason that these regimes in Eastern Europe had been imposed by alien armed forces"; some people in these countries had what Bohlen described as a "collective memory" of "democratic forms,"[23] a memory the Soviets did not have to deal with within their own borders.

A key element in Khrushchev's program for Eastern Europe was Yugoslavia, whose leader, Marshal Tito, had been excommunicated from the Soviet bloc by Stalin. The fence-mending had begun after Stalin's death, when Malenkov tried to normalize relations. Now Khrushchev traveled to Belgrade in late May of 1955 in what Bohlen thought was a bumbling effort to court Tito. In Belgrade the Soviet leader conceded that the satellites within the Soviet system could follow a course based on their own national interests, a policy Stalin had adamantly resisted. Bohlen, writing to the State Department on 3 June, was intrigued by the possibilities Khrushchev's admission presented. Although Yugoslavia did not rejoin the Soviet fold, the potential existed for a "new phase" in Soviet relations with other Communist states.[24]

As Khrushchev courted Yugoslavia, it appeared that he was also moving toward easing tensions with the West. The Geneva summit meeting of July 1955, followed by a session of the Council of Foreign Ministers in November, highlighted this erratic course of Soviet-American relations. Dulles had opposed Eisenhower's decision to meet with Khrushchev, but Bohlen encouraged it as a valuable opportunity for the president to gain some insight into Soviet attitudes, although Bohlen expected little of substantive value to result. The Soviets, he pointed out, had agreed to meet because they were worried about the massive arms proliferation, which strained the Soviet economy. The fear of war and economic deterioration may have made Khrushchev more willing to negotiate, but Bohlen suspected that the old Bolsheviks in the Kremlin who had retained their fear of the West limited his freedom to act.

As Bohlen predicted, the "spirit of Geneva" which prompted so much journalistic euphoria was devoid of substantive accomplishments. Eisenhower scored a public relations victory when he proposed an "open skies" disarmament arrangement, calling for aerial inspection of nuclear facilities. But the Soviets, ever suspicious of external meddling in their internal affairs, rejected Eisenhower's suggestion. Khrushchev, furthermore, refused even to discuss his control over Eastern Europe, and the German issue remained at a stalemate.

Meetings Bohlen had during this conference with the Soviet ambassador to the United States confirmed his appraisal of the Soviet position on West Germany. Bohlen discovered that the Soviets were intent upon keeping communications open. While they were unhappy about Germany's integration into NATO, they were resigned to it. In the short range, therefore, they sought a "modus vivendi" whereby the status quo would be accepted and the two military alliances could meet, try to settle disputes peacefully, and work to prevent any increase of troops stationed on foreign soil. Nevertheless, the Soviets' long-range goal, Bohlen realized, remained to eliminate the United States from Western Europe. The Kremlin leadership stuck to the hackneyed argument that Eastern Europe was still independent and not acting at the behest of the Soviet Union.[25]

Reflecting on what he had learned at Geneva, Bohlen confided to British Prime Minister Anthony Eden in 1956 that the Soviets wanted "peace at no price." They wanted to ease tensions in Europe, but were determined not to accept a German agreement. At the Geneva Council of Foreign Ministers, Molotov had spoken in a particularly brutal fashion against free elections in Germany, which appeared to Bohlen as a conscious effort to impress the West Germans with the "illogical, heedless, sheer power of Russia," and to drive them to negotiate with Moscow directly.[26]

Khrushchev, Bohlen believed, left the summit resigned to the fact that a stalemate would continue in Europe and consequently decided not only to continue to foster better relations with his satellites, but also to exploit third-world nationalism. Reconciling Soviet-American differences, therefore, would be more difficult, though not out of the question. Still, Bohlen apparently thought Soviet foreign policy was becoming more realistic. Despite the Kremlin's unhappiness with the status of West Germany, he did not foresee that the Soviets would be willing to resort to confrontation to forestall German independence.

Khrushchev's need to consolidate his power within the Soviet state was one factor which encouraged this restraint in Soviet foreign policy. As Bohlen had already learned, under collective rule efforts were made to link Communist doctrine with the prevailing situation. Clearly the major emphasis of much reform in the Soviet Union had been related to eliminating many of the more onerous aspects of Stalin's regime and justifying as much of this change as possible in ideological terms. But prior to the Twentieth Party Congress in 1956, care was taken to denigrate Stalin himself only obliquely.

The official party line as presented at this conference, especially Khrushchev's address attacking Stalin, convinced Bohlen of the "confidence and stability" extant in the Soviet system. The criticism of

Stalin caused some disruption in his native Georgia and encouraged some zealots to carry destalinization further than the party leaders intended, but it did not hamper external or internal Soviet development.[27] Initially Bohlen knew nothing of Khrushchev's devastating speech. He had learned from informants that Anastas Mikoyan, a member of the Praesidium, had criticized Stalin as a poor economist and a poor Marxian philosopher. But only after the congress adjourned did Bohlen hear rumors that Khrushchev had condemned the former dictator as a deviationist who had abused power. When the CIA in Warsaw obtained what was purported to be an accurate copy of Khrushchev's speech, Dulles asked Bohlen to authenticate it. Comparing the CIA document with other information, Bohlen corroborated it. In his customarily cautious style, he advised Dulles not to publish it. He granted that to do so would inform the public of events transpiring in the Soviet Union and would enlighten serious students of that country, but he worried that publishing the speech simply for its propaganda value might embarrass the Soviet leadership. It also might backfire and enhance Soviet prestige and credibility, for the theme of the speech—that there would be no repetition of Stalin's crimes—and the fact that the actual text was even more balanced than the leaks indicated, might convince many that the Soviet leadership had indeed "reformed."

Bohlen suggested that, if the decision were made to publish, the government should not be the agent, on the slight chance that the document might be fake. Dulles rejected Bohlen's advice, however, and released it on 4 June, a step Bohlen later conceded was correct since it removed lingering doubts in some circles that Khrushchev had actually made the speech.[28]

The speech may have enhanced the Soviet reputation, but coupled with efforts to defuse growing nationalist pressures in Eastern Europe by loosening old oppressive Stalinist controls, it also confronted the Kremlin with new crises in the form of disruptions in Poland and Hungary. As far as Bohlen was concerned, internal factors, not talk of liberation emanating from Eisenhower's foreign policy spokesmen, were predominantly responsible for these uprisings.[29]

With information tightly controlled in Moscow, Bohlen had trouble keeping abreast of Polish riots which erupted in June of 1956 and continued into the fall, forcing Bohlen's reports to Washington to be quite tentative. *Pravda* and *Izvestia* published typical accusations of outside agitation, adding to Bohlen's difficulties in obtaining an accurate perspective. At a meeting with Polish leaders in Warsaw during the fall Khrushchev decided not to use Soviet troops to suppress the revolts. Instead, Wladyslaw Gomulka, who had been imprisoned during

Stalin's era, took over the Polish Communist party and the government at the same time that the minister of defense, Konstantin Rokossovsky, a Soviet general of Polish descent, was removed from his post. Gomulka proceeded to institute reforms, while remaining continually cautious of the limits of Soviet tolerance.

Bohlen doubted that Gomulka gained power because the Soviets were unable to handle the situation in Poland. Rather, Bohlen thought that when the Soviet leaders went to Warsaw, they discovered that the revolt had the backing of the people, and more importantly, of the army and certain elements of the secret police. Gomulka survived, Bohlen emphasized, because Polish nationalism was strong and because Gomulka was astute enough to seek reform only to the extent that the Soviet Union would tolerate it.[30]

Such was not the fate of Hungary. When the insurrection broke out on 23 October, it appeared to Bohlen that the Soviet Union might pursue the same course it had in Poland. Imre Nagy, like Gomulka a Communist jailed under Stalin, was made premier. Bohlen suspected, but was not certain, that Nagy was the man who had asked for Soviet intervention. But Bohlen soon became confused about the revolt's direction. On 27 October, he informed the State Department that in a case like Hungary the Soviet Union would not use force because it was dealing with another Communist regime. Nonetheless, he cautioned, that assumption might not hold true if a pro-Soviet minority in the Hungarian party asked for intervention, a request he considered highly unlikely. Bohlen hesitated to advocate any form of American intervention, at least for the immediate moment. He conceded the possibility that the United States might achieve psychological and political advantage over the U.S.S.R. by taking the Hungarian issue to the United Nations, but he counseled Dulles to do so only after Nagy's relationship to the Soviet Union was clearly understood. If Nagy was heading in the same direction Yugoslavia had, the U.N. involvement might embarrass him and drive him closer to Moscow. If Nagy was simply following the Soviet line and had compromised himself, only then might the U.S. accrue benefits from such an appeal.

Bohlen's person-to-person encounters with Soviet leaders, including Zhukov and Khrushchev, yielded little to clarify the situation. At one point, he felt certain that the Soviet Union would liberalize its policy toward Eastern Europe; at another, the Soviet leaders seemed intent upon justifying their resort to force. Bohlen's confusion was alleviated when on 31 October Nagy, pressured by the revolutionary factors, asked for the removal of Soviet forces from his country, proclaimed an end to one-party rule, withdrew from the Warsaw Pact, and appealed to the United Nations for help.

Soviet officials were even less candid than usual with Bohlen until Khrushchev approached him at a reception for Syrian diplomats on 3 November. Probing, Bohlen asked Khrushchev what his government intended to do about Nagy's request for Soviet troop withdrawals. Khrushchev snapped that negotiations were proceeding and that things would be straightened out. When Bohlen mentioned reports of a Soviet troop buildup, Khrushchev angrily retorted that his government would use as many troops as were necessary and that Bohlen should realize that the Hungarian situation was no joke. Khrushchev's tone was ominous, prompting Bohlen to rush back to the American embassy and wire Washington that the Soviets were ready to invade; they did so on 4 November.

Bohlen lamented that, unlike the Poles, the Hungarians had gone too far. Further, he suspected that Khrushchev feared Hungary would eventually line up with the West as a hostile country, despite the fact that Dulles had sent Bohlen to Khrushchev specifically to impress upon him that the United States had no intention of seeking military allies among the Soviet satellites.[31]

Any propaganda advantage the United States might have derived from the Soviet invasion, however, was negated by the Middle East crisis of 1956. The Middle East was rapidly developing into one more arena of the cold war as both the Soviet Union and the United States concentrated their attention there.

In the beginning of 1956, Bohlen had pointed out to the State Department that one result of the Soviet regime's growing stability was an increased interest in the third world. The Soviet leaders, having weathered the transition from Stalin's rule, had become more confident, had made economic progress since 1953, and had improved their defense capabilities. Bohlen argued, in addition, that the Geneva summit had convinced them that the United States did not want war, making the Kremlin somewhat more optimistic about the future.

Thus, according to Bohlen, the Soviets were ready to step out and compete with the West in areas where they had not done so before. Still, he hastened to stress that their goals remained unchanged—strengthening Soviet power and influence wherever possible, at the same time weakening the position of the free world and hampering the growing western security system. While their goals remained constant, Bohlen perceived that their activities deviated from the traditional Communist concept of two camps, Communist and enemy, and now pragmatically included a third, the neutral camp.

This led Bohlen to predict that with the exception of disarmament talks the Soviet Union was abandoning negotiation as a diplomatic tool and was making anticolonialism not just a propaganda piece, but part of its policy. Anticolonialism, neutrality, and economic cooperation, particularly in the form of trade, were weapons the Kremlin could utilize to attract uncommitted countries in Asia, the Middle East, and Africa. Any of these countries seeking to maintain a policy of neutrality would receive support and assistance from the Soviet Union.

Bohlen conceded that the Soviet Union possessed certain advantages in this scheme. Posing as the champion of neutrality, it was supporting the existing policies and desires of a considerable number of countries. Furthermore, although Russia still could not compete economically with the West, the offer of trade without overt conditions of military or political pacts was attractive to the third-world countries. Bohlen insisted that this was a long-term trend. While not abandoning military threats and subversion as a tactic, the Soviets would subordinate these to diplomacy, he predicted. The West, therefore, had to recognize this new challenge and marshal its economic and technological superiority to oppose it.[32]

Bohlen now comprehended the diplomatic ramifications of third-world nationalism more than he had at the end of the Truman years. This trend in Soviet foreign policy played an unsettling role in the Suez crisis, which erupted in the fall. Acting, as Bohlen described it, on the "semispur of the moment," the Soviets exploited the unstable Middle Eastern situation. Previously suspicious of western military moves, a suspicion intensified by the formation of the Baghdad Pact in 1955, the Soviets endeavored to appeal to Arab nationalism by emphasizing anti-Zionism.[33] Their efforts were made even more effective by the fact that the Baghdad Pact had particularly angered Gamal Abdel Nasser, the Egyptian leader who had emerged as the spokesman for Arab nationalism. When Dulles withdrew economic support for Egypt's Aswan Dam project after Nasser purchased needed weapons from Czechoslovakia, Bohlen was shocked. This "tactless" American move played right into Soviet hands, Bohlen insisted, prompting Nasser to nationalize the Suez Canal in July of 1956.

The nationalization of the waterway triggered a crisis that could not be eased by a meeting in London of the canal users during August. Russia was not one of the sponsoring powers. Dulles, through Bohlen, asked the Russians to attend. But the secretary of state made it clear that, while he hoped for an amicable settlement, the U.S. was firmly behind the British and the French. He also linked hopes for progress on disarmament to the success of these talks. It was obvious to Bohlen that the secretary wanted to compel the Soviet Union to use its influence to persuade Nasser to relinquish control, but that the Soviets were not eager to do his bidding.[34]

Bohlen attended the London meetings, once again relegated to observer status. He disliked what he saw. Dulles, Bohlen thought, approached "downright trickery and dishonesty" in his manipulation of the parties involved. To the British and French, Dulles talked as if he favored them. To the Russians, he voiced anti-British and anti-French sentiment, consequently encouraging them in their policy of opposition to those western countries. The Kremlin exploited the situation to show its support for the Egyptians, a real propaganda boon.[35]

When negotiations failed, the Israelis invaded Egypt on 29 October in an attack coordinated with a British-French ultimatum and occupation of the Suez Canal on 30 October. The U.S.S.R. responded by threatening to send "volunteers" to aid Egypt and to unleash missiles on some of the western capitals. The Kremlin called upon the United States to join against the aggressor powers. Disturbed by these developments, Bohlen pressed the president to take every step necessary to achieve a cease-fire.

Eisenhower did not need to be reminded of the urgency of an American reponse. Dulles was hospitalized for cancer treatments, so the president intervened directly and instructed Bohlen to impress on the Soviets how seriously he viewed the situation and to encourage them to act prudently. The United States then worked through the United Nations to persuade the British and French to withdraw as a United Nations force moved into the canal zone.

America's misleading and indecisive policy, Bohlen acknowledged ruefully, both aroused the animosity of Arab nationalism and created cracks in the NATO alliance, especially when the United States found itself in the position of joining with the Soviets in the U.N. to force the British, French, and Israelis to withdraw. Buoyed by its gains in the Middle East, the U.S.S.R. expanded its support for countries turning against the West, regardless of their doctrinal persuasion.[36]

Bohlen's appraisal of the situation after these crises was far from a reaffirmation of the "spirit of Geneva." The Soviet position in Eastern Europe remained non-negotiable, and its stance on Germany had hardened even further. Overall, tensions may have relaxed, but Bohlen did not see therein the demise of the cold war. Rather, the lessening of immediate tensions meant keeping the "intensity within limits" in order to avoid "spilling over into a hot war." Soviet foreign policy was becoming more realistic; while based more on "common sense" as it tried to clean up many of Stalin's excesses, beneath the surface the basic Soviet attitude remained essentially the same.[37]

As Bohlen told the Senate Foreign Relations Committee in May 1957, however, there was some reason for hope, some real potential for making headway, especially on disarmament. The Soviet Union was hesitant to relinquish its World War II gains; however, it was equally determined to prevent another war. As a realist, Bohlen admitted that any agreement, "if it depended for its observance and fulfillment on Soviet good faith in honoring a pledged word," was of little value. But as long as agreements were to Russia's interest, he thought they would be kept. In addition, if agreements were self-implementing, or if they involved a good deal of inspection and control, with the consequences of violation outweighing the temptations to violate, then Bohlen was confident they were worth pursuing. The Soviet Union, he re-emphasized, was the "master" and not the "servant" of ideology. The preservation of the state took precedence over the extension of communism. The more Russia had to lose, the more seriously the possibility of discussing disarmament could be taken. Not only did the U.S.S.R. realize that an arms race might "spill over" into war, but it also understood the economic ramifications. Resources would have to be diverted to the military, creating even more of a strain on the Soviet economy.[38]

By 1957, Bohlen was feeling the frustration of his four years in Moscow. Soviet-American relations had followed a changing course, but were still strained. Few officials in Washington, he bemoaned, were eager to make any meaningful headway in improving relations. Nikita Khrushchev, looking back on Bohlen's tenure as ambassador, charged that Bohlen turned out to be a "shameless reactionary" who supported "all the most hateful policies then conducted by antagonistic forces in the United States." Rather than improving relations, Bohlen had, in Khrushchev's judgment, succeeded in "freezing them."[39] Such a scathing characterization could be attributed to Bohlen's personal pessimism that Soviet attitudes would ever change combined with the fact that, as ambassador, he was the official personification of the Dulles foreign policy, despite his personal differences with Dulles's approach.

Behind the official diplomatic facade, however, Bohlen's differences with Dulles had been magnified during his term in Moscow. Nevertheless, Bohlen was surprised when he received word from the secretary on 26 December 1956 of his removal from the ambassadorship on the pretext that he wanted to take up writing as a profession. Bohlen returned to the United States to clarify this misinformation, only to find that even Eisenhower had been told that this was his wish. Although Bohlen would have preferred to stay in Moscow for one more year, he was nonetheless willing to accept a transfer; four years was a long time to serve in the Soviet Union, and it had been a tense and eventful period. But Bohlen wanted another foreign post. He had received some offers to leave government service and join several research organizations studying Soviet-American relations, but such offers did not appeal to him.[40]

Bohlen's insistence upon remaining in government service presented Dulles with the dilemma of finding a suitable post for him, a difficult task since he doubted Bohlen's true commitment to the administration's foreign policy. He "did not like [Bohlen's] setting himself up in business here and criticizing us," Dulles told his brother Allen. "If he is in Washington he will work against us." The secretary was thus pressed to find an opening where Bohlen would be remote from the center of decision making. After considering Cuba, Pakistan, and a few other embassies, Dulles decided to send Bohlen to the Philippines, a Class I embassy where he thought Bohlen would be "adequately insulated" and could "do less harm." The major obstacle was to get Senate approval. Brooding about his predicament, Dulles told his brother that "if there is trouble we can withdraw and he will get out and there will be a stink because he has a big reputation in the press and we told him he could not be in Europe."[41] Dulles was greatly relieved that Senate opposition was scattered and Bohlen was easily confirmed.[42]

As for Bohlen, he remained the ultimate diplomat through the unpleasant transfer, disguising his feelings toward Dulles. He moved to the Philippines with mixed feelings of regret and anticipation. As he told James Byrnes, "while the choice was nil," he looked forward with great interest and pleasure to this "completely new experience," the change both "climatically and politically" from Moscow being about "as sharp as could be devised." He tried to convince himself that diplomatic developments, such as the negotiations over the air and naval bases, were making the Philippines of "considerable importance and interest."[43] But in the words of one reporter, Bohlen waited in the Philippines, "chafing over his inability to use his Russian knowledge garnered in 26 years."[44]

His "exile" in the Philippines had its pleasant side. He and his family enjoyed the chance to travel and see a new area of the world. The tropical climate permitted him to hone his golf game. But he could not escape from his obsession with Soviet affairs and tried to keep in direct contact with developments. His close friend and successor in Moscow, Llewellyn Thompson, and Christian Herter, Dulles's eventual successor as secretary of state—and even Dulles himself, sporadically checking on the accuracy of Thompson's reports—solicited Bohlen's expertise. But the secretary persisted in snubbing Bohlen's insights, particularly since they continued to clash with Dulles's own interpretations. What Bohlen observed from a distance did little to alter his perception of the Soviet Union's direction. When news reached him of the attempted ouster of Khrushchev in June of 1957, followed by the removal of Malenkov, Molotov, and Kaganovich from the Praesidium, Bohlen continued to deemphasize the personal power Khrushchev had attained. Bohlen pointed out that the Soviet leader had overcome his opposition by calling a meeting of the Central Committee, the body that had ostensibly elected him. This committee decided his fate, thus reaffirming the strength of the collective leadership.

Again, when Khrushchev assumed the premiership from Bulganin in 1958, Bohlen denied that the shift marked a return to one-man rule. He pointed out that the power play was just another step in the revival of governmental institutions and party leadership and was only secondarily a reflection of Khrushchev's personal ambition. Industrialization, Bohlen argued, had fostered a more educated Soviet society with a technician class that had to be brought under party control.

When the Russians launched Sputnik in 1957, Dulles gloated that the emphasis on space technologies exposed the inability of the Soviet economy to handle the development and production of manned bombers. Bohlen disagreed. The Russians had decided to leap over intermediate defenses and go straight to a missile program. He saw no indication that the Soviet economy could not handle manned bombers and missile production at the same time.

Berlin once again became an issue in 1958 when Khrushchev threatened to transfer authority over East Berlin, in essence abrogating all agreements on access to Berlin concluded between Russia and the United States. Bohlen wrote Thompson that the administration's best bet would be to free its ambassador to approach Khrushchev for direct discussions to determine the Soviet leader's true purpose. American strategy, he suggested, should be to get the West German government negotiating directly with the East Germans. He acknowledged the arguments about Communist discipline and organization versus "the looser set-up in any democracy"; but he pointed out that "50 million vigorous and prosperous Germans as against a group of East German Communists with a very insecure and uneasy hold on 17 million could not come out very badly for our side."[45] Thompson agreed, but Bohlen was in no position to press his point.

While the Soviet scene remained Bohlen's primary interest, it was not his major responsibility. His diplomatic skills were being taxed in Manila as he negotiated a new treaty for three naval and air bases, a treaty complicated by the American demand for jurisdiction over crimes committed by American servicemen stationed there. Disagreement with the Philippine government led to protracted talks lasting into 1959.[46]

When Bohlen had accepted the Manila post, his plan was to remain there for two years until he had accrued the maximum Foreign Service pension benefits, then to retire and seek a position in the private sector. On the one hand, he contemplated getting completely clear of the foreign policy field; on the other hand, he was tempted by several offers of research posts.[47] When Dulles resigned in April 1959 and was replaced by Christian Herter, Bohlen's plans changed. Herter appreciated Bohlen's expertise and made public his intention to bring Bohlen back to Washington, one of the few attractions which could have dissuaded Bohlen from retiring.

Several obstacles hindered his transfer, however. First, Bohlen's opponents were not totally silenced on Capitol Hill. Senators Everett Dirksen, Styles Bridges, and others adamantly opposed any substantive post for him. To sidestep this opposition, Herter decided to appoint Bohlen his special assistant, an office requiring no senatorial confirmation.[48]

Administration confusion, detected by the American press, was a further hindrance. Bohlen's transfer had been agreed upon in principle on 9 July 1959, and Herter had stated such at a news conference. But the effective date was postponed pending the completion of the Philippine treaty. At a news conference on 15 July, however, Eisenhower replied to a question on the Bohlen appointment by denying that there was any talk of bringing Bohlen back. He described Herter's report to him on the subject as "completely negative." The press interpreted this to mean that the president was "cool" to the appointment, setting off a flurry of speculation.

But confusion, not disenchantment with Bohlen, seemed to be the reason for Eisenhower's remarks. The president had misinterpreted Herter's decision to keep Bohlen in the Philippines pending the completion of the base negotiations. Some observers interpreted Eisenhower's remarks as a reflection of his irritation at the constant leaks emanating from the State Department. When Eisenhower discovered the response of the press, he quickly sent a personal apology to Bohlen expressing his confidence in him, and at a 22 July news conference, the president returned to the question and endeavored to clear up all misconceptions.[49]

After the confusion had been settled, Bohlen was officially offered the post in August. He approached his new assignment amid journalistic speculation of a shift away from the Dulles foreign policy. But where the shift would lead, no one seemed to know. To some reporters, Bohlen would be tough, but open to negotiate. To others, Bohlen represented a harder line. To such conservative publications as *Human*

Events, which catalogued Bohlen's past associations, the appointment was a great mistake. Herter was an "awfully nice fellow, but very weak," and had been misled by Bohlen's qualifications and by liberal columnists. To this publication, Bohlen's appointment meant an end to the "hold-the-line-against-Communism legacy" established by Dulles.[50]

Bohlen's return was not so seminal to foreign policy as had been speculated. He was happy to be back, feeling "like an old fire horse returning to his home station," and working for Herter was a pleasure. The secretary, on the surface a reserved and civilized man, down deep was a tough diplomat who did his homework. With Dulles gone, however, Bohlen conceded that Eisenhower was now running his own foreign policy.[51]

Bohlen was quickly in the thick of diplomatic activity. He accompanied Herter to Paris for a meeting of the NATO foreign ministers, who were attempting to deal with Charles de Gaulle's growing intransigence. Then in April of 1960, Bohlen was dispatched to Moscow to help prepare for Eisenhower's visit, which had been prompted by the improved relations between the two powers following Khrushchev's visit to the United States in 1959.[52]

A summit meeting in Paris had been planned to precede the president's trip to Moscow. Caught up in the euphoria of the recent contacts between the super powers, many in the State Department optimistically anticipated settlement of major disputes, including the ever-present conflict over Berlin, but Bohlen, returning from Moscow, did not share this optimism. He was convinced that Khrushchev himself was not in a very secure position. The Central Committee contained many critics of his foreign policy. Khrushchev, "the travelling salesman for Communism," as Bohlen caustically described him, struck a discordant note among his political opponents, who objected to the way he courted the capitalist countries.

Khrushchev, furthermore, appeared to be using Berlin for blackmail purposes; Bohlen advised Eisenhower to be resolute and show the Soviet leader that nothing could be gained by threatening a separate peace with East Germany. Bohlen feared that, although Khrushchev did not want war over Berlin, he would be forced to take a stand at some point or becoming the laughingstock of the Communist world. The United States could expect progress at the summit only if it approached the Soviet Union as a nation rather than an ideology, unlike the converse attitude so often evident in the Dulles years.[53]

Bohlen's predictions were never tested. A U-2 spy plane, shot down over the Soviet Union on 1 May 1960, doomed the summit. The facts surrounding this flight and Washington's response to its exposure disturbed Bohlen. In retrospect, he argued that the flights should never have been scheduled so close to the convening of the summit, and especially not on 1 May, an important Soviet holiday. Furthermore, after the fact, Eisenhower blundered by accepting responsibility for the flights. He should have pleaded "no comment," Bohlen suggested; the president's admission of blame put Khrushchev, who was under pressure within the Kremlin, in a very bad position. Since Khrushchev had gone against certain Kremlin hard-liners who had opposed his negotiating with the American president, Eisenhower's admission of responsibility gave ammunition to Khrushchev's political opponents. The president's stance, Bohlen further worried, damaged American prestige in the eyes of the rest of the world.[54]

A cloud of suspicion hung over the summit when it convened on 16 May. The American delegation, apprised in advance by the British and French of Khrushchev's plans to undermine the conference and publicly embarrass the president, wrestled with what approach to take. They learned that Khrushchev intended to demand that the United States meet several conditions: an apology for the U-2 flights; an agreement to terminate the flights; and punishment for those who had sanctioned them. Eisenhower had already stopped the flights, but found it impossible to comply with the other two conditions. Bohlen also agreed that the United States could not concede under pressure, but the members of the delegation decided that they could not unilaterally terminate the summit for lack of a convincing excuse. A confrontation was unavoidable, and when the summit formally began, there was a brief, but uncomfortable encounter. Bohlen was impressed with Eisenhower's self-discipline as he grew increasingly angry listening to Khrushchev's twenty-minute harangue presenting his expected demands. In the face of this diatribe, the president succeeded in maintaining his composure.

After Khrushchev finished, Prime Minister Harold Macmillan and President Charles de Gaulle spoke, affirming their support for the United States. Eisenhower followed; disguising his anger, he informed Khrushchev that he had ordered aerial spying stopped, but the president refused to issue an apology. This was not enough to satisfy the Russian leader. He left this session of the summit, and although the other leaders convened for one last meeting, Khrushchev did not return. The summit ended in failure.[55]

In briefing the press during the events at Paris and later before the Foreign Relations Committee, Bohlen tried to place the incident in a long-range perspective. The summit had not failed because of the U-2 incident alone, Bohlen surmised. Khrushchev originally had had two plans for the meeting. He intended either to scuttle it, or to compel America's allies to pressure the United States into accepting Soviet demands. Once again, Bohlen attributed these tactics to Khrushchev's internal political difficulties. If it became clear at the summit that no satisfactory accommodation could be reached on the Berlin issue, Khrushchev was preparing to blame the western allies. Based upon this analysis, Bohlen judged that nothing had been lost by the conference's failure. Furthermore, while hesitant to predict Soviet actions, he doubted that Soviet-American relations would change much as a result of the summit or the events preceding it. Despite the U-2 incident, Khrushchev did not want to return to the depths of the cold war.[56]

Bohlen stressed that the United States had to remain on guard, however. During the summer of 1960, the Soviet Union continued to show its dissatisfaction by withdrawing from disarmament talks and extending its offer of military assistance to regimes that served its purpose. Bohlen warned Eisenhower that, while some of the Soviet initiatives might be just words, offers of military assistance in particular might put them in a position where they would have to follow through. He contended that:

> While they may have no intention of acting on these threats, it is nevertheless possible that the Soviets, if they feel that this propaganda campaign is succeeding, might progressively commit themselves in future courses of action in the military field which would be extremely difficult for them to disavow if ever put to the test.

Bohlen worried that the absence of a strong response from the United States might create the appearance that the U.S.S.R. was in total command of the course of East-West relations. He thus advised that the president ask Congress for an additional $3 to $5 billion for the Defense Department and foreign military aid. Bohlen's advice coincided with the concerns of others who encouraged the president to promote such budget increases in Congress.[57]

For the remainder of Eisenhower's tenure in office, Bohlen accepted a number of roles—as acting assistant secretary of state for international organizations and as the American negotiator at a futile round of talks to settle the Soviet lend-lease debt from World War II. But the atmosphere since the end of the summit was not conducive to improved relations. Khrushchev was willing to wait for a new administration before he could contemplate any serious efforts to ease the tensions.

9.

THE LAST YEARS

The 1960 election ushered in John F. Kennedy's administration, and with it a new spirit and optimism in the country. Even Charles Bohlen, nearing the end of his career, fell under the spell of the Kennedy mystique. He admired the young, energetic president.

Bohlen had first met Kennedy in 1939 when, as a student, Kennedy had visited Moscow.[1] While the two had little contact in subsequent years, Kennedy was aware of Bohlen's reputation and experience. Soon after the election, Kennedy received a congratulatory note from Khrushchev. Uncertain how to respond, he turned to Bohlen and George Kennan. Both suggested that Kennedy unofficially send a personal note of thanks, indicating that if the Russians were serious about discussing outstanding differences, the president would be willing to do so. Both diplomats were not overly optimistic about this possibility. In fact, Theodore Sorensen, Kennedy's aide and confidante, recalled that Bohlen's proposed reply "seemed more curt than courteous," and that Kennedy responded more prudently than Bohlen had suggested.[2]

Not long after this incident, Kennedy's secretary of state-designate, Dean Rusk, informed Bohlen that he was considering him for one of the major European ambassadorships. Bohlen, however, asked to remain in Washington for a time in order to get a feel for the new administration's direction, and Rusk retained him as special assistant for Soviet affairs.[3]

Bohlen was impressed with Kennedy from the outset. The president appeared flexible and receptive to new ideas. Although the organization man in Bohlen made him a bit uneasy about Kennedy's tendency to by-pass official channels—Bohlen often would pick up his phone in the department to find the president personally calling him for advice—he applauded how receptive the president was to the insights of others.

Kennedy exuded a voracious desire to learn, and he turned to the experts for his information. Old hands at negotiating with the Soviet Union—Bohlen, Harriman, and Thompson—spent hours briefing Kennedy in detail on their perceptions of Soviet-American relations. Bohlen was flattered to be admitted to the inner circle as one of the elder statesmen.[4] In two days of meetings during February of 1961, for instance, the president sat back and listened, periodically posing questions to stimulate the proceedings. Bohlen and the others were one in their general impressions, with a few differences arising periodically. Bohlen, for example, argued that the influence of ideology on Soviet foreign policy was not yet dead, although it took a back seat to Soviet security concerns. On the contrary, Harriman stressed the personal nature of Khrushchev's rule, a factor which Bohlen, who had been so intent upon emphasizing the movement toward an institutionalized government and a collective society, gave less credit to. Despite these long sessions, Bohlen doubted that Kennedy ever really grasped the subtleties of the Communist doctrine. The president appeared to be more interested in the practical aspects of relations with the Soviet Union than with the nuances of theory.

In the course of these talks, several initiatives which would affect Kennedy's early foreign policy came up for discussion. During one session, Kennedy broached the possibility of a summit meeting. Bohlen seriously doubted, based upon his past experience, that summits were the proper place for decision making; still, he and Thompson agreed that the president would never clearly understand what he was up against until he had met Khrushchev face-to-face. Thus when Thompson returned to Moscow, he carried with him a letter for Khrushchev proposing a spring meeting at a neutral site such as Stockholm or Vienna.

Castro's takeover in 1959 and his subsequent swing toward communism had made Cuba a major concern also. Since Kennedy had injected Cuba as an issue in the 1960 campaign, he felt some compulsion to deal in strong terms with the Castro regime. Faced with the international and political realities, Kennan and Bohlen gave the president the same advice. Realizing the possible repercussions of an invasion, they warned that any action Kennedy might approve would have to be quick and successful. For a military movement against Cuba to drag on would be disastrous for America's diplomatic reputation unless the United States was willing to escalate it into a major confrontation.[5]

Despite the less-than-enthusiastic endorsement by Bohlen and Kennan, Kennedy pursued the plan for Cuba's invasion based primarily upon assurances of success from other advisors. Bohlen had been aware of the impending operation, the planning of which had begun while Eisenhower was still president, and his briefing with Kennedy was not the last time he was brought in on the preparations. Soon after briefing the president, he was once again called to the White House, this time for a meeting with CIA Director Allen Dulles and members of his organization. Bohlen was disturbed by talk of an invasion. He privately questioned its potential, especially since its success in part hinged on the CIA's erroneous claim that a U.S. military strike would trigger uprisings in the countryside. Bohlen knew that revolutionary fervor died slowly, making the likelihood of such a mass upheaval against the revolutionary government doubtful. However, during the meetings he kept his doubts to himself and adhered strictly to his narrow function of apprising the president of possible Soviet reactions to the invasion. Given the fact that Cuba was of no real strategic importance to the Soviet Union, Bohlen discounted the possibility that the U.S.S.R. would intervene militarily. Rather, the Kremlin would take advantage of the propaganda value of an American military action and protest loudly. Even if the conflict became protracted, the Soviet Union, in his estimation, would do no more than send arms and supplies to the Castro regime. His analysis encouraged rather than discouraged the invasion planners.

In early April, while returning from a meeting with the British prime minister in Key West, Kennedy again tried to discuss the Cuban venture with Bohlen, and again Bohlen side-stepped the issue by contending that he was not a Cuban expert.[6] Bohlen's reservations about the invasion were well-founded, making his failure to speak out the more disturbing and raising questions about his judgment. In retrospect Bohlen admitted that "like an idiot" he had passed up a chance to press his point of view. He pointed out that the invasion of Cuba was "almost inevitable," given the fact that publicly Kennedy had so strongly denounced the Eisenhower administration's failure to counter Castro's threat to Latin America; nonetheless, Bohlen's refusal to speak out cannot be defended.[7] Kennedy respected Bohlen as an advisor, and this was not an area totally alien to Bohlen's expertise; he had dealt first-hand in the past with Communist revolutionary fervor and he knew how slowly it died. Since the success of the plan was based on the CIA's miscalculation of the strength of revolutionary support for Castro's regime, had Bohlen expressed his concerns forthrightly he might have persuaded some of the planners to look more closely at their assumptions. However, evidently believing that the CIA plan was a foregone conclusion, given Kennedy's campaign promises, Bohlen neglected his duty and decided not to press his point regarding a course of action he judged he could not change.

But he was correct in assessing Khrushchev's reaction once the invasion began. The Soviet leader sent an angry letter to Kennedy, denouncing the invasion and expressing his intention to extend all necessary aid to the Cubans. Upon receipt of this communication, the president called upon Rusk, Bohlen, and Foy Kohler, deputy undersecretary of state for political affairs, to formulate an appropriate response. Bohlen drafted the letter, and Kennedy revised it. Aimed at countering Soviet propaganda, Kennedy's message informed Khrushchev that free people throughout the world did not recognize the historical inevitability of the Communist revolution. The great revolution in the world was that of those seeking to be free.

The president also had to explain the debacle to the American people and decided that a previously scheduled address to the American Society of Newspaper Editors on 20 April was an appropriate forum. Theodore Sorensen drafted the speech, then met with Bohlen and others to refine it. Its intent was to stifle demands for retaliation against Castro, to reassure America's allies, and to ensure that the Soviet Union did not misinterpret American restraint as a sign of weakness by emphasizing that that restraint was not inexhaustible.[8]

Kennedy's speech and his judicious handling of the failed invasion helped the U.S. stumble out of a bad situation, but the Bay of Pigs fiasco held long-range ramifications both within the administration and throughout the world. Nevertheless, even as the Kennedy administration was trying to minimize its losses, Khrushchev agreed to Kennedy's earlier invitation to meet at the summit. The conference was scheduled for June in Vienna.

Bohlen traveled to Vienna with the delegation and, with other close advisors, sat beside Kennedy as he came face-to-face with his Soviet counterpart. The proceedings developed as Bohlen expected. Khrushchev proved no more bellicose than in the past, and the discussions were unproductive, devoid of substance. The two leaders referred the Laos situation to a conference in Geneva, where the conferees ultimately assigned neutral status to that country. Disarmament negotiations made no headway, and in fact by early September the Soviets had broken the informal moratorium on nuclear tests in the atmosphere which had been in place since the Eisenhower administration. Germany, and particularly the status of Berlin, proved the most vexing issue, however. Khrushchev demanded a treaty recognizing the existence of an East and West Germany by the end of 1961; he threatened to sign a separate treaty with East Germany, leaving West Berlin in a precarious position, should that recognition fail to materialize.

Bohlen watched uncomfortably as the inexperienced president tried to argue ideology with Khrushchev. As Bohlen recalled, it was certainly not a "gay" occasion. The experienced Bohlen's judgment was that Khrushchev was no rougher than on other occasions, but the confrontation certainly had an impact on Kennedy.[9] Not only was this a frustrating meeting, but as Kennedy journeyed back to Washington via London, he wrestled within himself about the proper response to Khrushchev's Berlin challenge. Bohlen's admonition not to take Khrushchev's threats too seriously failed to sway the president.

In the wake of the Bay of Pigs, Kennedy felt he could not be intimidated concerning Berlin. But what to do was the question. Hardliners, particularly Dean Acheson, urged that Kennedy had to impress upon the Russians the gravity of the situation, which to Acheson entailed a general mobilization and even a declaration of a state of emergency. Bohlen, on the contrary, joined a more cautious group which opted for a more measured approach, avoiding the repercussions at home of full mobilization and preventing the impression abroad of a hysterical America. Kennedy borrowed something from both extremes. In July, he announced increased draft calls, mobilization of some reserve and National Guard units, and asked for additional congressional appropriations for the military. Bohlen, despite his fears of overexaggerating the Soviet position, considered this course of action "useful." It certainly sent Khrushchev a message.[10]

Khrushchev answered in August by ordering the erection of the Berlin Wall, ending the emigration from East to West Berlin. Once again Kennedy was careful, but firm. He sent 1,500 troops by road from West Germany to West Berlin to reinforce the city's garrison. To underline his determination he dispatched Vice-President Lyndon Johnson to Berlin, accompanied by Bohlen and Gen. Lucius Clay, former military commander of the city. Bohlen was favorably impressed with Johnson's willingness to accept advice and his success at lifting the morale of the Berliners.

The intense feelings of the West Berliners, who despised the wall's erection, particularly since the wall had been built by East Germans rather than Russians, profoundly affected the usually circumspect Bohlen. Upon his return, he told Kennedy that in the future any attempt by the Soviet Union to harass America's allies or erode their rights had to be met with swift, decisive action, even overreaction. The restrained American response to this provocation had seemingly increased the confidence of the Communists and consequently lowered the morale of the West Berliners who questioned U.S. determination to protect West Berlin. Although Johnson's visit had helped reassure the West Berliners, Bohlen believed that the U.S. government could not take a chance that its resolve might be questioned again in the future. Berlin, he was convinced, was of crucial importance to future Soviet-American relations. If the United States succumbed to blackmail, its bargaining position, in Bohlen's opinion, would be eroded.[11]

Subsequent assignments in later months reinforced Bohlen's worries. Close on the heels of the Berlin crisis, Bohlen accompanied Dean Rusk to Geneva in March 1962 for the reopening of arms limitations talks, stalled since the Soviet Union had resumed atmospheric testing in 1961. Any hope that Kennedy's stand in Berlin might make the Soviets more malleable and willing to make progress in arms questions proved futile.[12]

Throughout these critical months, Bohlen gained considerable insight into the intent and direction of the Kennedy administration so that when offered the French ambassadorship in 1962, he accepted willingly, in fact, eagerly. Not only were he and Avis particularly fond of Paris, but also he viewed dealing with French President Charles de Gaulle as a real political challenge. When Bohlen went to the White House on 17 October for his farewell visit, however, he found a somber president, immersed in the demands of another emergency. Kennedy showed Bohlen aerial photos of Soviet personnel placing medium- and intermediate-range ballistic missiles in Cuba. Bohlen needed no coaching to grasp the critical nature of this discovery. As it had been in Berlin, America was again being tested.

The president planned to gather a committee, the executive committee as it came to be called, to develop a reasoned response to this Soviet challenge. After the Bay of Pigs invasion, Kennedy had told Bohlen how disillusioned he was with the so-called "experts," particularly the military. He now was not going to act until he had considered all options.

Bohlen was present only at the executive committee meetings on 17 and 18 October before his departure for France. Kennedy had contemplated detaining him in Washington; but Bohlen dissuaded him, for any sudden change in plans, he argued, would jeopardize Kennedy's effort to keep the Soviet Union from guessing that he was aware of the missiles. Besides, Bohlen pointed out, Llewellyn Thompson had recently returned from Moscow and could provide as informed a perspective on the Soviet Union as he could.[13]

But before he departed, Bohlen made his position known. Perhaps he hoped to rectify the reticence he had exercised in the planning stages of

Bohlen's farewell visit to John F. Kennedy before departing as ambassador to France in 1962. (Courtesy John F. Kennedy Library.)

the Bay of Pigs invasion. Although he later declared that he admired the way Kennedy handled the missile crisis—combining in a masterful fashion a limited military response with the strongest possible diplomatic language—Kennedy's reaction did not totally coincide with Bohlen's preferred course of action. During the sessions of the executive committee that Bohlen attended, members evaluated both military and diplomatic options ranging from a limited air strike to a full air strike to an invasion to a blockade. By 18 October, two of the plans came to predominate—the "Rusk" and the "Bohlen approaches." Rusk opted for a limited or "surgical" air strike without prior warning, an action opposed by the diplomats present, by the military men who doubted that a limited air strike was possible, and by those advocating a blockade.

The "Bohlen approach" combined quiet diplomacy with a resolute, but prudent, challenge to Soviet moves. Bohlen, for so many years an advocate of reasonable military strength to complement diplomacy, argued for a blockade over an air strike. But he urged, both as he participated in the executive committee discussions and in a parting hand-written memorandum to Kennedy on 18 October, that any military decision, whether blockade or air strike, be preceded by private diplomatic correspondence with the Kremlin. In his memorandum, which he handed to Rusk for transmittal to the president, Bohlen admitted that missiles could not be tolerated in Cuba. Before the U.S. resorted to force, however, he proposed a stern letter to Khrushchev emphasizing that the United States "mean[t] business." Bohlen anticipated that the tone of Khrushchev's reply would betray his intentions. If the premier's answer was unsatisfactory and the decision to use force was made, Kennedy's letter would help establish America's case before its allies, for Bohlen was convinced that an air strike would certainly lead to war, not to a "neat disposal" of the bases. He thus concluded that the best course if all else failed was to seek a declaration of war against Cuba and force the missiles' removal.[14]

Bohlen's direct role in the crisis ended when he travelled to Paris to assume his new post. Back in Washington the "Bohlen approach" won at least partial support from the executive committee and the president. While Kennedy chose not to pursue quiet diplomacy at first, he did opt for a blockade—or quarantine—over an air strike. Faced with the quarantine, Khrushchev backed down, but the Soviet premier's reasons for provoking the United States with missiles in the western hemisphere puzzled Bohlen. Perhaps, he speculated, Khrushchev had underestimated Kennedy's resolve, drawing the wrong conclusions from the bungled Bay of Pigs invasion and thinking that the United States would take its case to the United Nations, consuming precious time that would allow the missiles to become a *fait accompli*.

Bohlen's traditional mode of analyzing the Soviet Union was to place events in the context of Soviet global policy. Potentially, the missiles accomplished two purposes for the Soviet Union. First, they could be used to force a settlement on Berlin and the division of Germany on terms favorable to the Russians. Second, standing in support of Cuba might counter Communist Chinese charges that the Soviet Union "had abandoned revolution in favor of comfortable deals with capitalistic powers."[15] The latter accomplishment would be particularly appealing to the Kremlin, given the growing competition between the Soviet Union and China for leadership of the Communist bloc.

The crisis, according to Bohlen, had far-reaching ramifications. It in part charted the course of future Soviet initiatives, particularly in Latin America. Ruminating on why Khrushchev had resorted to such a provocative move in the first place, Bohlen was reminded of how Lenin had once compared Russian national expansion to a bayonet thrust. "If you strike steel," Lenin was reported to have said, "pull back; if you strike mush, keep going." Bohlen speculated that if Khrushchev had invested a good deal of money and effort in nuclear hardware he hoped never to use in battle, he might want at least to use it for diplomatic blackmail.[16] As in so many incidents Bohlen had observed during his career, he once again saw the Kremlin probing for weak spots. In this instance, Khrushchev had obviously struck steel. Kennedy's response not only enhanced American prestige among its allies, it also undoubtedly contributed to Khrushchev's fall from power.

France had openly supported the United States during the missile crisis. But Franco-American relations as a whole were less amicable. Bohlen's five years in Paris, therefore, proved trying. Dealing with de Gaulle, a man Bohlen admired as one of the few truly great men he had met, was particularly difficult. Relations were at their high point immediately after Bohlen's arrival; from there they deteriorated, culminating in French withdrawal from the NATO military structure in 1966.[17]

De Gaulle officially informed the United States in March of his intention to withdraw. He insisted that all U.S. troops be removed from French soil and all NATO bases be closed by 10 April 1967. Immediately Bohlen was called to Washington to consult with the State Department and Congress. Appearing before a subcommittee of the Senate Foreign Relations Committee, he remarked that the only surprise was the suddenness of de Gaulle's move, which was expected, but not until 1968 or 1969. Bohlen granted that the situation was serious, but denied that the whole NATO structure was now in "disarray." De Gaulle had not withdrawn from the treaty itself, and the integrated military command acted only in times of conflict anyway.

Bohlen interpreted de Gaulle's actions not as anti-American, but rather pro-French. He surmised that de Gaulle believed that with French forces being a part of NATO, French interests were inevitably subordinated to those of the United States, something the French president could not accept since close association with the U.S. might suck France into an unwanted conflict outside of Europe, as in Vietnam. The Cuban missile crisis had made de Gaulle acutely conscious of this possibility. Bohlen also realized that de Gaulle operated under the illusion that France had certain qualities which would allow it to play an important role in world affairs, a role it could not perform if its freedom of action were restricted by ties with the United States. Bohlen noted that the nation-state was all-important to the French leader. With more independence, he could approach the Soviet Union, although de Gaulle,

Bohlen thought, had seriously underestimated ideology as a motivating force for the Soviet Union. The French leader mistakenly prophesied that ideology was a passing phenomenon, whereas the nation was long lasting.

De Gaulle's misperceptions aside, Bohlen concluded that the French president was a shrewd diplomat and had not acted precipitously in withdrawing from NATO. De Gaulle knew full well that between France and the Soviet Union lay West Germany, a nation the United States was still bound to defend, certainly a potent protective barrier for France.

As the French component in NATO was dismantled, Bohlen was witnessing the reversal of American efforts pursued through the 1950s to integrate the military command in Western Europe. It had been so difficult to get French acceptance. Now French nationalism reasserted itself, creating a division in the western defense structure, and Bohlen, typically calm in his assessment, considered it counterproductive for the United States to oppose the French steps.[18]

Bohlen, who would not remain in France long enough to observe the long-range repercussions of de Gaulle's actions, would have been content to finish his career in France, retiring after the 1968 presidential elections. He and his wife immersed themselves in the social and cultural life of Paris, a fitting reward for a long and arduous career. But Dean Rusk informed Bohlen in 1967 that Lyndon Johnson, who had succeeded the assassinated Kennedy, had different plans. After offering him a second tour as ambassador to the Soviet Union, a position Bohlen respectfully declined, Rusk designated him deputy undersecretary of state for political affairs. The Senate confirmed his nomination in December of that year.[19]

Bohlen returned to the United States and an administration consumed by the escalating conflict in Vietnam. Bohlen's attitude toward this ubiquitous dilemma combined reasoned caution with a learned consideration of its historic development. As an authority on the Soviet Union and in his other government posts over the preceding decades, he had touched upon the subject of Vietnam peripherally and had come to believe that at times America's approach hampered rather than promoted possible solutions. In 1954, when Geneva discussions were held on Vietnam and Korea, Bohlen had written to Dulles arguing that, if the United States and its allies stood firm, the Soviet Union might prevail upon the Chinese and consequently the North Vietnamese to reach a settlement favorable to western interests. With the Soviet leaders preoccupied with making collective leadership work, Bohlen predicted that they were not eager to get involved in another conflict. He also thought that Ho Chi Minh wanted to end the fight. Later, Bohlen lamented that Dulles had ignored his advice and that the United States had not been firm enough.

While Bohlen was ambassador to France, America's Vietnam policy, particularly Johnson's decision to bomb the North, again disturbed him. If Johnson thought the bombing would force Ho to negotiate, Bohlen suspected that he was sadly mistaken. Considering the Communist view of history, overt pressure would not lead to negotiations, for to give in on these terms would lead to more pressure and more concessions. Using Korea as his example, Bohlen pointed out that the Communists extended no peace feelers that he knew of during the Inchon landing when they were on the defensive. Rather, they waited until the conflict was stalemated and then only when coaxed by indirect threats—such as Dulles's suggestion that he might use the atomic bomb—not by direct confrontation. The Communists, Bohlen said, perceived the struggle with the capitalist world as a fight to the finish.[20] His advice on Vietnam closely followed his past advocacy of a firm, but reasoned, response accompanied by a willingness to negotiate. But the beleaguered Johnson administration was not open to Bohlen's proposals.

Despite the prevalence of the Vietnam issue, Bohlen still continued to concentrate primarily on the persistence of Soviet control over its sphere of influence in Eastern Europe. He remained certain that the United States held an advantage over the Soviet bloc, particularly in foreign trade. He testified before the House Foreign Affairs Committee soon after his return to Washington in February 1968 that in contrast with the Soviet effort to reinforce control over Eastern Europe, nationalism and national boundaries endured as factors which could potentially weaken the Soviet hold. Anything the United States did to help the Eastern bloc nations reestablish their autonomy would be beneficial to the American position. Expanding trade was one means to this end. The resultant markets and diversification would loosen the hold of the Communist parties in the Eastern countries.

Bohlen judged that it was always to America's benefit to have these countries acting in their own self-interest, determining their own policies rather than being dictated to by the Soviet Union. Foreign competition from expanded trade would compel the Communist party to respond to the needs of the marketplace and the wishes of consumers, which would in the long run erode monopolistic control directed from Moscow.[21]

Bohlen's testimony corresponded with his long-held belief that Eastern European nationalism would ultimately threaten Soviet control. Before his retirement, the 1968 Czechoslovak revolt exposed the validity of this position. The revolt began in 1967 when rebellious students protested at the University of Prague, seeking redress of two complaints—the country's economic breakdown and the continued use of Stalinist repression by the government. The students wanted to liberalize the Communist party's restrictive policies. By the spring of 1968, insurrections had grown to crisis proportions. The Czechoslovak Communist party responded by appointing a new leader, Alexander Dubcek, who favored economic reforms and some liberalization. But soon dissident demands escalated to include a multiparty system, one thing the Soviet Union could not tolerate. By the middle of the summer, when Soviet troops mobilized on the border, Bohlen was seriously alarmed. He warned Rusk that Soviet military preparation was "somewhat excessive for a war of nerves, and it could be that in addition to making final preparations for a move in Czechoslovakia the Soviets are preparing for any eventuality which might arise."[22]

His concern eased a bit after members of the Politburo went to Cierna at the end of July to meet with Dubcek and other Czechoslovak leaders. A pivotal meeting, in Bohlen's estimation, the Soviets had journeyed there under the illusion that the masses backed them, only to find the Czechoslovaks supporting Dubcek and his reforms. Realizing the Czechs' sentiments, the Soviets decided to compromise, settling for a guarantee from Dubcek that the polemical attacks in the Czechoslovak press would end—a guarantee Bohlen doubted that Dubcek could fulfill—and Dubcek's assurance that his country would accept the dominance of the Communist party.

From Cierna, the Soviet leaders proceeded to a meeting of the Warsaw Pact at Bratislava where the Czechoslovaks reaffirmed their fidelity to the pact and the Russians reassured the concerned Poles and East Germans. By the middle of August, Bohlen's outlook had changed. He told Rusk that, although troops remained mobilized along Czechoslovakia's border, there was no sign of any imminent action. "It rather appears now that the Soviet pressure will be continued through the maintenance of troops on the borders of Czechoslovakia, and I would presume a considerable amount of Soviet activity within Czechoslovakia, in the endeavor to help bring about the formation of some pro-Soviet group." He doubted any spectacular changes for the rest of August.[23]

But he was wrong. In a sudden decision, the Soviets aided by their satellites invaded Czechoslovakia on 20 August. Bohlen was quick to caution against American overreaction. The best course he could see for the U.S. was to remain low-key and only register indignation. He advised Johnson to cancel a planned trip to the Soviet Union (the invitation had been extended only two days previously by the Soviet ambassador). Diplomatic protest was the only viable and realistic American option in the face of the Soviet determination to maintain control of these areas of vital interest.

Czechoslovakia showed that Soviet concern for its borders and spheres of influence was as alive in 1968 as it had been at the end of World War II. Why had the Russians invaded? Bohlen believed Dubcek was ready to preside over the liquidation of the Soviet system in his country, weakening the buffer zone so essential to Soviet security. Dubcek's actions, furthermore, threatened the stability of East Germany, and there was some apprehension that the liberal trends might even spread East into the Ukraine.[24] Thus Bohlen's final counsel, as so often during his career, was premised on a careful analysis of the Soviet mind.

Bohlen retired in 1969 with the honor, as the senior Foreign Service officer in the department, of serving as acting secretary of state until William Rogers, Richard Nixon's nominee for that post, was sworn in.[25] With that recognition, Bohlen left government service, having spent his final years as the elder sage of Soviet affairs. He had held important and prestigious posts, and his insights were usually sought, if not always heeded. To the end he remained suspicious of the Soviet Union, yet cautious in his advocacy of a U.S. policy toward it.

CONCLUSION

Charles E. Bohlen's career provides a significant perspective through his style, his approach to diplomacy, and his insights and observations into an important era in United States history. Having survived in the State Department for nearly forty years, he left his subtle mark on the direction of American foreign policy. Unlike his colleague, George Kennan, who carved a place in history with his "Mr. X" article, Bohlen, with the exception of his encounter with Joseph McCarthy, wielded his influence primarily behind the scenes.[1]

Bohlen was more the diplomatic technician than the theoretical scholar. John Ensorr Harr in *The Professional Diplomat* identified the "elite nucleus" among the professional diplomats in the State Department, men who, while remaining within the bounds of conventional forms, were capable of taking risks and were willing to innovate. They pursued basically unconventional careers within the framework of the professional service, acquiring new and broader perspectives and additional skills, which ultimately resulted in their attaining positions of importance. Bohlen was one of these "elite." Harr reports that in a poll of State Department professional personnel in the late 1960s, when asked to identify the "ideal diplomat," Bohlen was their choice.[2]

Bohlen began his career in an unconventional fashion for his day, choosing to be an area specialist rather than a generalist. Through good fortune, ability, and knowledge of the workings of the system, he rose through the ranks to positions of influence. Throughout, he adhered to the norms of professional etiquette, keeping his disagreements from the public eye, even during the Dulles years when he was sorely tempted to confront his superior. When in 1953 he likened an ambassador to a military officer who is bound to implement the orders of the president and secretary of state, he was not rationalizing his viewpoint just to receive the ambassadorship to the Soviet Union; rather, the statement was in character with his diplomatic demeanor.[3]

Conforming to these self-imposed standards, Bohlen nevertheless aired his views within department channels. Beginning in World War II, especially after Hopkins introduced him into the White House circle, and continuing into the postwar years, Bohlen analyzed and on occasion criticized diplomatic moves and developing policies: he warned Franklin Roosevelt against giving Winston Churchill unqualified American endorsement when Churchill proposed a meeting with Stalin in Moscow during October of 1944; he voiced his reservations about the shape of the evolving North Atlantic Pact and NSC-68; he delivered a circumspect assessment of the future of collective security after Stalin's death.

But on occasion Bohlen was, unfortunately, too circumspect, even timid, in pressing his position. His caution compelled him to reject certain opportunities to challenge department policies that he questioned. This reticence to speak out was particularly evident when he begged off expressing his doubts about the impending Bay of Pigs invasion, even though President Kennedy had solicited his judgment. Undoubtedly Bohlen savored the prominence and influence his postwar positions brought him, but this does not adequately explain his willingness at times to be so amenable to official policy, even when he had doubts about it. Other considerations were also influential. For one, Robert Kelley, in training the early Soviet experts, had taught that good diplomatic reporting should be based on established fact or direct information, a warning which Bohlen incorporated into his own approach to diplomacy. His experiences over the years convinced him of the wisdom of this advice. Furthermore, in many respects Bohlen agreed with the prevailing suspicion of the Soviet Union and believed that the United States would have to pursue a firm policy to counter this perceived threat. As he remarked in critiquing a draft of NSC-68, it was better "to over-simplify in the direction of greater urgency" than "to over-simplify the side of complacency when dealing with Soviet intentions."[4] He clearly fit into the wartime and postwar State Department mind set, always suspicious of the Soviet Union and doubtful of the possibility of any really close relationship. He was schooled from the very beginning to be wary of this nation dominated by communism, and in that sense he was a cold warrior and part of the establishment. Although he often disagreed with policies and assumptions prevalent in the government, he concurred with the broad aim of combating the Soviet Union.

But one also has to acknowledge that Bohlen cannot be viewed simply as a cold warrior. Suspicion of the Soviet Union had its varying degrees of intensity and different reasons for existence. Daniel Yergin described Bohlen as an advocate of the "Riga Axioms," a set of diplomatic principles which portrayed the Soviet Union as driven by Communist ideology and intent upon world conquest. Adherents to these axioms, Yergin argues, concluded that the United States must take a firm and hostile stand toward the Soviet Union.[5] But Bohlen is too complex a figure to be so simply characterized. He was not rigid in his outlook. In fact, he once remarked to Arthur Schlesinger, Jr. that nothing would clarify the discussion of American policy toward the Soviet Union more than the elimination of the words "hard" and "soft" from the language.[6] More appropriately, some historians have begun to view Bohlen as a diplomat who, while not naïve about Soviet intent, advocated working toward an equitable modus vivendi with Russia.[7] Although his outlook was consonant with those who in the World War II and postwar period perceived the Soviet Union as a threat, he adamantly maintained that that threat had to be kept in the proper perspective. The "precipice of panic," he once opined, should be avoided as much as "the more gentle but equally lethal slope of complacency."[8]

This aspect of Bohlen's diplomatic philosophy has often been obscured by the fact that he was a "company man." Bohlen's sometimes ambiguous attitude toward the U.S.S.R. has led Martin Weil, for example, to charge him with opportunism, a contention based on the manner in which Bohlen moved from the mainstream of the generally suspicious Soviet experts in the State Department to his heady influential position in the Roosevelt White House under the patronage of Harry Hopkins. Weil asserts that Bohlen was willing to compromise himself for the sake of personal advancement.[9] Such an assertion ignores the numerous times Bohlen defended what he believed in despite possible adverse effects on his career, as in the brouhaha over his nomination as ambassador to the Soviet Union and later in his disputes with John Foster Dulles.

Bohlen was a man of action. His advice was grounded in his assessment of past events, his grasp of the Soviet mind, and his evaluation of the demands of the present situation. At times the latter criterion led him to overlook some of the long-range implications of policy decisions; he was often more concerned about the immediate moment and the effective diplomatic process than with conceptualizing and developing profound theories.

Here the contrast between him and his fellow Russian expert, George

Kennan, comes into clearer focus. Bohlen was a doer, Kennan a theorist. In analyzing the exchanges between the two through the years, one is struck by their agreement on the Soviet Union and its intentions. Both, having been schooled in Kelley's program and having observed the Soviet Union from the time of recognition, were less than optimistic about the future course of Soviet-American relations during the war and foresaw difficult times afterward. Both have been called realists. But Bohlen was more the pragmatic realist and Kennan the theoretical realist. Kennan was more the pessimist, particularly from the time he judged that the Roosevelt administration was pursuing a naïvely conciliatory course toward the U.S.S.R. Disdainful of having to execute diplomacy in a democracy, Kennan as a consequence often ignored the influence of public opinion and the ballot box in the diplomatic process. Still, he was adept at measuring immediate actions against their long-range impact. He was prescient, for example, in espousing a blunt acceptance of spheres of influence even prior to the Yalta Conference, believing that this could facilitate breakthroughs in Soviet-American discussions later.

Bohlen was more the optimist in that he maintained some hope for diplomacy and, for better or worse, conceded that a democracy imposed certain restraints on American freedom of action. He warned that, despite one's doubts, the American response to Soviet machinations could not outrun the immediate moment. Thus he had been thinking along the lines of spheres of influence as a solution to postwar differences even before Yalta. He had distinguished between "open" and "closed" spheres, acknowledging that the former was possibly acceptable. But in 1945 the timing was inopportune. Other options had to be pursued first, if only because America's moral leadership, which provided this country with a distinct propaganda advantage over the Soviet Union, would be damaged if the onus of aggravating the cold war fell on America. Furthermore, when the proper moment came for Bohlen in 1946, he was content to accept these spheres tactily rather than to declare their existence as a fact, an admission which could prove disastrous in a country with an electorate comprising a large number of East European descendants.

Kennan's and Bohlen's differences were matters of personality, degree, and timing—the brilliant pessimistic theorist versus the more optimistic and pragmatic technician. Kennan had a profound impact on events during the late 1940s and then found himself ostracized from the Foreign Service following John Foster Dulles's accession to the secretaryship. Bohlen, in his typical fashion, continued to function as a diplomat, despite his personal and policy differences with the secretary of state, and finally found his patience rewarded at the end of the Eisenhower years.

But the two men, despite their differences in approach, were not that far apart on their assessment of the Soviet Union. When Kennan penned "The Sources of Soviet Conduct" in 1947, an article he later admitted was not sufficiently clear regarding his conception of the Soviet Union, the work provoked a reply by noted political analyst Walter Lippmann, who worried that Kennan had exaggerated ideology's role in shaping Soviet foreign policy. To Lippmann, the U.S.S.R. could better be understood as a nation pursuing a policy rooted in national interests extending as far back as the tsarist period. Treating the Soviet Union as a nation and structuring diplomacy accordingly could lead to meaningful agreements, whereas Kennan's call to contain communism would lead to confrontation. These contrasting perceptions exemplify two sides of a question which troubled many within the government. How one interpreted Soviet motives had a profound influence on the policy one advocated.

As Kennan pointed out in his memoirs, he had not meant to convey the interpretation Lippmann derived. Nonetheless, his lack of clarity obscured his point that the Soviet Union's ideology had to be considered along with both its traditional national interests and the demands of the dictatorship, particularly under Stalin, when trying to evaluate Soviet impulses. On this count, Bohlen agreed with Kennan. Like Kennan, he had a sophisticated perception of the Soviet Union which rejected simple answers, but he saw Soviet motivation as a mix of different factors. In the postwar years, however, Bohlen, although constantly reminding the policy makers of the presence of ideology as a complicating element, tended toward Lippmann's admonition that the Soviet Union was a nation with interests which could be satisfied. On this point, Bohlen remained essentially consistent throughout.[10] He never doubted that the Soviet Union presented a threat, a threat created by a unique combination of ideology and national interest. But he especially saw it as a nation, leading him to believe that limited accommodations were possible. Within the parameters of ideological constraints, the Soviet Union was coldly pragmatic in its pursuit of national security.

The U.S.S.R. to Bohlen could never discard its ideology. Communism's influence had been more pronounced in the formative years of the state. But even after the war's end, it persisted. As he pointed out in *The Transformation of American Foreign Policy,* a distinction had to be made between Russian nationalism and Soviet nationalism.[11] Many of the Soviet concerns corresponded to the tsarist period, such as its preoccupation with secure borders, yet ideology provided a unique perspective from which Soviet leaders interpreted the actions of other nations and new instruments for pursuing foreign policy. Communism was both a means to attract discontented groups throughout the world and a rationalization which emphasized that the desired ends of the Soviet state justified the means. The Kremlin since Stalin's accession had utilized the Comintern, the Cominform, and various national Communist parties as tools to accomplish these goals.[12]

Although ideology could not be ignored, Bohlen constantly stressed that the Soviet Union gave precedence to national interests and did not promote revolution haphazardly. It seized proffered opportunities rather than manufacturing them. From Stalin's time, Bohlen portrayed the Kremlin as cautious and responsive to counter force.[13] To deal with the Soviets effectively, he urged that the United States maintain its strength in order to compel them to realize that their best interests would be served by diplomatic discussion. Bohlen meant political, economic, and moral, as well as reasonable military, strength. In doing so, the United States had to avoid needlessly provoking the Soviet Union by precipitous actions or decisions based on ill-founded suspicion of Soviet expansionism. No matter how strong the Soviet Union and how great its capability, he chose to stress basing policy on Soviet intent and not its capability. His perception of this intent was far more reserved than other diplomats'.

Bohlen pessimistically granted that the Soviet Union often acted as a cause rather than a nation. But at the same time, it could be reckoned with, although his expectations were limited. Despite urging that diplomacy never be abandoned, he admitted that it was an illusion to believe that normal relations were possible.[14] Contrary to what revisionist historians saw in the American policy he had a part in shaping, Bohlen saw "enlightened self-interest—a cooperative venture with the rest of the world to fulfill realistic expectations and to implement the American commitment to genuine democracy."[15] Containment to him was a poor word to describe American policy since it tended to stress the negative aspect of the confrontation with the U.S.S.R. and failed to give proper emphasis to the assistance rendered Western Europe and the rest of the free world.[16]

Bohlen's advice was tailored to the moment, as befit a pragmatist. He disdained undue confrontation and threat, but had little in common with those who would blindly pursue accommodation with the Soviet Union. Even in retirement he persisted in this vein. *Witness to History*, the memoirs of a consummate diplomat, stands as an essentially consistent and accurate statement of his perceptions, erring only in omission.[17] Not only did Bohlen continue to defend his past viewpoints, as in his justification of the Yalta agreements, but he applied the same long-held standards to developing diplomatic situations.[18] In June of 1969, he and his colleague, Llewellyn Thompson, took it upon themselves to visit President Richard Nixon. Worried about plans to ease trade restrictions with Communist China, they warned Nixon not to use China against the U.S.S.R., a tactic which might have serious repercussions for Soviet-American relations.[19] They insisted that the United States should avoid needlessly provoking the Soviet Union. On another occasion, when asked his assessment of the Soviet invasion of Czechoslovakia, a crisis which he had been preoccupied with during his final months in the State Department, he could not resist criticizing the emerging "detente" policy, which he feared was moving toward conciliating the Soviet Union and popularizing the false belief that normal relations with that power were feasible. The invasion of Czechoslovakia, he declared, had done away with the "illusion of detente."[20]

When asked to speak on the relationship between the United States and Europe before a group at the National War College in January of 1971—at a time when Willy Brandt, chancellor of West Germany, was pursuing his policy of Ostpolitik—Bohlen put the situation into perspective by asserting that the Soviet Union in the past and at the present was intent upon perpetuating a divided Germany. The United States, on the other hand, had always advocated a reunited Germany, even though circumstances had militated against its implementation. He suggested that in pursuing its German policy, the United States was not only promoting its own interests, but its "attitude toward that key question was very much dictated by the attitude of the European countries themselves." He still distrusted the Soviet Union, believing that although there was much of benefit in Brandt's overtures, he was omitting some key factors, most particularly the future of Berlin. The Soviet Union, in Bohlen's opinion, was exploiting Brandt's omissions.[21]

Bohlen died on New Year's Day, 1974. His funeral was attended by a long list of notable dignitaries, including his old mentor, Averell Harriman, and the incumbent secretary of state, Henry Kissinger.[22] Clearly Bohlen was a respected authority on the Soviet Union. But the question of the extent of his influence on American foreign policy may never be conclusively answered, largely because in keeping with the role he saw for the professional diplomat, he stood essentially in the background, dispensing his advice quietly and carrying out his duties and obligations.

Bohlen's career presents a unique perspective on the development of American foreign policy. He was always in the second echelon within the State Department, more often consulted regarding the motives and reactions of the Soviet Union than the specific policies which the United States should pursue. Unlike George Kennan, who in his capacity as head of the Policy Planning Staff found himself in the enviable position of devising policy, Bohlen dealt more often with the potential efficacy of a policy which had already been conceptualized or with probable Soviet reactions to policy decisions under consideration or already implemented. His insights were often merged with those of others to shape American foreign policy.

Since Bohlen in many respects mirrored the prevailing outlook in the Department of State, since he was committed to being a diplomat who worked within the confines of his office, and since his advice was often blended with other recommendations as a particular policy was thought through to its final delineation, his impact on Soviet-American relations is not always clearly evident. However, he did have the confidence of those in positions of power, from Harry Hopkins through John Kennedy. As a respected authority on the Soviet Union, Bohlen could not help but affect the direction of American foreign policy as this country came to grips with its own status as a world power and with the establishment of its relationship with the Soviet Union, a relationship in which Bohlen played a lengthy and significant role.

NOTES

Preface

1. Barton Bernstein, "The Week We Almost Went to War," pp. 12–21; Eduard Mark, "Charles E. Bohlen and the Acceptable Limits of Soviet Hegemony in Eastern Europe," pp. 201–13; Robert Messer, "Paths Not Taken," pp. 297–319; and Daniel Yergin, *Shattered Peace,* are a few of these more recent works which have concentrated more on Bohlen's role.

2. Joyce and Gabriel Kolko, *The Limits of Power,* p. 2.

3. To one degree or another, Arthur Schlesinger, Jr., "The Origins of the Cold War," pp. 22–52, and Herbert Feis, *From Trust to Terror,* stand as examples of the more orthodox interpretation which accepts the presence of an ideological threat from the Soviet Union.

4. Carl W. Strom, "The Office of Counselor of the Department of State," p. 15. Emphases are in the original.

5. Messer, "Paths Not Taken," p. 297.

1. The Education of a Diplomat

1. Quoted in Joseph and Stewart Alsop, *The Reporter's Trade,* p. 43.

2. Bohlen was variously described in different sources. Ralph Block said he had "pretenses" about himself, letting his hair grow down his back "à la parisien"; Ralph Block Oral History (HSTL). *Newsweek* reporters described him as "the most unpressed man in the foreign service," one who abandoned striped pants and never carried a cane, "The Expert at Ike's Elbow," *Newsweek,* 18 July 1955, p. 33.

3. Martin Weil, *A Pretty Good Club,* pp. 156–62. Weil describes Bohlen as an opportunist who sometimes compromised his principles for his ambitions.

4. Bohlen's German ancestry caused some problems at the time of World War II and after, especially since one of his relatives married into the influential Krupp family. But the relationship was distant. Bohlen was the third generation in his family to be born in the United States. Bohlen to Miss Chase, 27 Aug. 1947, Bohlen Papers (NA), Box 8.

5. Charles E. Bohlen, *Witness to History,* p. 4.

6. St. Paul's School Directory, p. 53.

7. Cleveland Amory, *The Proper Bostonians,* p. 300; Harvard University, *Harvard Nineteen Twenty-Seven Class Album,* p. 170; *The New York Times,* 2 Jan. 1974, p. 42.

8. Bohlen, *Witness,* pp. 4–7.

9. Daniel Yergin, *Shattered Peace,* pp. 17–41, believes that this training program had a major influence in the course of Soviet-American relations from the time the United States recognized the Soviet Union into the postwar years. Diplomats trained by Kelley, including Bohlen, he argues, were part of a department clique which espoused what he labeled the "Riga Axioms"—the belief that the Soviet Union was an ideologically motivated and aggressive nation, bent on expansion and domination. Eschewing any real effort at cooperation, these diplomats opted for a strong posture to confront this nation. Although Yergin oversimplified Bohlen's approach (an oversimplification discussed in Daniel Harrington, "Kennan, Bohlen, and the Riga Axioms," pp. 423–37), it is significant that he correctly recognized the importance of this training program for the future outlook of Bohlen, Kennan, and the others. Frederic L. Propas, "Creating a Hard Line Toward Russia," presents a detailed account of this program and Kelley's intent.

10. The termination of the program after only seven officers had been trained led to a critical shortage of Russian experts at the end of World War II; Louis Halle, *The Cold War as History,* pp. 104–5, discusses the significance of the shortage.

11. Bohlen, *Witness,* p. 17; Bohlen, interview with the author, 5 May 1973; interview with Bohlen cited in C. Ben Wright, "George Kennan: Scholar-Diplomat," pp. 6–7, 81, and 442; George F. Kennan, *Memoirs: 1925–1950,* pp. 64–65.

12. Bohlen, *Witness,* pp. 8 and 37–39. Weil, *A Pretty Good Club,* pp. 156–57, goes so far as to say that Bohlen "just wanted to get ahead."

13. Charles Thayer, *Diplomat,* p. 132.

14. A. C. Frost, Report to Department Concerning Vice-Consul Charles E. Bohlen, undated, NA, RG 59, 123 Bohlen, C.E./38.

15. Bohlen, *Witness,* pp. 9–13.

16. Bohlen, *The Transformation of American Foreign Policy,* pp. 16–17. Bohlen viewed recognition as a tactical diplomatic move which foreshadowed America's emergence from isolationism. It was a move dictated by mutual advantage and compelled by Hitler's rise and Japan's expansion in Asia, developments that concerned both the Soviet and American governments.

17. Bohlen, *Witness,* pp. 15–16. Bohlen later concluded that Bullitt had been used by Lenin. However the leaders at Versailles responded to the proposal, the Bolsheviks could realistically expect to benefit. On the one hand, since the White Russians controlled most of the territory at the time, the territorial advantage would have gone to them. But a cease-fire would have given the Bolsheviks the chance to recoup. On the other hand, a rejection of the peace plan would create the impression among the Russian people that the Bolsheviks were the party of peace.

18. Ibid., pp. 32–35.

19. Diary entry, 7 Mar. 1934,Thayer Papers, Box 6.

20. Bohlen, *Witness,* pp. 18–26; Thayer, *Bears in the Caviar,* pp. 85–86 and 145–50.

21. Bohlen, *Witness,* pp. 26–27.

22. Ibid., p. 37; John Hazard to Samuel Harper, 2 Mar. 1935, Samuel Harper Papers, Box 19. Hazard predicted that "in forty years or less" Bohlen would be the embassy counselor.

23. Bohlen, *Witness,* pp. 37–38.

24. Ibid., pp. 39–41; Kennan, *Memoirs: 1925–1950,* pp. 87–89.

25. Bohlen, *Witness,* pp. 44–45.

26. Ibid., pp. 47–55. Stalin's overriding influence and the disruption and turmoil were certainly evident to Bohlen. See, for example, Kirk to Secretary (prepared by Bohlen), 30 Sept. 1938, NA, RG 59, 861.00/11800. This letter was attached to the testimony of Louis K. Steiner, an American Communist seeking to return to the United States. His testimony depicted a U.S.S.R. torn by dissent and Stalin's tightening grip. Although Bohlen did not agree with Steiner's assessment of Soviet foreign policy, he did concur with the "broad outlines" of his description of the internal political and economic situation.

27. Memorandum by the Second Secretary in the Soviet Union (Bohlen), 2 Feb. 1938, *FRUS: The Soviet Union, 1933–1939,* pp. 509–14.

28. Dispatch to Secretary of State from Kirk (drafted by Bohlen), 22 June 1938, NA, Moscow Post Records, 1938, 800-B.

29. Dispatch to Secretary of State from Kirk (drafted by Bohlen), 17 June 1938, ibid.

30. Bohlen, *Witness,* pp. 45 and 56–58.

31. Kirk to State Department (drafted by Bohlen), 22 June 1938, *FRUS: The Soviet Union, 1933–1939,* pp. 584–85.

32. Henderson to Secretary (drafted by Bohlen), 18 Feb. 1938, NA, RG 59, 761.00/293.

33. Ibid.
34. Ibid.
35. Ibid.; see also Kirk to State Department (drafted by Bohlen), 22 June 1938, *FRUS: The Soviet Union, 1933–1939*, pp. 587–88, which discusses a speech by Kalinin stressing the capitalist encirclement theme; Bohlen, *Witness*, p. 58.
36. Dispatch to Secretary of State (drafted by Bohlen), 24 Sept. 1938, NA, Moscow Post Records, 1938, 800-Part II.
37. Kirk to Secretary of State (drafted by Bohlen), 31 Oct. 1938, *FRUS: The Soviet Union, 1933–1939*, pp. 591–92; Bohlen, *Witness*, pp. 60–61.
38. Ibid., pp. 60–63; Kirk to State Department, 30 Mar. 1939 and 6 Apr. 1939, *FRUS: The Soviet Union, 1933–1939*, pp. 747–53.
39. Bohlen, *Witness*, pp. 64–65; Kirk to State Department, 4 May 1939, *FRUS: The Soviet Union, 1933–1939*, pp. 758–59.
40. Grumman to State Department, 17 May 1939, *FRUS: 1939*, 1:318–19.
41. Grumman to State Department, 20 May 1939, 1:319–21; ibid., 22 May 1939, 1:321–22.
42. Grumman to Secretary of State, 1 July 1939, ibid., 1:327–29.
43. Grumman to Secretary of State, 6 Aug. 1939, ibid., 1:332–33.
44. Steinhardt to Secretary of State, 16 Aug. 1939, ibid., 1:334–35.
45. Steinhardt to Secretary of State, 24 Aug. 1939, ibid., 1:342–43. Bohlen's recollections of this series of events is found in Bohlen, *Witness*, pp. 67–84. Leonard Mosley, *On Borrowed Time*, pp. 229, 343–44, and 374–77, gives an account of these intrigues. At certain points—such as his description of how Bohlen listened in at the German embassy while the two representatives were finalizing the agreement—his account is more embellished than Bohlen's recollections.
46. Bohlen, *Witness*, p. 84.
47. Ibid., pp. 85–86.
48. Steinhardt to Secretary (memorandum drafted by Bohlen), 15 Apr. 1940, NA, RG 59, 761.62/661. Bohlen persisted in this interpretation in future analyses. See, for example, Bohlen, *Witness*, pp. 84–86; Bohlen, *Transformation*, pp. 61–62; Bohlen to W. W. Rostow, 11 June 1952, Bohlen Papers (FOI).
49. Bohlen to Steinhardt, undated, Steinhardt Papers, Box 33.
50. Bohlen to Grew, 16 June 1941, Department of State, Tokyo Consular and Diplomatic Correspondence.
51. John M. Allison, *Ambassador from the Prairie*, pp. 69–70.
52. In the past, historians have misunderstood the place Bohlen saw for ideology in Soviet thinking. Beatrice Farnsworth, *William C. Bullitt and the Soviet Union*, p. 150, for example refers to three major hypotheses Foreign Service officers expounded to explain Soviet actions during the 1930s: Soviet behavior was shaped by power politics; while power played a role, equal weight should be given to ideology; and the Soviet regime was an experiment in the right direction. Farnsworth places Bohlen, Kennan, and Loy Henderson in the second group, which gave equal value to ideology and power. Bohlen's analyses, however, did not view ideology as that all-determining, although he

stressed it could not be overlooked. Daniel Yergin, *Shattered Peace,* with his discussion of the Riga Axioms and Bohlen's adherence to them also seems to exaggerate this aspect of Bohlen's thinking. Hugh De Santis, *The Diplomacy of Silence,* pp. 27–44, more appropriately places Bohlen in the context of the numerous Foreign Service officers puzzling over the changes and machinations of Soviet policy. De Santis points out that Bohlen was one who was coming to see Soviet policy as the result of the "amoral realpolitik" in Stalin's thinking (p. 39).

2. Into the Inner Circle

1. Charles E. Bohlen, *Witness to History,* pp. 115–17; Max Hill, *Exchange Ship,* pp. 231–32; Questionnaire, 5 Sept. 1942, NA, RG 59, 123 Bohlen, Charles E./231.

2. Memorandum by Cordell Hull, 26 July 1943, NA, RG 59, 123 Bohlen, Charles E./231.

3. Bohlen, *Witness,* p. 121.

4. Bohlen to Atherton, 24 June 1943, NA, RG 59, 740.0011/EW '39/29898-1/2.

5. Bohlen to Dunn and Atherton, 23 Feb. 1943, NA, RG 59, 861.415/80; Bohlen, *The Transformation of American Foreign Policy,* pp. 66–67; for Bohlen's critique of Roosevelt and FDR's promise of a second front to Molotov in June of 1942, see Bohlen, *Witness,* pp. 123–24. Although Bohlen had not yet returned from Japan at the time this promise was made, he lamented that Roosevelt had allowed himself to be maneuvered into overpromising in order to foster friendship with the Russians, a situation which only became worse since the second front did not materialize until 6 June 1944.

6. See, for example, Bohlen to Matthews and Acheson, 15 Sept. 1943, NA, RG 59, 861.24/1676; draft letter of transmittal of Third Protocol, 7 June 1943, ibid., 861.24/1508-5/13. Another example of Bohlen's suspicion of Soviet intent includes Bohlen to Dunn, 19 May 1943, ibid., 701.6112/85. Here Bohlen reported on the appointment of Constantin Oumansky, a former head of TASS, as ambassador to Mexico, an appointment Bohlen described as more intended to exploit his "left-wing contacts in the United States" than to use his diplomatic expertise; see also Dunn, 27 Aug. 1943, Hull Papers, Box 52, in which Bohlen reported on the furor raised in the Soviet press during the summer of 1943, when the United States asked a Soviet official to postpone his visit to Algiers and the French Committee of Liberation because the campaign against Sicily was impending and Washington did not want to focus on the political situation until the military moves had been completed. Although Washington ultimately withdrew its objections on 14 August, Bohlen stressed that the Soviet press made much of the incident.

7. Bohlen to Dunn, 7 Sept. 1943, commenting on a letter from Samuel Cross to Dunn of 30 Aug. 1943, ibid., Box 52.

8. Bohlen, *Witness,* pp. 132–33; "Dramatis Personae," *Time,* 18 Oct. 1943, p. 28; Stettinius to Roosevelt, 28 Oct. 1943, NA, RG 59, 123 Bohlen, Charles

E./244; Stettinius notes in his memo book on 6 October 1943 that "I had a frank talk with him [Roosevelt] about Chip"; Stettinius Papers, Box 237.

9. W. Averell Harriman and Elie Abel, *Special Envoy to Churchill and Stalin*, p. 225; Harriman to Hopkins, 1 Dec. 1943, Hopkins Papers, Box 139; Harriman to Hopkins, 13 Dec. 1943, ibid., Box 96; Memo Book, 27 Oct. 1943, Stettinius Papers, Box 237; Stettinius to Bohlen, 2 Nov. 1943, NA, RG 59, 123 Bohlen, Charles E./242; Harriman to Hopkins, 13 Dec. 1943, Roosevelt Papers, Map Room Files, Box 13; "Changes in the Embassy Staff" and "Harriman Comments on Feis Notes," Feis Papers, Box 91; Hull to Stettinius, 31 Oct. 1943, *FRUS: Cairo and Teheran*, p. 59.

10. Bohlen Memorandum, 9 Nov. 1943, *FRUS: Cairo and Teheran*, pp. 74–76; Bohlen Memorandum, 16 Nov. 1943, ibid., pp. 201–3; Bohlen Memoranda, 5 Nov. 1943, *FRUS: 1943*, 3:720–21 and 781–86; Bohlen, *Witness*, pp. 134–35; Harriman, *Special Envoy*, p. 256.

11. Bohlen, *Witness*, pp. 134–35.

12. A. H. Birse, *Memoirs of an Interpreter*, p. 156, mentions how Bohlen was initially halting and stumbling, especially in interpreting some technical military terms.

13. Memorandum by Bohlen, 15 Dec. 1943, *FRUS: Cairo and Teheran*, pp. 845–48; see also Bohlen, *Witness*, pp. 153–54, for a brief retrospective comment on the memorandum; Bohlen, *Transformation*, p. 25; Bohlen continued to develop the political ramifications of Teheran in early 1944, Bohlen, "Current Problems in Relations with the Soviet Union," 24 Mar. 1944, Bohlen Papers (NA), Box 3; Bohlen, "Soviet War Aims," Mar. 1944, ibid.

14. Hugh De Santis, *The Diplomacy of Silence*, pp. 101–7.

15. Bohlen, *Witness*, p. 122.

16. Robert Sherwood, *Roosevelt and Hopkins*, p. 774.

17. Bohlen, *Witness*, pp. 122–23; Sherwood, *Roosevelt and Hopkins*, pp. 774–75.

18. "Changes in the Embassy Staff" and "Harriman Comments on the Feis Notes," Feis Papers, Box 91; Winant to Hopkins, 21 Jan. 1944, Roosevelt Papers, Map Room Files, Box 13; Harriman to Hopkins, 21 Jan. 1944, Hopkins Papers, Box 96; Stettinius to Harriman, 7 Mar. 1944, Stettinius Papers, Box 722. Bohlen was instrumental in settling the situation for Harriman. He brought Harriman and Kennan together at a dinner during the spring of 1944; the association eventually led to Kennan's transfer to Harriman's staff during the summer of that year; George F. Kennan, *Memoirs, 1925–1950*, p. 190.

19. Bohlen's colleagues recalled that he was unofficially performing liaison duties as early as the beginning of 1944; see, for example, Kennan, *Memoirs, 1925–1950*, p. 190; Harriman Comments on Feis Notes, Feis Papers, Box 91. Bohlen himself admitted that upon his return from Moscow he had an "in" at the White House and was "gradually cut in on many more confidential bits of business," Bohlen, *Witness*, p. 156. See also Calendar Notes, 27 Nov. 1944, Thomas Campbell and George Herring, eds., *The Diaries of Edward R. Stettinius, Jr., 1943–1946*, pp. 185–86; Sherwood, *Roosevelt and Hopkins*, pp. 774–75; diary of Adm. William Leahy (LC), 4 Dec. 1944, p. 112.

20. Martin Weil, *A Pretty Good Club*, p. 291n.

21. Bohlen, *Witness*, p. 165; Bohlen to Simpson, 20 July 1960, cited in Smith Simpson, *Anatomy of the State Department*, pp. 261–62n.

22. "Fish and Chip," *Time*, 5 June 1944, p. 38.

23. Bohlen, "United States-Soviet Relations, 1933–1944," 11 Dec. 1944, Bohlen Papers (NA), Box 8.

24. Bohlen, "Current Problems in Relations with the Soviet Union," 24 Mar. 1944, Bohlen Papers (NA), Box 3.

25. Memorandum by Bohlen, 3 Feb. 1944, *FRUS: 1944*, 4:811–13.

26. Bohlen, "Recent Developments in Regard to Religion in the Soviet Union," 5 July 1944, NA, RG 59, 861.404/7-544.

27. Harley Notter, *Postwar Foreign Policy Preparation*, pp. 209–12. A Policy Committee dealt with current problems, and a Postwar Programs Committee tackled postwar planning. With all of their subcommittees and overlapping interests, Notter notes that as time passed the two became virtually indistinct.

28. Bohlen to Stettinius, 16 May 1944, Stettinius Papers, Box 216.

29. Lynn Etheridge Davis, *The Cold War Begins*, pp. 103–9.

30. Memorandum of conversation by Bohlen, 24 May 1944, *FRUS: 1944*, 3:1272–73.

31. Diary entry, 13 June 1944, Campbell and Herring, *Stettinius Diaries*, pp. 85–86.

32. Bohlen to Stettinius, 10 June 1944, NA, RG 59, 760c. 61/6–1044.

33. Roosevelt to Stalin, 19 June 1944, U.S.S.R., Ministry of Foreign Affairs, *Correspondence Between the Chairman of the Council of Ministers of the U.S.S.R. and the Presidents of the U.S.A. and the Prime Ministers of Great Britain During the Great Patriotic War of 1941–45*, 2:146; Stalin to Roosevelt, 24 June 1944, ibid., 2:148.

34. Stalin to Roosevelt, 9 Aug. 1944, ibid., 2:154–55.

35. Subcommittee on Problems of European Organization, 3 Mar. 1944, Notter Files, Box 84; see also Davis, *The Cold War Begins*, pp. 135–37; Thomas Paterson, *On Every Front*, p. 43.

36. Policy Committee Meetings, 13 and 25 October 1944, cited in Davis, *The Cold War Begins*, p. 154; Bohlen, "British Suggestions on the Polish State-ment," 18 Dec. 1944, NA, RG 59, 860c.01/12–1844; Bohlen, Memorandum on conversation, 11 Nov. 1944, *FRUS: 1944*, 3:1332–33.

37. Bohlen to Hopkins, 3 Oct. 1944, Hopkins Papers, Box 141; see also Bohlen to Sherwood, 8 July 1948, Sherwood Papers, which clears up the chronology of these events; Bohlen, *Witness*, pp. 162–63; Sherwood, *Roosevelt and Hopkins*, pp. 832–33.

38. Bohlen, *Witness*, p. 163; Roosevelt to Harriman, and Roosevelt to Churchill, 4 Oct. 1944, *FRUS: Yalta*, pp. 6–8; Bohlen interview with Sherwood, 14 Jan. 1947, Sherwood Papers, contains a remark by Bohlen that this shift by Roosevelt strained U.S.-British relations and led to Hopkins's mission to London prior to the Yalta Conference to try to mend the rift.

39. Bohlen, *Witness*, pp. 163–64; Winston Churchill, *Triumph and Tragedy*,

p. 227, contends that he did pass this percentage agreement to Stalin on a half sheet of paper during their meeting.

40. Bohlen, interview with the author, 5 May 1973; Bohlen, *Witness*, p. 160. Arthur Schlesinger, Jr., "Origins of the Cold War," pp. 27, 29, and 36–39, notes that Bohlen was one of the ;"universalist" supporters of an international organization and credited Kennan among those with the "minority" view which opposed the universalist approach and advocated a sphere of influence solution. This generalization ignores both Bohlen's pessimism about Soviet intentions as well as his position, not that the U.N. was the answer, but that at that point it might at least be worth a try.

41. Bohlen, *Witness*, p. 159.

42. Diary entry, 8 Sept. 1944, Campbell and Herring, *Stettinius Diaries*, pp. 130–31; Edward R. Stettinius, Jr., *Roosevelt and the Russians*, p. 21; Extract from Stettinius's diaries, 4 and 8 Sept. 1944, *FRUS: 1944*, 1:778–82 and 784–88; Roosevelt to Harriman, 8 Sept. 1944, ibid., 1:788–89; Stalin to Roosevelt, 14 Sept. 1944, U.S.S.R., *Correspondence*, 2:160.

43. Kennan to Bohlen, 26 Jan. 1945, Bohlen Papers (LC), Box 5.

44. Bohlen to Kennan, undated, ibid.; for a discussion of this exchange of views, see Bohlen, *Witness*, pp. 175–76; John L. Gaddis, *Strategies of Containment*, pp. 14–15.

45. Bohlen, *Witness*, pp. 176–77; interview with Bohlen, cited in C. Ben Wright, "George F. Kennan: Scholar-Diplomat," p. 291. This interview stresses the argument that Communist parties could still be used by the Kremlin despite any agreement to accept spheres of influence. See also Bohlen to Hopkins, 14 Sept. 1944, Hopkins Papers, Box 142 as one example of how powerful the domestic support for Poland was.

46. Samuel Rosenman, *Working with Roosevelt*, p. 480, mentions Bohlen working on drafts of a Roosevelt campaign speech delivered in New York City on 21 October 1944. Bohlen, in *Witness*, p. 167, takes credit for authoring a portion of Roosevelt's 1945 State of the Union Address.

3. Yalta to Potsdam

1. James Byrnes, *Speaking Frankly*, p. 67; William Leahy, *I Was There*, p. 299; Edward R. Stettinius, Jr., *Roosevelt and the Russians*, p. 103. Stettinius points out specifically that Bohlen was an advisor on "substantive" matters in his official capacity as advisor to the secretary of state. But his close relationship with Hopkins and the fact that as interpreter he was one of the only other Americans present when Roosevelt met with Stalin gave him added perspective. The Yalta Papers bear his distinct mark, since he had the additional responsibility of keeping the minutes.

2. Charles E. Bohlen, *Witness to History*, pp. 167–70.

3. Ibid., pp. 171–72.

4. Ibid., p. 174.

5. Ibid., p. 201.

6. Ibid., p. 178.

7. Bohlen to Rosenman, 18 Feb. 1945, Rosenman Papers (FDRL), Box 27; see also Bohlen, *Witness,* p. 193.

8. Bohlen, *Witness,* p. 181.

9. Ibid., p. 193.

10. Bohlen to Rosenman, 11 July 1949, Rosenman Papers (FDRL), Box 32; see also Bohlen to Sherwood, 8 July 1948, Sherwood Papers, Box 94.

11. Bohlen to Rosenman, 11 July 1949, Rosenman Papers (FDRL), Box 32; Bohlen to Sherwood, 8 July 1948, Sherwood Papers, Box 94.

12. Bohlen to Hopkins, 30 Mar. 1945, Hopkins Papers, Box 142.

13. Bohlen, *Witness,* pp. 184–86. This was not the only time Bohlen dealt with Roosevelt's animosity toward de Gaulle. De Gaulle had agreed with Hopkins's suggestion that he meet with Roosevelt on his return trip from Yalta, on French soil in Algiers. However, when word reached Roosevelt on board the *Quincy* en route to Algiers that de Gaulle was cancelling the meeting, the president composed a vituperative reply. Hopkins, too sick to leave his cabin, intercepted the reply and sent Bohlen to dissuade Roosevelt from persisting. Roosevelt seemed immune to Bohlen's arguments until Bohlen agreed that de Gaulle was "one of the biggest sons of bitches who ever straddled a pot." "Tickled" by this, Roosevelt allowed Bohlen and Hopkins to draft a less hostile response; Bohlen, *Witness,* pp. 204–5; interview with Bohlen by Robert Sherwood, 14 Jan. 1947, Sherwood Papers.

14. Although the question of Poland's western boundary remained in doubt, the United States had essentially agreed to accept Russian demands for the Curzon line as the boundary between the Soviet Union and Poland. See, for example, Bohlen to Hickerson, 9 Jan. 1945, NA, RG 59, 501.BC/1-945 CS/W.

15. The Chargé to the Polish Government in Exile to the secretary of state, 27 Jan. 1945, *FRUS: 1945,* 5:115–21; see also Edward Rozek, *Allied Wartime Diplomacy,* pp. 336–37; Bohlen, *The Transformation of American Foreign Policy,* pp. 39–40.

16. Roosevelt to Stalin, 6 Feb. 1945, U.S.S.R., Ministry of Foreign Affairs, *Correspondence Between the Chairman of the Council of Ministers of the U.S.S.R. and the Presidents of the U.S.A. and the Prime Ministers of Great Britain During the Great Patriotic War of 1941–45,* 2:187–89; Bohlen, *Witness,* pp. 188–90.

17. Bohlen, *Witness,* pp. 190–92. Among loopholes which Bohlen mentioned was an interpretation of the phrase "in the first instance." The Russians took it to mean that the first meeting would be held in Moscow with only the Lublin government. The English translation clearly specified only that the first meeting of all parties should be in Moscow rather than Warsaw.

Interestingly enough, one of Bohlen's pet peeves was a preoccupation with being precise when negotiating with the Russians. Even the concept of democracy could have different meanings. He rather cynically told C. L. Sulzberger that in the Soviet lexicon a " 'democratic government' is one with at least 20 percent Communists in its composition. A 'progressive democratic government' is one with at least 40 percent Communists in its make up. A 'people's democratic government' is a Communist dictatorship"; diary entry, 31 Jan. 1954, C. L. Sulzberger, *A Long Row of Candles*, p. 957. Thus it paid to be precise as to what "democratic" meant when dealing with the Soviet Union.

18. Bohlen to Rosenman, 18 Feb. 1945, Rosenman Papers (FDRL), Box 27.

19. Bohlen, *Witness*, p. 193. Bohlen was surprised that the declaration prepared in the State Department met with only token opposition from Stalin. Roosevelt's advocacy of this declaration was a clear indication, in Bohlen's opinion, that FDR was not promoting a spheres-of-influence settlement at Yalta; Bohlen to Rosenman, 11 July 1949, Rosenman Papers (FDRL), Box 32.

20. Bohlen, *Transformation*, pp. 34–36; Bohlen to Sherwood, 8 July 1948, Sherwood Papers; Bohlen to Rosenman, 11 July 1949, Rosenman Papers (FDRL), Box 32; Statement by W. Averell Harriman, 13 July 1951, Roosevelt Papers, Personal File. The secrecy was maintained even at the upper levels of the State Department. James Byrnes, when he became secretary of state, asked Bohlen about the agreement and then told President Truman what Bohlen had told him. Truman thereupon removed the signed agreement on China from Admiral Leahy's safe in the White House and deposited it in the State Department; James Byrnes, *All in One Lifetime*, pp. 268–269.

21. Bohlen, *Witness*, pp. 196–98. Bohlen remarked that Roosevelt was "obviously . . . bothered by what he was doing."

22. *The New York Times,* 14 Feb. 1971, 4:11; 8 Feb. 1970, p. 28; U.S. Congress, Senate, Committee on Foreign Relations, *The Nomination of Charles E. Bohlen to be United States Ambassador Extraordinary and Plenipotentiary to the Union of Soviet Socialist Republics,* pp. 34, 60, 67, and 95.

23. Draft message prepared for Roosevelt by Bohlen and Leahy, 15 Mar. 1945, Roosevelt Papers, Map Room Files, Box 31; for further discussion of the exchange of views between Churchill and Stalin, see Winston Churchill, *Triumph and Tragedy*, pp. 422–29.

24. Bohlen to Stettinius, 17 Apr. 1945, *FRUS: 1945*, 5:228–29.

25. Bohlen, *Witness*, p. 212.

26. Calendar Notes, 13 Apr. 1945, Campbell and Herring, *Stettinius Diaries*, pp. 317–18.

27. Memorandum by Bohlen, 20 Apr. 1945, NA, RG 59, 760c.61/4-2045; see also Bohlen, *Witness*, pp. 212–13.

28. Bohlen to Stettinius, 19 Apr. 1945, *FRUS: 1945*, 5:832–38.

29. James Dunn and Charles Bohlen, Memorandum for the President, 23 Apr. 1945, NA, RG 59, 860c.01/4-2345; see also Lynn Etheridge Davis, *The Cold War Begins*, pp. 222–23.

30. Harry Truman, *Year of Decisions,* pp. 74–76; Memorandum of conversation by Bohlen, 22 Apr. 1945, *FRUS: 1945*, 5:235–36.

31. Forrestal diaries, 23 Apr. 1945, Forrestal Papers; Walter Millis, ed., *The Forrestal Diaries,* pp. 50–51; Truman, *Year of Decisions*, pp. 76–82; Memorandum by Bohlen, 23 Apr. 1945, *FRUS: 1945*, 5:252–55; Memorandum of conversation by Bohlen, 23 Apr. 1945, ibid., 5:256–58; Truman, *Year of Decisions,* pp. 79–82; Bohlen, *Witness*, p. 213.

32. Bohlen, *Witness*, p. 215; W. Averell Harriman and Elie Abel, *Special*

Envoy to Churchill and Stalin, 1941–1946, p. 450; Robert Sherwood, *Roosevelt and Hopkins,* pp. 885–87; Truman, *Year of Decisions,* pp. 257–58.

33. Gar Alperovitz, *Atomic Diplomacy, Hiroshima and Potsdam,* pp. 270–74, denies that Bohlen and Harriman initiated the Hopkins mission, asserting that this was a reversal of Truman's "firm policy" which had been so characteristic in April. This shift was purportedly due to Henry Stimson's 25 April advocacy of delay in order to avoid confrontation until the atomic bomb had been tested and it could then be employed as a useful diplomatic tool. Alperovitz bases his argument on the belief that both Harriman and Bohlen were advocates of a tough stand toward the U.S.S.R., an attitude he saw as inconsistent with supporting Hopkins's mission. Secondly, he cites references to a planned mission in Truman's memoirs which dated from 30 April when he was also ready to send Joseph Davies to London.

Indeed, there is another reference in Truman's memoirs that he asked Hopkins on the train en route to Roosevelt's funeral to undertake the mission; Truman, *Year of Decisions,* p. 257. But Hopkins pleaded poor health. Nevertheless he accepted on 4 May; at this time, Truman links Hopkins's acceptance to Harriman's advice.

Arthur Schlesinger, Jr., "Origins of the Cold War," p. 24n, contends that Bohlen and Harriman did suggest the Hopkins mission. But he argues that, contrary to attempting to reverse the Roosevelt policy by taking a firm stance, they wanted to show the continuity of American policy. Also, Larry Bland, "W. Averell Harriman: Businessman and Diplomat," p. 405, disagrees with Harriman's assertion that he and Bohlen conceived the idea of the trip.

Schlesinger's position seems closer to the truth than Alperovitz's. Bohlen, although suspicious of Soviet intent, had not yet abandoned the hope for accommodation. At the time, his most important concerns were the immediate obstacles to the United Nations and other disagreements hampering Soviet-American relations. Hopkins was the logical choice to emphasize American good will and to make personal diplomacy work. Bohlen certainly knew this.

34. Bohlen, Minutes of meeting between Hopkins and Stalin, 26 May–6 June 1945, *FRUS: Potsdam,* 1:24–57 and 60.

35. Bohlen, *Witness,* p. 223.

36. Bohlen to Harriman, 13 June 1945, Feis Papers, Box 80.

37. Memorandum by Joseph Grew, 15 May 1945, *FRUS: Potsdam,* 1:12–15; Joseph Grew, *The Turbulent Era,* 1:1463; Bohlen, *Witness,* p. 217.

38. Ibid., p. 227.

39. Bohlen's remark about the Soviet Union stripping Germany can be found in Forrestal's diary entry for 29 July 1945, in Millis, *The Forrestal Diaries,* p. 79. Bohlen's impressions of these proceedings are found in *Witness,* pp. 231–35.

40. Memorandum by Bohlen, 28 Mar. 1960, *FRUS: Potsdam,* 2:1582–87.

41. Bohlen recalled that he did not accompany Truman around the table because the president wanted to maintain a casual air; Bohlen recollection, 26 Jan. 1960, *FRUS: Potsdam,* 2:378n; Bohlen, *Witness,* p. 237. But James Byrnes, *All in One Lifetime,* p. 300, and A. H. Birse, *Memoirs of an Interpreter,* p. 210, recall that he accompanied the president to speak with Stalin.

42. Bohlen, *Witness*, p. 238.

43. Diary entry, 6 July 1945, Millis, *Forrestal Diaries*, pp. 73–74.

44. U.S. Congress, Senate Committee on Foreign Relations, *The Nomination of Charles E. Bohlen*, p. 114.

45. Proclamation Calling for the Surrender of Japan, 26 July 1945, *FRUS: Potsdam*, 2:1474–76.

46. U.S. Congress, Senate Committee on Foreign Relations, *The Nomination of Charles E. Bohlen*, p. 114.

4. The Futility of Diplomacy

1. Charles E. Bohlen, *Witness to History*, pp. 245, 256; W. Averell Harriman and Elie Abel, *Special Envoy to Churchill and Stalin, 1941–1946*, p. 509, also mentions that beginning with the final days of the London Council of Foreign Ministers, Byrnes "overcame his disinclination to seek advice," and proceeded to mention Bohlen as one of those the secretary turned to; see also Robert L. Messer, *The End of an Alliance*, p. 8.

2. Report on the Tripartite Conference of Berlin, 2 Aug. 1945, *FRUS: Potsdam*, 2:1500–1501.

3. Patricia Dawson Ward, *The Threat of Peace*, pp. 31–32; Lloyd Gardner, *Architects of Illusion*, pp. 92–93; Ronald W. Pruessen, *John Foster Dulles*, p. 281.

4. Squires to Schoenfeld, 11 Oct. 1945, *FRUS: 1945*, 4:886–87; James Byrnes, *All in One Lifetime*, p. 338.

5. Bohlen to Byrnes, 12 Oct. 1945, Bohlen Papers (NA), Box 4.

6. Bohlen, draft memorandum discussing what faced the Soviet government, undated, Bohlen Papers (NA), Box 1. Judging from the content, this draft was part of the same analysis which follows, dealing with policies the United States should pursue. Both are undated, but appear to have been written following the London conference.

7. Bohlen, draft memorandum, undated, ibid.

8. Bohlen memorandum, 18 Oct. 1945, ibid., Box 4.

9. Bohlen, *Witness*, pp. 175–77; Eduard Mark, "Charles E. Bohlen and the Acceptable Limits of Soviet Hegemony in Eastern Europe," pp. 201–13, points to Bohlen's involvement in spheres of influence alternatives as far back as World War II. See, for example, a document, "Soviet Attitudes on Regional Organizations in Eastern Europe," 23 Sept. 1943, NA, Notter Files, Box 119, a report by a policy group with which Mark notes Bohlen was involved.

10. Bohlen memorandum, 18 Oct. 1945, Bohlen Papers (NA), Box 4.

11. Mark, "Charles E. Bohlen and the Acceptable Limits," p. 201, attributes a remark Byrnes made in a 31 October 1945 address, in which he expressed willingness to accept a Soviet sphere of influence of a certain kind in Eastern Europe, to such advice as that given by Bohlen. In a 1947 State Department lecture, in fact, Bohlen, while denying authorship, cites Byrnes's speech as an example of department thinking regarding the proper Soviet relationship to

Eastern Europe; Bohlen, "U.S. Relations with the Curtain States," 10 July 1947, Bohlen Papers (NA), Box 6. See also Bohlen to Lippmann, 17 Feb. 1948, Lippmann Papers, Box 57.

12. "The Capabilities and Intentions of the Soviet Union As Affected by American Policy," 10 Dec. 1945, NA, RG 59, 711.61/12–1045 (reproduced in *Diplomatic History,* Fall 1977, pp. 389–99); Robert L. Messer, "Paths Not Taken," pp. 297–319, discusses this report, pointing out how the department was not of one mind in assessing Soviet postwar policy. At what might be viewed as the opposite pole from Kennan's get-tough containment policy was the position of Cloyce K. Huston, chief of the Division of Southern European Affairs, who, according to Messer, saw the Soviet Union attempting to prevent a recurrence of a cordon sanitaire in Eastern Europe, which had preceded the war. The United States, he contended, should thus support Soviet aims in Eastern Europe rather than act as a watchdog; Huston to Matthews and Hickerson, 24 Oct. 1945, NA, RG 59, 711.61/10–2445.

13. Bohlen to Matthews, 14 Feb. 1946, NA, RG 59, 711.61/2–1446.

14. Messer, "Paths Not Taken," pp. 311–13, gives an insightful discussion of why the conclusions of the report had little influence.

15. James Byrnes, *Speaking Frankly,* p. 109; Bohlen, *Witness,* p. 247, concurs with Byrnes's statement that Byrnes conceived of this idea alone. In fact, Bohlen was somewhat concerned about excluding France. But Robert Murphy, *Diplomat Among Warriors,* p. 300, suggests that the Moscow meeting was Bohlen's idea, for Bohlen believed that personal contact with Stalin might remove obstacles. Certainly Bohlen's advice on the Hopkins mission might have reinforced Murphy's erroneous belief. Messer, *The End of an Alliance,* p. 135, argues that Byrnes conceived the idea while still at the London meetings.

16. Memorandum of conversation, 19 Dec. 1945, *FRUS: 1945,* 2:680–87; Bohlen, *Witness,* pp. 247–49; Byrnes, *Speaking Frankly,* pp. 113–15; Messer, *The End of an Alliance,* pp. 152–53.

17. Byrnes, *All in One Lifetime,* p. 314; Daniel Yergin, *Shattered Peace,* p. 127.

18. Memorandum of conversation, 23 Dec. 1945, *FRUS: 1945,* 2:750–58; Norman A. Graebner, *Cold War Diplomacy, 1945–1960,* p. 26; Graebner, ed., *An Uncertain Tradition,* pp. 233–34; Byrnes, *Speaking Frankly,* pp. 116–21; Harriman, *Special Envoy,* p. 525; Ward, *The Threat of Peace,* pp. 62–63. Regarding the overall evaluation of the Moscow arrangements, Byrnes, *Speaking Frankly,* p. 122, argues that Bohlen and Harriman agreed with him that they had reached a much more specific agreement than that made at Yalta. He was, therefore, surprised that some of the press chose to portray his efforts as "appeasement." Byrnes may have overstated Bohlen's and Harriman's optimism.

19. Bohlen, *Witness,* p. 250.

20. Bohlen to Dunn, 24 Oct. 1944, NA, RG 59, 761.91/10–2444.

21. Messer, *The End of an Alliance,* p. 198; Bruce R. Kuniholm, *The Origins of the Cold War in the Near East,* pp. 321–22.

22. Bohlen, *The Transformation of American Foreign Relations,* pp. 79–80.

23. Ibid., pp. 75–76. Bohlen also mentions an April 1945 article by French Communist Jacques Duclos, condemning the actions of American Communist Earl Browder, as another origin of the cold war.

24. Bohlen memorandum, 13 Mar. 1946, Bohlen Papers (NA), Box 4.

25. Memorandum from Division of European Affairs, 20 Sept. 1946, NA, RG 59, 711.66/9–2046. See also Bohlen to Lovett, 6 Sept. 1947, Bohlen Papers (FOI). In this note, Bohlen pleads for funds to assist the NCL in order to further American interests.

26. C. L. Sulzberger, *A Long Row of Candles,* p. 366, notes that in a 4 November 1947 discussion, James Byrnes told him that Bohlen had worked to support the Social Democratic Party in Germany, but Byrnes had rejected this because it would be interfering in the internal affairs of a nation and it might not work out practically, especially if other German parties were to come to power.

27. Bohlen, *Witness,* p. 252; Byrnes, *Speaking Frankly,* p. 257; Joseph and Stewart Alsop, *The Reporter's Trade,* p. 15; *The New York Times,* 9 Nov. 1946, p. 4.

28. U.S. Department of State, *Making the Peace Treaties, 1941–1947,* pp. 137–38.

29. Memorandum of conversation, 25 Nov. 1946, *FRUS: 1946,* 2:1264–69; Byrnes, *Speaking Frankly,* pp. 153–55; Byrnes, *All in One Lifetime,* pp. 382–83; Bohlen, *Witness,* pp. 255–56; Ward, *The Threat of Peace,* pp. 262–63. Byrnes's account even differs with Bohlen's on the point of who visited whose hotel room. Byrnes recalled Molotov visiting him.

30. U.S. Department of State, *Making the Peace Treaties,* pp. 138–41.

5. Forging a Policy

1. Donald C. Blaisdell Oral History (HSTL).

2. Charles E. Bohlen, *Witness to History,* p. 270.

3. Ibid., pp. 258–60; J. P. Williams Oral History (CUL); see also Carl W. Strom, "The Office of Counselor of the State Department," pp. 14–15.

4. Minutes of Executive Sessions, Senate Committee on Foreign Relations, *FRUS: 1947,* 2:169; Matthews to Byrnes, 11 Feb. 1947, Byrnes Papers, Folder 593.

5. Charles P. Kindelberger Oral History (HSTL); Bohlen, "Basic Issues at Moscow Conference," 11 Feb. 1947, Bohlen Papers (NA), Box 4.

6. Bohlen memorandum, 15 Apr. 1947, *FRUS: 1947,* 2:337–44; see also Bohlen, *Witness,* p. 263.

7. Bohlen Interview, 16 Feb. 1953, Price Papers; Bohlen, *The Transformation of American Foreign Policy,* pp. 87–89; Bohlen Oral History (PUL).

8. Marshall to Acheson, 7 Mar. 1947, *FRUS: 1947,* 5:100–101; Bohlen, *Witness,* p. 261; Bohlen, *Transformation,* p. 87.

9. George C. Marshall Interview, 30 Oct. 1952, Price Papers; George F. Kennan, *Memoirs: 1925–1950,* pp. 342–43.

10. Kennan to Acheson, 23 May 1947, *FRUS: 1947,* 3:223–30; Memorandum by Clayton, 27 May 1947, ibid., 3:230–34; Kennan, *Memoirs,* pp. 342–59.

11. Summary of discussion on problems of relief, rehabilitation, and reconstruction of Europe, 29 May 1947, *FRUS: 1947,* 3:235.

12. Ibid., 3:234–36.

13. Bohlen Interview, Price Papers; Carlisle Humelsine memorandum, undated, Jones Papers, Box 2; Bohlen, *Witness,* pp. 263–64; Dean Acheson, *Present at the Creation,* pp. 232–34. Acheson helped insure a European response by alerting some European journalists to the significance of Marshall's proposal.

14. Bohlen, *Witness,* pp. 264–65; Bohlen Interview, Price Papers.

15. Ibid.

16. Bohlen, "U.S. Relations with the Curtain States," 10 July 1947, Bohlen Papers (NA), Box 6.

17. Bohlen, "Certain Aspects of the European Recovery Program," 5 Mar. 1948, Department of State Press Release no. 170.

18. Bohlen Interview, Price Papers; Bohlen, "Certain Aspects of ERP"; Bohlen, "American Aid in Restoring the European Community," *The Department of State Bulletin* 18 (18 Jan. 1948), pp. 80–81; Bohlen, "Europe and the United States," ibid., 59 (15 July 1968), p. 72.

19. Bohlen memorandum, 30 Aug. 1947, *FRUS: 1947,* 1:763–64.

20. Bohlen, "United States Foreign Policy," 28 Apr. 1948, Bohlen Papers (NA), Box 6.

21. Bohlen, "Basic Objectives of American Foreign Policy," 27 Apr. 1948, ibid., Box 7.

22. Bohlen to Lovett, 22 Apr. 1948, Bohlen Papers (NA), Box 2; Bohlen, *Witness,* pp. 276–77; diary entry, 23 Apr. 1948, Walter Millis, ed., *The Forrestal Diaries,* p. 424.

23. Bohlen to Lovett, 22 Apr. 1948, Bohlen Papers (NA), Box 2; Kennan, *Memoirs,* pp. 364–65; Bohlen, *Witness,* p. 277.

24. Marshall to Moscow Embassy, 29 Apr. 1948, *FRUS: 1948,* 4:840–41.

25. Smith to Marshall, 4 May 1948, NA, RG 59, 711.61/5–448; Smith to Marshall, 10 May 1948, *FRUS: 1948,* 4:854–57; Bohlen, *Witness,* p. 277.

26. Memorandum of Press Conference, 11 May 1948, Bohlen Papers (NA), Box 2; for an analysis of this incident, see J. Samuel Walker, "No More Cold War," pp. 75–84.

27. Memorandum of conference by John Foster Dulles, 19 July 1948, Dulles Papers (PUL), Box 115.

28. Bohlen revision of telegram from Marshall to U.S. Embassy in the United Kingdom, 20 July 1948, *FRUS: 1948,* 2:971–73.

29. Bohlen, *Witness,* pp. 277–78.

30. Ibid., pp. 278–80; diary entry, 3 Aug. 1948, Millis, *Forrestal Diaries,* p. 469; for a full account of the trip to Europe, see Lucius Clay, *Decision in Germany,* pp. 368–69.

31. Bohlen, *Witness,* p. 278; Smith to Marshall, 3 Aug. 1948, *FRUS: 1948,* 2:1006–7; Bohlen memorandum, 4 Aug. 1948, ibid., 2:1013–14; diary entry, 3 Aug. 1948, Millis, *Forrestal Diaries,* p. 469. On this date, Forrestal overstated

Bohlen's optimism, describing Bohlen as presenting a "glowing account" of the Soviet position.

32. Diary entry, 10 Aug. 1948, *Forrestal Diaries,* p. 470.

33. Bohlen to Marshall, 30 Aug. 1948, Truman Papers, President's Secretary's File, Box 188.

34. Bohlen, "Possible Soviet Strategy and Tactics in Security Council," undated, Bohlen Papers (NA), Box 1.

35. Bohlen to Marshall, 8 Oct. 1948, *FRUS: 1948,* 2:1214–16.

36. Bohlen memorandum, 12 Oct. 1948, NA, RG 59, 501.BC/10–1248 TSF; Bohlen to Jessup, 16 Oct. 1948, *FRUS: 1948,* 2:1223–25; Bohlen to Marshall, 8 Oct. 1948, ibid., 2:1214–16.

37. Draft memorandum by Kennan, 4 Oct. 1948, Bohlen Papers (NA), Box 5.

38. Bohlen to Kennan, 25 Oct. 1948, ibid.

39. Bohlen, "Soviet Aims in Berlin Situation," undated, ibid., Box 7.

40. Princeton Seminars, 8–9 July 1953, Acheson Papers, Box 74; Meeting in Department of State, 17 Mar. 1949, *FRUS: 1949,* 3:698–700; Acheson, *Present at the Creation,* pp. 267–74; Bohlen, *Witness,* pp. 283–85.

41. Lord Inverchapel to Marshall, 13 Jan. 1948, *FRUS: 1948,* 3:3–6; Hickerson memorandum, 21 Jan. 1948, ibid., 3:9–12; Bohlen, *Witness,* pp. 266–67; Bohlen, *Transformation,* pp. 92–93.

42. John D. Hickerson, director of the Office of European Affairs, and Theodore Achilles, chief of the Division of Western European Affairs, were leading proponents of the treaty from the outset. For their views on the treaty negotiations and their perceptions of Bohlen's and Kennan's positions, see Hickerson and Achilles Oral Histories (HSTL).

43. Bohlen, *Witness,* p. 267.

44. Bohlen also expressed concern about such technical matters as what countries should be included—such as the proposed membership of the Scandinavian countries and the failure to include Greece, Turkey, and Iran in the planning; see Escott Reid, *Time of Fear and Hope,* pp. 106–12, and Geir Lundestad, *America, Scandinavia, and the Cold War,* pp. 297–317.

45. Kennan to Lovett, 29 Apr. 1948, *FRUS: 1948,* 3:108–9. Some of the participants described Bohlen's and Kennan's position as outright opposition to the treaty. See, for example, Reid, *Time of Fear and Hope,* pp. 106–12. Reid focuses at one point on the very correspondence mentioned here to exemplify their opposition. See also Theodore Achilles Oral History (HSTL).

46. Memorandum of third meeting of working group participating in the Washington Exploratory Talks on Security, 15 July 1948, *FRUS: 1948,* 3:184–85.

47. Fifth meeting of the Washington Exploratory Talks on Security, 9 July 1948, ibid., 3:177.

48. Memorandum of the fourth meeting of the working group participating in the Washington Exploratory Talks on Security, 20 July 1948, ibid., 3:193.

49. Kennan to Marshall, 20 Jan. 1948, ibid., 3:7–8.

50. Memorandum of third meeting of the working group participating in the Washington Exploratory Talks on Security, 15 July 1948, ibid., 3:185.

51. Ibid., 3:184–87.

52. Lovett to Marshall, 2 Nov. 1948, ibid., 1 (pt. 2): 648–50; Bohlen to Marshall S. Carter, 7 Nov. 1948, ibid., 1 (pt. 2): 652–53.

53. Bohlen to Carter, 7 Nov. 1948, "Draft Reply" attached, ibid., 1 (pt. 2): 653–55.

54. Secretary of State to Acting Secretary of State, 8 Nov. 1948, ibid., 1 (pt. 2): 655; for a discussion of this episode, see Timothy P. Ireland, *Creating the Entangling Alliance*, pp. 124–25.

55. Undersecretary's meeting, Department of State, 15 Apr. 1949, *FRUS: 1949*, 1:284.

56. Bohlen testimony, "Extension of the European Recovery Program," 15 Feb. 1949, U.S. Congress, House Committee on International Relations, *Selected Executive Session Hearings of the Committee, 1943–1956*, 4:45; see also memorandum of third meeting of the working group participating in the Washington Exploratory Talks on Security, 15 July 1948, *FRUS: 1948*, 3:186.

57. Bohlen memorandum, 8 Feb. 1949, *FRUS: 1949*, 4:70.

58. Bohlen to Kennan, 19 Sept. 1952, Bohlen Papers (FOI). Here he contends that no one had any exaggerated ideas of the "imminence of a Russian attack." The treaty intended to give the Europeans some sense of confidence and security "which left to themselves they clearly lacked."

59. Bohlen, "Collective Security in the North Atlantic Area," 18 Mar. 1949, Bohlen Papers (NA), Box 6.

60. Bohlen to Acheson, 8 Feb. 1949, NA, RG 59, 840.20/2–849.

61. Minutes of meeting with Connally and Vandenberg, 3 and 5 Feb. 1949, *FRUS: 1949*, 4:64–65; also 14 Feb. 1949, ibid., 4:108–10; Bohlen to Acheson, 18 Feb. 1949, Bohlen Papers (NA), Box 1.

62. Bohlen, "Consistency of U.S. Policy," 14 Apr. 1949, *FRUS: 1949*, 1:277–78.

63. Bohlen, "Charge That Our Policies Are Undermining the United Nations," undated, ibid., 1:278–81; Bohlen statement, press conference, 29 Mar. 1949, Bohlen Papers (NA), Box 6.

64. Bohlen, *Witness*, pp. 285–86; Kennan, *Memoirs*, pp. 468–69. Western news reports of contemplated American troop reductions in Europe complicated Bohlen's efforts to reassure the allies and coordinate the western stance.

65. Bohlen, "An Estimate of Possible Soviet Intentions at the Forthcoming CFM," 18 May 1949, Bohlen Papers (NA), Box 5; Bohlen memorandum, 6 June 1949, *FRUS: 1949*, 3:960–62; Bohlen, "Analysis of Possible Soviet Proposals at CFM," 23 May 1949, Bohlen Papers (NA), Box 5.

66. Minutes, U.S. Delegation to CFM, 6th session, 27 May and 15 June 1949, NA, RG 43, Box 309.

67. Bohlen to Acheson, 9 June 1949, Bohlen Papers (NA), Box 1.

68. Princeton Seminars, 15–16 July 1953, Acheson Papers, Box 74.

6. Growing Confrontation

1. Charles E. Bohlen, *Witness to History*, p. 288; J. T. Williams Oral History (CUL); Theodore Achilles Oral History (HSTL). Achilles contends that

Bohlen was transferred to get him out of the way because he was a treaty opponent. This is questionable since the Senate had already ratified the treaty by the time Bohlen was transferred and since Acheson had relied on Bohlen to help "sell" the treaty to Vandenberg and Connally.

2. Bohlen, *Witness,* p. 289; Bohlen to Acheson, 20 Oct. 1949, NA, RG 59, 840.20/10-2849; James Webb memorandum for the president, 14 Nov. 1950, Truman Papers, Official File; *The Department of State Bulletin* 21 (Dec. 1949), pp. 950–51.

3. Bohlen to Kennan, 6 Oct. 1949, Bohlen Papers (NA), Box 3.

4. Kennan to Bohlen, 12 Oct. 1949, ibid.

5. Meeting of ambassadors at Rome, 21 Oct. 1949, *FRUS: 1949,* 4:493; Bohlen to Kennan, 29 Oct. 1949, Bohlen Papers (NA), Box 3.

6. Meeting of U.S. ambassadors in Rome, 22–24 Mar. 1950, *FRUS: 1950,* 3:800.

7. Ibid., 3:815–16.

8. Bohlen to Acheson, 15 Oct. 1950, ibid., 3:377–80.

9. Bohlen statement before the Voorhees group, 3 Apr. 1950, ibid., 3:1369–72.

10. Bohlen to Marshall S. Carter, 7 Nov. 1948, *FRUS: 1948,* 1:652–54.

11. Informal summary of Bohlen's remarks on intentions and capabilities of Soviets, undated, Bohlen Papers (NA), Box 6.

12. For draft report, see Report to the President Pursuant to the President's Directive of 31 Jan. 1950, 7 Apr. 1950, *FRUS: 1950,* 1:235–92.

13. Bohlen to Nitze, 5 Apr. 1950, *FRUS: 1950,* 1:221; Paul Y. Hammond, "NSC 68: Prologue to Rearmament," pp. 316–17.

14. Discussion of U.S. delegation at tripartite preparatory meeting for 1950 London Foreign Ministers Conference, 27 Apr. 1950, *FRUS: 1950,* 3:841.

15. Bohlen to Nitze, 5 Apr. 1950, ibid., 1:222.

16. Ibid.; for Acheson's reaction to Bohlen's criticisms of NSC-68, see Dean Acheson, *Present at the Creation,* p. 347.

17. Bohlen to Nitze, 5 Apr. 1950, *FRUS: 1950,* 1:223–25; for a detailed discussion of Bohlen's concerns about NSC-68, see Hammond, "NSC 68," pp. 308–21.

18. Bohlen, *Witness,* pp. 291–92.

19. Bruce to Acheson, 26 June 1950, *FRUS: 1950,* 7:174–75; Acheson, *Present at the Creation,* p. 408.

20. Webb to Acheson, 28 June 1950, Webb Papers.

21. F. E. Nolting Memorandum, 30 June 1950, *FRUS: 1950,* 7:258–59; Kennan to Acheson, 8 Aug. 1950, ibid., 1:363; Bohlen, *Witness,* pp. 292–94; George F. Kennan, *Memoirs: 1950–1963,* pp. 24, 49; Kennan Oral History (PUL).

22. Bohlen to Matthews, 7 July 1950, *FRUS: 1950,* 7:325–27.

23. Bohlen memorandum, 13 July 1950, *FRUS: 1950,* 1:342–44; ibid., 4:1220–21.

24. Minutes of meeting held by representatives of France, the United Kingdom, and the United States in Paris, 3 Aug. 1950, *FRUS: 1950,* 7:519–24; Princeton Seminars, 10–11 Oct. 1953, Acheson Papers, Box 75; David S.

McLellan, *Dean Acheson: The State Department Years,* pp. 353–54.

25. Bohlen, *Witness,* pp. 294–95; Kennan, *Memoirs,* 2:26, 34–35; Acheson, *Present at the Creation,* pp. 476–77; McLellan, *Dean Acheson,* p. 297. Also, for Bohlen's remarks on the Chinese position, see Minutes of a meeting of representatives of France, the United Kingdom, and the United States, 4 Aug. 1950, *FRUS: 1950,* 6:420; diary entry, 1 Dec. 1950, C. L. Sulzberger, *A Long Row of Candles,* p. 194.

26. Diary entries, 21 Dec. 1950, 2 Jan. 1951, and 30 Aug. 1951, Sulzberger, *A Long Row of Candles,* pp. 598–600 and 667–68; Sulzberger, "Foreign Affairs: Peacemaking a la Russe," *The New York Times,* 26 June 1970, p. 40. Sulzberger attributes Malik's discussions with Jessup in the U.N. and his ultimate speech on peace in Korea to the Bohlen-Zhukov discussions. Acheson, *Present at the Creation,* pp. 532–33, discusses the other informal contacts which ultimately helped construct a cease-fire.

27. Bohlen to Secretary of State, 5 Apr. 1951, *FRUS: 1951,* 7 (pt. 1): 304–5; Ambassador Bruce to Secretary of State, 23 Apr. 1951, ibid., 7 (pt. 1):376.

28. Bohlen, *Witness,* pp. 296–97.

29. Ibid., pp. 298–300; Memorandum by Bohlen, 4 Oct. 1951, *FRUS: 1951,* 7 (pt. 1):990.

30. Bohlen, *Witness,* pp. 291–92; Department to Bohlen, 22 Feb. 1951, Truman Papers, White House Central Files, Confidential Files, Box 38; Dulles to Eisenhower, 20 Mar. 1957, Eisenhower Papers, Official File, 8-F; Phillip Jessup, *The Birth of Nations,* p. 135.

31. Memorandum for National Security Council by the Executive Secretary, 12 July 1951, *FRUS: 1951,* 1:101; Directive by President to National Security Council, 12 July 1951, ibid., 1:102.

32. Bohlen to Nitze, 28 July 1951, *FRUS: 1951,* 1:106–9; Memorandum by Bohlen, 22 Aug. 1951, ibid., 1:164–66; Memorandum by Bohlen, 21 Sept. 1951, ibid., 1:170–72; Bohlen to Secretary of State, 25 Sept. 1951, ibid., 1:177–78; Bohlen to Secretary of State, 9 Oct. 1951, ibid., 1:180–81.

33. Policy Planning Staff Memorandum, 22 Sept. 1951, *FRUS: 1951,* 1:172–76.

34. For drafts of this document, see Report to the President by NSC: Preliminary Report by the NSC on Status and Timing of Current U.S. Programs for National Security (NSC 114/1), 8 Aug. 1951, *FRUS: 1951,* 1:127–57; Report to NSC by Acting Executive Secretary: United States Programs for National Security, 12 Oct. 1951, ibid., 1:182–92.

35. Bohlen, "Creating Situations of Strength," *The Department of State Bulletin* 27 (4 Aug. 1952), p. 169; Bohlen to Kennan, 19 Sept. 1952, Bohlen Papers (FOI).

36. Bohlen, *Witness,* p. 312.

37. Bohlen memorandum, undated, Bohlen Papers (FOI).

38. These observations by Bohlen were scattered throughout a series of essentially repetitive briefing sessions he gave to groups in the Department of Defense; 15 Oct. 1951, 20 Dec. 1951, 31 Mar. 1952, 29 May 1952, 25 Sept. 1952, 13 Nov. 1952, Bohlen Papers (FOI). Bohlen's perceptions of French involve-

ment in Indochina impeding the integration of Germany into Europe's defense community are also found in Memorandum of conversation by Bohlen, 7 Feb. 1952, *FRUS: 1952–54*, 5 (pt. 1):610–11.

7. A Defeat for McCarthy

1. Memorandum by Bohlen, 23 Jan. 1953, Bohlen Papers (LC), Box 12; Charles E. Bohlen, *Witness to History*, pp. 312–13.
2. Bohlen Oral History (CUL); Dwight D. Eisenhower Oral History (PUL); Dwight D. Eisenhower, *Mandate for Change*, p. 212.
3. Bohlen Oral History (PUL); diary entry, 31 Jan. 1954, C. L. Sulzberger, *A Long Row of Candles*, p. 958; Bohlen Oral History (CUL).
4. Bohlen Oral History (PUL); Bohlen, *Witness*, pp. 309–10.
5. Bohlen, "Estimation of the International Political Situation," Defense Department Briefing, 25 Sept. 1952, Bohlen Papers (FOI); see also, Bohlen, "Bases of Soviet External Action and Possible U.S. Counter-action," 30 Oct. 1952, ibid.
6. Bohlen, *Witness*, pp. 309–10.
7. George F. Kennan, *Memoirs, 1950–1963*, pp. 171–75; Bohlen to Acheson, 7 Jan. 1952, Bohlen Papers (FOI); Bohlen memorandum, 23 Jan. 1953, Bohlen Papers (LC), Box 12. Bohlen was sufficiently aware of the storm raised by Kennan's address that when he met with Dulles to discuss the possibility of his being nominated as ambassador, he pointed out that he had approved the speech. But Dulles brushed it aside.
8. Eisenhower, *Mandate for Change*, p. 212; James N. Rosenau, *The Nomination of "Chip" Bohlen*, pp. 3–4. For examples of Dulles's intention to remove Bohlen from a policy-making position, see telephone conversation with Congressman Judd, 6 Mar. 1953; with Senator Knowland, 7 Mar. 1953; with Governor Byrnes, 16 Mar. 1953; with General Persons, 16 Mar. 1953; Dulles Papers (DDEL), Box 10; U.S. Congress, Senate Committee on Foreign Relations, *Hearings on the Nomination of Charles E. Bohlen to be United States Ambassador Extraordinary and Plenipotentiary to the Union of Soviet Socialist Republics*, pp. 103–5.
9. Roderic L. O'Connor, Special Assistant to the Secretary to Charles F. Willitt, 26 Feb. 1953, Eisenhower Papers, Official File, Box 151.
10. Bohlen, *Witness*, pp. 313–14.
11. Rosenau, *The Nomination of "Chip" Bohlen*, p. 4; James T. Patterson, *Mr. Republican*, p. 596; Sherman Adams, *Firsthand Report*, pp. 24, 94; Drew Pearson, *Diaries, 1949–1959*, p. 259.
12. U.S. Congress, Senate Committee on Foreign Relations, Hearings, 2 Mar. 1953, *The Nomination of Charles E. Bohlen*, pp. 1–100.
13. Report by the undersecretary of state, 5 Mar. 1953, U.S. Congress, Senate Committee on Foreign Relations, *Executive Sessions of the Senate Foreign Relations Committee: 1953*, 5:247–48; Bohlen to Dulles, 4 Mar. 1953, Bohlen Papers (FOI).
14. Examples of Dulles's own phone conversations criticizing the Bohlen

nomination included conversations with Congressman Judd, 6 Mar. 1953; with Senator Knowland, 7 Mar. 1953; with Sherman Adams, 13 Mar. 1953; Dulles Papers (DDEL), Box 10. On the other hand, Byrnes's support for Bohlen was expressed in a conversation, 16 Mar. 1953, ibid. Byrnes also wrote to Bohlen suggesting that if he had a letter from Senator Vandenberg expressing sincere regard for him, Bohlen should give it to some of Vandenberg's friends in the Senate, 16 Mar. 1953, Byrnes Papers. Wiley predicted that Bohlen would be confirmed, conversation, 16 Mar. 1953, Dulles Papers (DDEL), Box 10.

15. Dulles conversation with Lourie, 16 Mar. 1953, Dulles Papers (DDEL), Box 1; John R. Beal, *John Foster Dulles,* pp. 142–43.

16. Phone conversations, Dulles with Taft, with Byrnes, with Bohlen, 16 Mar. 1953, Dulles Papers (DDEL), Box 10. Political expediency on one occasion had to be argued to prevent even Dulles from abandoning the nomination. See Emmet J. Hughes, *The Ordeal of Power,* p. 93.

17. For examples of news coverage of the affair, see *The New York Times,* 16 Mar. 1953, pp. 1 and 16; 18 Mar. 1953, p. 1; 19 Mar. 1953, p. 1; 21 Mar. 1953, p. 4; "The Bohlen Case," *Time,* 30 Mar. 1953, p. 14; "An Ambassador is Confirmed," *Time,* 6 Apr. 1953, pp. 27–28; "Chip on the Old Block," *Newsweek,* 23 Mar. 1953, pp. 23–24; "The Bohlen Blowup," *Newsweek,* 30 Mar. 1953, p. 26; "Ike's Victory with Bohlen Reduces McCarthy Influence," *Newsweek,* 6 Apr. 1953, pp. 21–23; "The Bohlen Fuse," *U.S. News and World Report,* 27 Mar. 1953, pp. 58, 60.

18. U.S. Congress, Senate Committee on Foreign Relations, Hearings, 18 Mar. 1953, *The Nomination of Charles E. Bohlen,* pp. 100–112.

19. Ibid., pp. 112–28. The question of Bohlen's remark about Yalta appears on p. 123. It refers to Bohlen, "US Relations with the Curtain States," 10 July 1947, Bohlen Papers (NA), Box 6. The transcript of Bohlen's remarks contains no reference to such "glorious diplomatic triumphs."

20. Eisenhower news conferences, 19 and 26 Mar. 1953, U.S., *Public Papers of the Presidents of the United States: Dwight D. Eisenhower, 1953,* pp. 109 and 130–32; Bohlen Oral History (CUL): Bohlen Oral History (PUL).

21. Telephone conversation, Dulles with Eisenhower, 17 Mar. 1953; Dulles with Stephens, 18 Mar. 1953, Dulles Papers (DDEL), Box 10.

22. Hughes, *The Ordeal of Power,* p. 85; telephone conversations, Dulles with Wiley, 20 Mar. 1953, with Kahn, 20 Mar. 1953, with Wiley, 21 Mar. 1953, with Brownell, 21 Mar. 1953, all in Dulles Papers (DDEL), Box 10.

23. D. Norton-Taylor correspondence with the author, 16 Apr. 1979. In his letter, Norton-Taylor quoted pertinent passages from correspondence he received from Whittaker Chambers on 23 Mar. 1953. Portions of this letter were cited in Allen Weinstein, *Perjury,* pp. 536–37.

24. Report by the undersecretary of state, Walter Bedell Smith, 5 Mar. 1953, U.S. Congress, Senate Committee on Foreign Relations, *Executive Sessions: 1953,* pp. 248–50. This volume contains the statement Wiley was referring to. Smith testified to Bohlen's competence and expressed his concern that Bohlen be sent to Moscow as quickly as possible, given the situation following Stalin's death.

25. U.S. Congress, Senate, 83d Cong., 1st sess., 23 Mar. 1953, *Congressional Record*, pp. 2187–2208.

26. Telephone conversations, Dulles with Brownell, with Taft, with Wiley, 23 Mar. 1953, Dulles Papers (DDEL), Box 10; with Wiley, with Hoover, 24 Mar. 1953, ibid., Box 1; Dulles to Wiley, 24 Mar. 1953, Bohlen Papers (FOI).

27. Minutes of committee meeting, 24 Mar. 1953; U.S. Congress, Senate Committee on Foreign Relations, *Executive Sessions: 1953*, p. 268.

28. Summary of FBI Investigation of Charles E. Bohlen, 16 Mar. 1953, Files of the Federal Bureau of Investigation (FOI).

29. Notes taken by Taft, Taft Papers, Box 485; John Sparkman Oral History (PUL).

30. Committee Meeting, 25 Mar. 1953, U.S. Congress, Senate Committee on Foreign Relations, *Executive Sessions: 1953*, pp. 269–78.

31. U.S. Congress, Senate, 83d Cong., 1st sess., 25 Mar. 1957, *Congressional Record*, pp. 2277–2300.

32. Ibid., 27 Mar. 1953, pp. 2374–2392. With Taft's help, the White House got a large margin of victory. Yet Eisenhower was a bit perturbed by some who voted against Bohlen. In particular, he had believed that Senators Dirksen and Goldwater were "a bit more intelligent" than the others who sought to defend their position with the "most spurious kind of excuse and the most misleading kind of argument"; see Robert Ferrell, ed., *Eisenhower Diaries*, p. 234.

33. Athan Theoharis, *Seeds of Repression*, pp. 184–86.

34. David M. Oshinsky, *A Conspiracy So Immense*, p. 288n; Bohlen, *Witness*, p. 323.

35. Bohlen Oral History (CUL); Bohlen Oral History (PUL); Bohlen, *Witness*, pp. 335–36.

36. Bohlen, *Witness*, p. 335.

37. Bohlen Oral History (CUL).

8. Return to Moscow

1. Thomas Whitney, *Russia in My Life*, p. 288.

2. Charles E. Bohlen Oral History (PUL).

3. Avis Bohlen to Charles Thayer, 21 May 1956, Thayer Papers, Box 1. Bohlen's wife expressed her husband's frustration when she wrote that, on one visit to Washington, Bohlen had seen the president for twenty minutes "and for your *very* private information—*no* repeat—he *saw* JFD for a total of 15 minutes!!!" Indeed, according to the presidential appointment book, Bohlen only met with the president seven times after his departure for Moscow, four of these being official meetings during the Geneva summit, one a "formal" protocol visit; President's Appointment Book, Eisenhower Papers. Harrison Salisbury Oral History (CUL) mentions Bohlen's frustration at trying to convey the changes taking place in the U.S.S.R. when he returned to Washington to report. He would meet with the president only briefly, and Eisenhower would ask no questions. Then Dulles's reception would be cool. They discussed nothing of substance.

4. An example of how Bohlen was described in his ambassadorial role is found in "The Expert at Ike's Elbow," *Newsweek,* 18 July 1955, p. 33.

5. Briefing by Bohlen, 20 May 1957, U.S. Congress, Senate Committee on Foreign Relations, *Executive Sessions of the Senate Foreign Relations Committee: 1957,* 9:489–90; Charles E. Bohlen, *Witness to History,* pp. 339, 352–53, 357–58; Bohlen address, National War College, 11 Apr. 1956, Bohlen Papers (FOI).

6. Bohlen, "America's Position Abroad," 21 Mar. 1952, Bohlen Papers (FOI); Bohlen, *Witness,* pp. 369–72; diary entry, 8 Oct. 1953, C. L. Sulzberger, *A Long Row of Candles,* p. 898.

7. Bohlen remarks, 20 May 1957, U.S. Congress, Senate Committee on Foreign Relations, *Executive Sessions: 1957,* 9:490–93; Bohlen address, National War College, 1 May 1957, Bohlen Papers (FOI); Bohlen, *Witness,* p. 358; diary entry, 8 Oct. 1953, Sulzberger, *A Long Row of Candles,* p. 898.

8. Bohlen, *Witness,* pp. 355–56; diary entry, 11 July 1953, Sulzberger, *A Long Row of Candles,* p. 887. Although it was evident that Bohlen was just guessing that Beria had been arrested and he was thus truly unalarmed, newspapers at the time speculated that the administration had some inside information and had conveniently sent Bohlen to France under the guise of a vacation so that he could return quickly to the United States to consult. See, for example, *The New York Times,* 11 July 1953, pp. 1, 3; *Time,* 20 July 1953, p. 11.

9. Bohlen, *Witness,* pp. 356–58; diary entry, 10 July 1953, Sulzberger, *A Long Row of Candles,* pp. 886–87, 917; Bohlen address, National War College, 11 Apr. 1956, Bohlen Papers (FOI).

10. Bohlen to Hughes, 9 Mar. 1953, Bohlen Papers (FOI); Emmet J. Hughes, *The Ordeal of Power,* p. 102.

11. Bohlen to O'Connor, 1 Apr. 1953, Dulles Papers (DDEL), Draft Correspondence and Speech Series, Box 1.

12. Eisenhower address, "The Chance for Peace," 16 Apr. 1953, U.S., *Public Papers of the Presidents of the United States: Dwight D. Eisenhower, 1953,* 1:179–88.

13. Bohlen to secretary, 17 Apr. 1953; 25 Apr. 1953, Eisenhower Papers, White House Central Files-Confidential File, Box 61.

14. Bohlen, *Witness,* p. 349.

15. Bohlen to Department of State, 24 May 1953, *FRUS: 1952–54,* 15 (pt. 1):1095–96; Bohlen, *Witness,* p. 350.

16. Bohlen to Department of State, 28 May 1953, *FRUS: 1952–54,* 15 (pt. 1):1109–11; 3 June 1953, ibid., 15 (pt. 1):1133–34; Bohlen, *Witness,* pp. 350–51.

17. Notes on Bohlen's activities, *The Department of State Bulletin,* 31 (4 Oct. 1954), pp. 486–89; Council on Foreign Relations, *The United States in World Affairs: 1954,* pp. 421–23; Sherman Adams, *Firsthand Report,* pp. 111–13; Robert Donovan, *Eisenhower,* pp. 183, 190; Bohlen address, National War College, 1 May 1957, Bohlen Papers (FOI). On the issue of adequate checks, Bohlen remarked that the Soviets were still leery of accepting what the United States might view as adequate inspection because of the nature of their society.

18. Bohlen to Dulles, 10 June 1955, Eisenhower Papers, International Series, Box 45.

19. Diary entry, 27 Jan. 1954, Sulzberger, *A Long Row of Candles,* pp. 953–54; Bohlen, *Witness,* pp. 362–63; Livingston Merchant Oral History (CUL). The only concrete outcome of the conference was the agreement to convene a meeting in Geneva to discuss Vietnam and Korea. Bohlen interpreted for Dulles at the meeting when these later discussions were agreed to.

20. Bohlen to Department of State, 21 Oct. 1954, *FRUS: 1952–54,* 5 (pt. 2):1459–61; Bohlen to French Embassy, 17 Dec. 1954, ibid., 5 (pt. 2):1510–13; Bohlen, *Witness,* p. 366.

21. Diary entry, 29 Nov. 1955, C. L. Sulzberger, *The Last of the Giants,* pp. 221–23; Bohlen, *Witness,* pp. 363–69, 393–95.

22. Bohlen, *Witness,* pp. 366, 374–77; diary entry, 9 May 1955, Sulzberger, *The Last of the Giants,* pp. 171–72.

23. Bohlen address, National War College, 1 May 1957, Bohlen Papers (FOI).

24. Bohlen, *Witness,* pp. 348, 376–77, 379.

25. Memorandum by Bohlen, 19 July 1955, Eisenhower Papers, White House Official File, Office of Staff Secretary: International Trips and Meetings, Box 1; Bohlen, *Witness,* pp. 378, 381–82, 386–89; Bohlen Oral History (CUL).

26. Anthony Eden, *Memoirs,* p. 367; diary entry, 13 Nov. 1955, Sulzberger, *The Last of the Giants,* p. 216.

27. Bohlen address, National War College, 11 Apr. 1956, Bohlen Papers (FOI).

28. Bohlen, *Witness,* pp. 394–400; Bohlen Oral History (CUL). So important were the events of this congress that Bohlen was called home to brief the president on 20 April 1956; President's Appointment Book, Eisenhower Papers.

29. Bohlen, *Witness,* pp. 402–4, 423.

30. Ibid., pp. 407–9; Bohlen address, National War College, 1 May 1957, Bohlen Papers (FOI).

31. Bohlen address, National War College, 1 May 1957, Bohlen Papers (FOI); Bohlen, *Witness,* pp. 409–18; Bohlen Oral History (CUL).

32. Bohlen to Dulles, 27 Jan. 1956, Eisenhower Papers, Anne Whitman File, International Series, Box 45.

33. Briefing by Bohlen, 20 May 1957, U.S. Congress, Senate Committee on Foreign Relations, *Executive Sessions: 1957,* 9:516–18; Bohlen address, National War College, 1 May 1957, Bohlen Papers (FOI); Bohlen Oral History (CUL); Bohlen, *Witness,* pp. 425–26.

34. Bohlen, *Witness,* pp. 425–29; Bohlen Oral History (CUL); Dulles to Bohlen, 6 Aug. 1956, Eisenhower Papers, Anne Whitman File, International Series, Box 47.

35. Bohlen, *Witness,* pp. 429–30; Press Release, 16 Aug. 1956, Eisenhower Papers, Official File, Box 155.

36. Hughes, *The Ordeal of Power,* p. 224; J. R. Beal, *John Foster Dulles,* pp. 263, 286–87; Bohlen Oral History (CUL); Bohlen, *Witness,* pp. 431–38;

diary entry, 28 Nov. 1955, Sulzberger, *The Last of the Giants*, p. 221.

37. Bohlen address, National War College, 1 May 1957, Bohlen Papers (FOI).

38. Briefing by Bohlen, 20 May 1957, U.S. Congress, Senate Committee on Foreign Relations, *Executive Sessions: 1957*, 9:496–505.

39. Nikita Khrushchev, *Khrushchev Remembers: The Last Testament,* pp. 359–60. Khrushchev's remark was made in regard to Bohlen's effort to discourage Konrad Adenauer from moving closer to the Soviet Union. Khrushchev believed that Bohlen was acting on his own, not at the behest of the State Department.

40. See, for example, Bohlen to Max Milliken, 4 Feb. 1957, which discusses a position at the Massachusetts Institute of Technology Center for International Studies; Paul Nitze to Bohlen, 24 Sept. 1956; Bohlen to Nitze, 15 Oct. 1956, which discusses a position within the Foreign Service Educational Foundation; Robert B. Stewart to Bohlen, 26 Nov. 1957, which offered Bohlen a position at the Fletcher School of Law and Diplomacy; all letters in Bohlen Papers (FOI). Bohlen, *Witness,* pp. 441–43, discusses his plans and points out that he wanted another foreign post so he could accrue the maximum pension before his retirement.

41. Telephone conversations, Dulles with Allen Dulles, 23 Jan. 1957, Dulles Papers (DDEL), Box 6; with General Persons, 5 Mar. 1957, ibid., Box 12. Alan Stang, *The Actor*, pp. 317–18, and E. T. E. Smith, *The Fourth Floor*, p. 119, refer to Bohlen's possible transfer to Cuba. The telephone conversation with Persons also refers to an abandoned plan to secure a Latin American assignment. Bohlen, *Witness,* pp. 442–43, mentions that he was offered the post in Pakistan.

42. Bohlen testimony, 30 Apr. 1957, U.S. Congress, Senate Committee on Foreign Relations, *Hearings on the Nomination of Charles E. Bohlen to Be Ambassador to the Philippines;* U.S. Congress, Senate, 85th Cong., 1st sess., 15 Apr. and 15 May 1957, *Congressional Record*, pp. 6180, 6542.

43. Bohlen to Byrnes, 26 Apr. 1957, Byrnes Papers, Folder 637(3).

44. "Bohlen Survived Knives, Wields Censor's Scissors," *Detroit News,* 29 May 1960, Republican National Committee News-clipping File (DDEL).

45. Bohlen, *Witness,* pp. 453–56; Bohlen Oral History (PUL); Llewellyn Thompson Oral History (PUL); Thompson to Bohlen, 12 Mar. 1958; Bohlen to Thompson, 22 Mar. 1958; Bohlen to Thompson, 2 Apr. 1959, all three letters in Bohlen Papers (FOI); Herter to Bohlen, 13 July 1957; Bohlen to Herter, 25 July 1957; Herter to Bohlen, 3 Aug. 1957, all three letters in Herter Papers (DDEL), Box 19.

46. Bohlen, *Witness,* pp. 451–52.

47. Nitze to Bohlen, 25 Mar. 1959 and Bohlen to Nitze, 29 May 1959, Bohlen Papers (FOI); Avis Bohlen to Thayers, 19 Jan. 1957; Avis Bohlen to Charles Thayer, 16 Apr. 1958; Charles Bohlen to Thayer, 10 Dec. 1958, all in Thayer Papers, Box 1.

48. Herter to Dillon, 13 May 1959; Dillon to Bohlen, 21 July 1959; Herter to Bohlen, 27 July 1959, all in Herter Papers (DDEL), Box 21; telephone con-

versation between Senator Alexander and Dillon, 10 July 1959, Herter Papers (DDEL), Box 12. Herter had originally planned to appoint Bohlen as counselor or special ambassador-at-large.

49. Bohlen to Herter, 9 July 1959; Herter to Eisenhower, 16 July 1959; Dillon to Bohlen, 16 July 1959; Bohlen to Herter, 6 Aug. 1959, all in Herter Papers (DDEL), Box 21; Eisenhower news conferences, 15 July and 22 July 1959, U.S., *Public Papers of the Presidents, Eisenhower: 1959,* pp. 527–28, 545; Eisenhower to Bohlen, 16 July 1959; Bohlen to Eisenhower, 29 July 1959, Eisenhower Papers, Anne Whitman File, Administrative Series, Box 7. For newspaper comments, see, for example, *The New York Times,* 16 July 1959 and *Providence Journal,* 17 July 1959, Republican National Committee Newsclipping File (DDEL), Box 115.

50. See, for example, Neal Sanford, "Herter Bid to Bohlen Echoes Wildly," *Christian Science Monitor,* 13 July 1959; Jack Steele, "Bohlen Is Regarded as Top Expert on the Soviet Union," *Washington Daily News,* 22 Sept. 1959; *New York Herald Tribune,* 8 Nov. 1959, all in Republican National Committee Newsclipping File (DDEL), Box 115; "Dulles Betrayal," *Human Events,* 8 July 1959, p. 1.

51. Bohlen to William Stoneman, 10 Oct. 1959, Stoneman Papers; diary entry, 23 Nov. 1959, Sulzberger, *The Last of the Giants,* p. 618.

52. Bohlen Oral History (CUL); Bohlen, *Witness,* pp. 461–63.

53. Bohlen, *Witness,* p. 467; diary entry, 29 Apr. 1960, Sulzberger, *The Last of the Giants,* pp. 665–66.

54. Bohlen, *Witness,* pp. 465–66; Bohlen Oral History (CUL).

55. Bohlen, *Witness,* pp. 468–69; Bohlen Oral History (CUL); Memorandum of a conference with president, by A. J. Goodpaster, 16 May 1960, Eisenhower Papers, Anne Whitman File, Box 39.

56. Press conference, 18 May 1960, Hagerty Papers, Box 30; U.S. Congress, Senate Committee on Foreign Relations, *Events Incident to the Summit Conference: Hearings,* p. 94.

57. Bohlen, *Witness,* pp. 471–72.

9. The Last Years

1. Charles E. Bohlen Oral History (JFKL); Charles E. Bohlen, *Witness to History,* p. 476.

2. George F. Kennan Oral History (JFKL); Bohlen, *Witness,* p. 474; Theodore Sorensen, *Kennedy,* p. 231.

3. Bohlen, *Witness,* pp. 474–75.

4. Bohlen Oral History (JFKL); Avis Bohlen to Thayer, 22 Feb. 1961, Thayer Papers, Box 1. Mrs. Bohlen wrote how delighted her husband was to have spent seven hours briefing the president, "just about twice as much time as Eisenhower gave to Tommy (Thompson) and Chip combined in eight years!" John L. Gaddis, in *Strategies of Containment,* pp. 199–200, has noted that Bohlen was one of the State Department officers Kennedy listened to because he found his views "congenial."

5. Arthur Schlesinger, Jr., *A Thousand Days*, pp. 304–5; Sorensen, *Kennedy*, pp. 541–42; Bohlen Oral History (JFKL); Bohlen, *Witness*, p. 479; Kennan Oral History (JFKL).

6. Bohlen, *Witness*, pp. 476–78; Bohlen Oral History (JFKL); Schlesinger, *A Thousand Days*, pp. 275–77, 287; Theodore Sorensen Oral History (JFKL).

7. Bohlen, *Witness*, p. 478.

8. Ibid., pp. 478–79; Bohlen Oral History (JFKL).

9. Bohlen Oral History (JFKL); Bohlen, *Witness*, pp. 480–83; Schlesinger, *A Thousand Days*, p. 374.

10. Bohlen, *Witness*, pp. 482–84; Bohlen Oral History (JFKL).

11. Bohlen, *Witness*, pp. 484–86; Bohlen Oral History (JFKL); Schlesinger, *A Thousand Days*, pp. 379–405.

12. Bohlen, *Witness*, p. 487.

13. Bohlen, *Witness*, pp. 489–91; Bohlen Oral History (JFKL); Elie Abel, *The Missile Crisis*, p. 56.

14. Bohlen, *Witness*, pp. 491–92; Sorensen memorandum, 18 Oct. 1962, Kennedy Papers. Barton Bernstein in two persuasive articles contends that this memorandum, along with other evidence, shows that there was an option short of confrontation—Bohlen's diplomatic approach—which was discarded by the administration. See Barton Bernstein, "The Week We Almost Went to War," pp. 16, 17, 21, and "Courage and Commitment," p. 10. It seems, however, that Bohlen was not at odds with those who advocated a firm response, but rather wanted to see Khrushchev's reply before finally deciding to act. Bohlen was one with the others on the committee who saw this as a true crisis.

15. Bohlen, *Witness*, p. 495.

16. Sorensen, *Kennedy*, pp. 676–77.

17. Diary entry, 30 Nov. 1962, C. L. Sulzberger, *The Last of the Giants*, p. 936.

18. Bohlen testimony, 17 Mar. 1966, U.S. Congress, Senate Subcommittee of the Committee on Foreign Relations, *The Crisis in NATO*, pp. 1–12; Bohlen, *Witness*, pp. 499–513; diary entry, 18 May 1967, C. L. Sulzberger, *Age of Mediocrity*, p. 344.

19. U.S. Congress, Senate, 90th Cong., 1st sess., 15 Dec. 1967, *Congressional Record*, p. 37125.

20. Bohlen, *Witness*, pp. 521–25; diary entries, 11 Feb. 1966 and 12 Aug. 1966, Sulzberger, *Age of Mediocrity*, pp. 227, 282. In Richard Nixon, *The Memoirs of Richard Nixon*, p. 406, Nixon refers to similar advice that Bohlen, Thompson, and Harriman gave Lyndon Johnson prior to the bombing halt in 1968. They argued that the U.S.S.R. could do nothing as long as the U.S. was bombing a fellow socialist country. But the U.S.S.R. would be active with its help if the U.S. stopped. Nixon gloated that the halt was agreed upon, yet the U.S.S.R. did nothing.

21. Bohlen testimony, 20 Feb. 1968, U.S. Congress, House Foreign Affairs Committee, *Hearings Before the Subcommittee on Europe: East-West Trade*, pp. 75–76, 84–85.

22. Bohlen to Rusk, 26 July 1968, Bohlen Papers (LC), Box 12; Bohlen, *Witness*, pp. 529–30.

23. Bohlen to Rusk, 13 Aug. 1968, Bohlen Papers (LC), Box 12; Bohlen, *Witness*, pp. 531–32.

24. Bohlen, *Witness*, pp. 532–33.

25. *The New York Times*, 26 Jan. 1969, p. 76.

Conclusion

1. Despite Bohlen's low profile, occasionally some journalists did note his increasing importance. See, for example, George F. Eliot, "Who Really Runs the World?" pp. 425–27, an article in 1949 which listed Bohlen as one of the eight men running the world from the background. Also see "The Analysis by Mr. X: It's America Vs. Russia . . . Until Russia is Forced to Cooperate or Collapse," *Newsweek*, 21 Jan. 1947, pp. 16–17; "Messrs. Bohlen and Kennan, Authors of a Firm Policy to Russia: How They Reached the Conclusion That the U.S.S.R. Will Not Co-operate," *U.S. News and World Report*, 8 Aug. 1947, pp. 50–51.

2. John Ensorr Harr, *The Professional Diplomat*, pp. 317–19.

3. U.S. Congress, Senate, *Hearings on the Nomination of Charles E. Bohlen to be United States Ambassador Extraordinary and Plenipotentiary to the Union of Soviet Socialist Republics*, pp. 6 and 126; Charles E. Bohlen, Memorandum, 23 Jan. 1953, Bohlen Papers (LC).

4. Bohlen to Nitze, 5 Apr. 1950, *FRUS: 1950*, 1:222.

5. Daniel Yergin, *Shattered Peace*, pp. 17–41.

6. Arthur Schlesinger, Jr., *A Thousand Days*, p. 386.

7. Daniel Harrington, "Kennan, Bohlen, and the Riga Axioms," pp. 423–37; Robert Messer, "Paths Not Taken," pp. 297–319.

8. "The Expert at Ike's Elbow," *Newsweek*, 18 July 1955, p. 33.

9. Martin Weil, *A Pretty Good Club*, pp. 156–62.

10. George Kennan, "The Sources of Soviet Conduct," pp. 566–82; Walter Lippmann, *The Cold War;* Kennan, *Memoirs, 1925–1950*, pp. 379–80.

11. Bohlen, *The Transformation of American Foreign Policy*, pp. 104–5.

12. For expressions of this viewpoint, see Bohlen, *The Transformation of American Foreign Policy*, pp. 101–21; Bohlen, *Witness to History*, pp. 537–38; Bohlen, "Key Characteristics of the Communist Threat," *The Department of State Bulletin*, 24 Oct. 1960, p. 637; Bohlen, "Bases of Soviet External Action and Possible US Counteractions," 30 Oct. 1952, Bohlen Papers (FOI); Bohlen address, School of Advanced International Studies, Brookings Institution, 23 Jan. 1962, Bohlen Papers (LC), Box 3.

13. See, for example, Bohlen, *Transformation*, pp. 104–5.

14. Bohlen, *Witness*, p. 541.

15. Bohlen, "Creating Situations of Strength," *The Department of State Bulletin*, 4 Aug. 1952, pp. 167–68.

16. U.S. Congress, Senate, *Hearings on Bohlen Nomination*, pp. 4, 71; Bohlen, "Creating Situations of Strength," pp. 168–70.

17. One glaring instance of omission is his failure to discuss his reservations about the North Atlantic Treaty, choosing to stress only his final assessment that the treaty was "simply a necessity"; Bohlen, *Witness,* p. 267.

18. See, for example, *The New York Times,* 8 Feb. 1970, p. 28 and 14 Feb. 1971, p. 28.

19. Henry Kissinger, *White House Years,* pp. 189–90. As Kissinger describes the meeting, Nixon implied sympathy with the diplomats while they were there, then mocked their "softheadedness" when they had left.

20. *The New York Times,* 14 Mar. 1969, p. 57.

21. Bohlen, "The United States and Europe," 29 Jan. 1971, Bohlen Papers (LC), Box 3.

22. *The New York Times,* 2 Jan. 1974, pp. 1, 42 and 5 Jan. 1974, p. 30.

BIBLIOGRAPHY

NOTE: The sources listed in this bibliography are divided into categories that appear in the following order:
Manuscripts
Oral Histories
Correspondence
Published Document Collections
Periodicals and Newspapers
Published Memoirs and Diaries
Secondary Works, Books
Secondary Works, Articles
Dissertations

Manuscripts

Clemson University Library
James F. Byrnes Papers

Dwight D. Eisenhower Library
John Foster Dulles Papers
Dwight D. Eisenhower Papers: Ann Whitman File
Central File
Confidential File
General File
Official File
James Hagerty Papers
Christian Herter Papers
Republican National Committee: Newsclipping Files

Harvard University Library
    1927 Class Album, Harvard University
    Christian Herter Papers
    Robert Sherwood Papers

John F. Kennedy Library
    John F. Kennedy Papers: White House Files

Library of Congress
    Charles E. Bohlen Papers
    Joseph E. Davies Papers
    Herbert Feis Papers
    Cordell Hull Papers
    William D. Leahy Diaries
    Laurence Steinhardt Papers
    Robert Taft Papers

National Archives
    Record Group 84: Diplomatic and Consular Post Records:
                     Moscow (1935–38, 1943–44), Paris (1931–33),
                     Prague (1929–30); Tokyo (1940–41)
    Record Group 59: Charles E. Bohlen Papers
                     Decimal File
                     Harley Notter File
                     123 File
    Record Group 43: Records of International Conferences

Princeton University Library
    John Foster Dulles Papers
    James Forrestal Diaries
    James Forrestal Papers
    George F. Kennan Papers

Franklin D. Roosevelt Library
    Adolph Berle Papers
    Harry L. Hopkins Papers
    Eleanor Roosevelt Papers
    Franklin D. Roosevelt Papers: Map Room File
                               President's Official File
                               President's Personal File
                               President's Secretary's File
    Samuel Rosenman Papers

St. Paul's School
    Class Directory

Harry S Truman Library
Dean Acheson Papers
William L. Clayton Papers
Clark Clifford Papers
Democratic National Committee: Newsclipping Files
George Elsey Papers
Paul G. Hoffman Papers
Joseph M. Jones Papers
Harry B. Price Papers
Samuel Rosenman Papers
Charles Thayer Papers
Harry S Truman Papers: Central Files: Confidential File
                                        Official File
                                        Permanent File
                                        President's Personal File
                          Map Room File
                          President's Secretary's File
James E. Webb Papers

U.S. Department of Justice
Charles E. Bohlen, Summary of Federal Bureau of Investigation Security Investigation, 16 March 1953 (FOI)

U.S. Department of State
Charles E. Bohlen, Official Files (FOI). These files are part of the Bohlen materials not yet transferred to the National Archives.

University of Chicago Library
Samuel N. Harper Papers

University of Michigan Library
William S. Stoneman Papers
Arthur Vandenberg Papers

University of Virginia Library
Edward R. Stettinius, Jr. Papers

Oral Histories

Charles E. Bohlen. Interview with the author, 5 May 1973, Washington, D.C.

Columbia University Library
Charles E. Bohlen
Ernest Gross

Livingston Merchant
Harrison Salisbury
United Nations Conference
James T. Williams

John F. Kennedy Library
Dean Acheson
Charles E. Bohlen
Roswell Gilpatric
Roger Hilsman
George F. Kennan
Ong Yoke Lin
Press Panel
Sir Patrick Reilly
Theodore Sorensen
Llewellyn E. Thompson

Princeton University Library
Charles E. Bohlen
Dwight D. Eisenhower
George F. Kennan
Robert D. Murphy
John Sparkman
Llewellyn E. Thompson

Harry S Truman Library
Theodore Achilles
William L. Batt, Jr.
Donald Blaisdell
Ralph Block
John D. Hickerson
Charles Kindelberger

Correspondence (all to author and in author's possession)

Charles E. Bohlen, 26 March 1973
Benjamin V. Cohen, 29 September 1972
Eldridge Durbrow, 6 November 1972
W. Averell Harriman, 12 September 1972
Robert F. Kelley, 19 November 1972
Foy D. Kohler, 17 October 1972
Carl Marcy, 18 October 1972
H. Freeman Matthews, 15 September 1972
Livingston Merchant, 17 September 1972
Robert Murphy, 11 December 1972

Duncan Norton-Taylor, 16 April 1979
C. L. Sulzberger, 19 October 1972
Willard L. Thorp, 18 October 1972

Published Document Collections

The New York Times. The Pentagon Papers. New York: Quadrangle Books, 1971.

U.S.S.R. Ministry of Foreign Affairs. *Correspondence between the Chairman of the Council of Ministers of the U.S.S.R. and the Presidents of the U.S.A. and the Prime Ministers of Great Britain During the Great Patriotic War of 1941–45.* Vol. 1, *Stalin's Correspondence with Churchill and Attlee, 1941–1945.* Vol. 2, *Stalin's Correspondence with Roosevelt and Truman, 1941–1945.* Moscow: Foreign Language Publishing House, 1957.

U.S. Congress. *Congressional Record.*

———. House. Committee on Appropriations. *First Deficiency Appropriations Bill for 1948.* Hearings. 80th Cong., 1st sess., 1948.

———. House. Committee on Foreign Affairs. *The Crisis in NATO.* Hearings. 89th Cong., 2d sess., 1966.

———. House. Committee on Foreign Affairs. *Hearings Before the Subcommittee on Europe: East-West Trade.* 90th Cong., 2d sess., 1968.

———. House. Committee on Foreign Affairs. *United States Foreign Policy for a Post-War Recovery Program.* GPO: 1948.

———. House. Committee on International Relations. *Selected Executive Session Hearings of the Committee, 1943–50,* Vol. 4, *Foreign Economic Assistance Programs.* GPO: 1976.

———. Senate. Committee on Foreign Relations. *Background Documents on Events Incident to the Summit Conference.* 86th Cong., 2d sess., 1960.

———. Senate. Committee on Foreign Relations. *Events Incident to the Summit Conference.* 86th Cong., 2d sess., 1960.

———. Senate. Committee on Foreign Relations. *Executive Sessions of the Senate Committee on Foreign Relations.* Vol. 5, 83d Cong., 1st sess., 1953. Historical Series, 1977.

———. Senate. Committee on Foreign Relations. *Hearings in Executive Session: Foreign Relief Assistance Act of 1948.* 80th Cong., 2d sess., 1948. Historical Series, 1973.

———. Senate. Committee on Foreign Relations. *The Nomination of Charles E. Bohlen to be United States Ambassador Extraordinary and Plenipotentiary to the Union of Soviet Socialist Republics.* 83d Cong., 1st sess., 1953.

———. Senate. Committee on Foreign Relations. *On the Nomination of Charles E. Bohlen to Be Ambassador to the Philippines.* 85th Cong., 1st sess., 1957.

U.S. Department of State. *Foreign Relations of the United States: 1940–1952/54.* Washington, D.C.: GPO, 1955–84.

———. *Foreign Relations of the United States: The Conference at Berlin*

(Potsdam). 2 vols. Washington, D.C.: GPO, 1960.

——. *Foreign Relations of the United States: The Conferences at Cairo and Teheran, 1943*. Washington, D.C.: GPO, 1961.

——. *Foreign Relations of the United States: The Conferences at Malta and Yalta, 1945*. Washington, D.C.: GPO, 1955.

——. *Foreign Relations of the United States: The Soviet Union, 1933–1939*. Washington, D.C.: GPO, 1952.

——. *Making the Peace Treaties, 1941–1947*. Washington, D.C.: GPO, 1947.

U.S. Government. *Public Papers of the Presidents of the United States, Dwight D. Eisenhower*. 8 vols. Washington, D.C.: GPO, 1958–61.

——. *Public Papers of the Presidents of the United States, Harry S Truman*. 8 vols. Washington, D.C.: GPO, 1961–66.

Periodicals and Newspapers

The Department of State Bulletin, 1940–74.
The New York Times, 1929–74.
Newsweek, 1940–74.
Time, 1940–74.
U.S. News and World Report, 1940–74.

Published Memoirs and Diaries

Acheson, Dean. *Present at the Creation: My Years in the State Department*. New York: W. W. Norton, 1969.

Adams, Sherman. *Firsthand Report: The Story of the Eisenhower Administration*. New York: Harper and Brothers, 1961.

Allison, John M. *Ambassador from the Prairie: Or Allison Wonderland*. Boston: Houghton Mifflin, 1973.

Alsop, Joseph and Stewart. *The Reporter's Trade*. New York: Reynal and Co., 1958.

Birse, A. H. *Memoirs of an Interpreter*. New York: Coward-McCann, 1967.

Blum, John M., ed. *From the Morgenthau Diaries*. 3 vols. Vol. 1, *Years of Crisis, 1928–1938*. Vol. 2, *Years of Urgency, 1938–1941*. Vol. 3, *Years of War, 1941–1945*. Boston: Houghton Mifflin, 1959–67.

——. *The Price of Vision: The Diary of Henry A. Wallace, 1942–1946*. Boston: Houghton Mifflin, 1973.

——. *Roosevelt and Morgenthau*. Boston: Houghton Mifflin, 1970.

Bohlen, Charles E. *The Transformation of American Foreign Policy*. New York: W. W. Norton, 1969.

——. *Witness to History, 1929–1969*. New York: W. W. Norton, 1973.

Byrnes, James F. *All In One Lifetime*. New York: Harper and Bros., 1958.

——. *Speaking Frankly*. New York: Harper and Bros., 1947.

Campbell, Thomas M., and Herring, George C., eds. *The Diaries of Edward R. Stettinius, Jr., 1943–1946*. New York: New Viewpoints, 1975.

Churchill, Winston S. *The Second World War.* 6 vols. Vol. 1, *The Gathering Storm.* Vol. 2, *Their Finest Hour.* Vol. 3, *The Grand Alliance.* Vol. 4, *The Hinge of Fate.* Vol. 5, *Closing the Ring.* Vol. 6, *Triumph and Tragedy.* Boston: Houghton Mifflin, 1948–53.

Clay, Lucius D. *Decision in Germany.* Garden City, N.Y.: Doubleday, 1950.

Davies, Joseph E. *Mission to Moscow.* Garden City, N.Y.: Garden City Publishing Co., 1943.

Deane, John R. *The Strange Alliance: The Story of Our Efforts at Wartime Cooperation with Russia.* New York: Viking, 1947.

Dobney, Frederick J., ed. *Selected Papers of Will Clayton.* Baltimore: The Johns Hopkins Univ. Press, 1971.

Eden, Anthony. *The Memoirs of Anthony Eden.* 2 vols. Vol. 1, *The Reckoning.* Vol. 2, *Full Circle.* Boston: Houghton Mifflin, 1960–65.

Eisenhower, Dwight D. *Crusade in Europe.* Garden City, N.Y.: Doubleday, 1948.

———. *The White House Years.* 2 vols. Vol. 1, *Mandate for Change: 1953–1956.* Vol. 2, *Waging Peace: 1956–1961.* Garden City, N.Y.: Doubleday, 1963–65.

Ferrell, Robert, ed. *The Eisenhower Diaries.* New York: W. W. Norton, 1981.

Galbraith, John K. *Ambassador's Journal: A Personal Account of the Kennedy Years.* Boston: Houghton Mifflin, 1969.

Grew, Joseph C. *Ten Years in Japan: A Contemporary Record Drawn from the Diaries and Private and Official Papers of Joseph C. Grew.* New York: Simon and Schuster, 1944.

———. *Turbulent Era: A Diplomatic Record of Forty Years.* 2 vols. Boston: Houghton Mifflin, 1952.

Harriman, W. Averell, and Abel, Elie. *Special Envoy to Churchill and Stalin, 1941–1946.* New York: Random, 1975.

Hill, Max. *Exchange Ship.* New York: Farrar and Rinehart, 1942.

Hull, Cordell. *The Memoirs of Cordell Hull.* 2 vols. New York: Macmillan, 1948.

Hughes, Emmet J. *The Ordeal of Power: A Political Memoir of the Eisenhower Years.* New York: Atheneum, 1963.

Jessup, Philip C. *The Birth of Nations.* New York: Columbia Univ. Press, 1974.

Johnson, Lyndon B. *The Vantage Point: Perspectives of the Presidency, 1963–1969.* New York: Holt, Rinehart, and Winston, 1971.

Kennan, George F. *Memoirs.* 2 vols. Vol. 1, *1925–1950.* Vol. 2, *1950–1963.* Boston: Little, Brown, 1967–72.

Kennedy, Robert F. *Thirteen Days: A Memoir of the Cuban Missile Crisis.* New York: W. W. Norton, 1969.

Khrushchev, Nikita. Translated and edited by Strobe Talbott. *Khrushchev Remembers.* Boston: Little, Brown, 1970.

———. *Khrushchev Remembers: The Last Testament.* Boston: Little, Brown, 1974.

Kissinger, Henry. *White House Years.* Boston: Little, Brown, 1979.

Lane, Arthur Bliss. *I Saw Poland Betrayed: An American Ambassador Reports to the American People.* Indianapolis: Bobbs-Merrill, 1948.

Leahy, William D. *I Was There: The Personal Story of the Chief of Staff to Presidents Roosevelt and Truman Based on His Notes and Diaries Made at the Time*. New York: McGraw-Hill, 1950.

Mikolajczyk, Stanislaw. *The Rape of Poland: Pattern of Soviet Aggression*. New York: Whittlesey House, 1948.

Millis, Walter, ed. *The Forrestal Diaries*. New York: Viking, 1951.

Murphy, Robert. *Diplomat Among Warriors*. Garden City, N.Y.: Doubleday, 1964.

Nixon, Richard M. *The Memoirs of Richard Nixon*. New York: Grosset and Dunlap, 1978.

Pearson, Drew. *Diaries, 1949–1959*. Edited by Tyler Abell. New York: Holt, Rinehart, and Winston, 1974.

Reid, Escott. *Time of Fear and Hope: The Making of the North Atlantic Treaty, 1947-1949*. Toronto: McClelland and Stewart, 1977.

Rosenman, Samuel I. *Working with Roosevelt*. New York: DeCapo Press, 1972.

Ross, Irwin. *The Loneliest Campaign: The Truman Victory of 1948*. New York: New American Library, 1968.

Sherwood, Robert. *The White House Papers of Harry L. Hopkins*. 2 vols. London: Eyre and Spottiswoode, 1949.

Smith, Earl E. T. *The Fourth Floor: An Account of the Castro Communist Revolution*. New York: Random, 1962.

Smith, Jean E., ed. *The Papers of General Lucius D. Clay: Germany, 1945–1949*. 2 vols. Bloomington: Indiana Univ. Press, 1974.

Smith, Walter B. *My Three Years in Moscow*. Philadelphia: J. B. Lippincott, 1950.

Sorensen, Theodore C. *Kennedy*. New York: Harper and Row, 1965.

Standley, William H., and Ageton, Arthur A. *Admiral Ambassador to Russia*. Chicago: Henry Regnery Co., 1955.

Stettinius, Edward R., Jr. *Roosevelt and the Russians: The Yalta Conference*. Edited by Walter Johnson. Garden City, N.Y.: Doubleday, 1949.

Stimson, Henry L., and Bundy, McGeorge. *On Active Service in Peace and War*. New York: Harper and Bros., 1948.

Sulzberger, C. L. *An Age of Mediocrity: Memoirs and Diaries, 1963–1972*. New York: Macmillan, 1973.

———. *The Last of the Giants: Memoirs and Diaries, 1954–1963*. New York: Macmillan, 1970.

———. *A Long Row of Candles: Memoirs and Diaries, 1934–1954*. New York: Macmillan, 1969.

Thayer, Charles W. *Bears in the Caviar*. Philadelphia: J. B. Lippincott, 1951.

Truman, Harry S. *Memoirs*. 2 vols. Vol. 1, *Year of Decisions*. Vol. 2, *Years of Trial and Hope*. Garden City, N.Y.: Doubleday, 1955–56.

Truman, Margaret (Daniel). *Harry S Truman*. New York: William Morrow, 1972.

Vandenberg, Arthur H., Jr., ed. *The Private Papers of Senator Vandenberg*. Boston: Houghton Mifflin, 1952.

Whitney, Thomas P. *Russia In My Life*. New York: Reynal and Co., 1962.

Secondary Works, Books

Abel, Elie. *The Missile Crisis.* Philadelphia: J. B. Lippincott, 1968.

Adams, Henry H. *Harry Hopkins: A Biography.* New York: G. P. Putnam's Sons, 1977.

Alperovitz, Gar. *Atomic Diplomacy, Hiroshima and Potsdam: The Use of the Atomic Bomb and the American Confrontation with Soviet Power.* New York: Simon and Schuster, 1965.

Amory, Cleveland. *The Proper Bostonians.* New York: E. P. Dutton, 1947.

Beal, John R. *John Foster Dulles: 1888–1959.* New York: Harper and Row, 1959.

Bennett, Edward M. *Recognition of Russia: An American Foreign Policy Dilemma.* Waltham, Mass.: Blaisdell Publishing, 1970.

Bishop, Donald. *The Roosevelt-Litvinov Agreements: The American View.* Syracuse, N.Y.: Syracuse Univ. Press, 1965.

Browder, Robert P. *The Origins of Soviet-American Diplomacy.* Princeton: Princeton Univ. Press, 1953.

Burns, James MacGregor. *Roosevelt: The Soldier of Freedom.* New York: Harcourt, Brace, Jovanovich, 1970.

Campbell, Thomas M. *Masquerade Peace: America's U.N. Policy, 1944–1945.* Tallahassee: Florida State Univ. Press, 1973.

Clemens, Diane Shaver. *Yalta.* New York: Oxford Univ. Press, 1970.

Council on Foreign Relations. *The United States in World Affairs, 1953–1965.* 13 vols. New York: Harper and Row, 1955–66.

Curry, George. *James F. Byrnes.* New York: Cooper Square Publishers, 1965.

Daniels, Jonathan. *The Man of Independence.* Philadelphia: J. B. Lippincott, 1950.

Davis, Lynn Etheridge. *The Cold War Begins: Soviet-American Conflict Over Eastern Europe.* Princeton: Princeton Univ. Press, 1974.

Davidson, W. Phillips. *The Berlin Blockade: A Study in Cold War Politics.* Princeton: Princeton Univ. Press, 1958.

DeSantis, Hugh. *The Diplomacy of Silence: The American Foreign Service, the Soviet Union, and the Cold War, 1933–1947.* Chicago: The Univ. of Chicago Press, 1979.

Divine, Robert A. *Eisenhower and the Cold War.* New York: Oxford Univ. Press, 1981.

———. *The Reluctant Belligerent: American Entry into World War II.* New York: John Wiley and Sons, 1965.

———. *Roosevelt and World War II.* Baltimore: The Johns Hopkins Univ. Press, 1969.

Donovan, Robert J. *Conflict and Crisis: The Presidency of Harry S Truman, 1945–1948.* New York: W. W. Norton, 1977.

———. *Eisenhower: The Inside Story.* New York: Harper and Brothers, 1956.

———. *Tumultuous Years: The Presidency of Harry S Truman, 1949–1953.* New York: W. W. Norton, 1982.

Druks, Herbert. *Harry S Truman and the Russians, 1945–1953*. New York: Robert Speller and Sons, 1966.

Eayrs, James. *In Defence of Canada: Growing Up Allied*. Toronto: Univ. of Toronto Press, 1980.

Farnsworth, Beatrice. *William C. Bullitt and the Soviet Union*. Bloomington: Indiana Univ. Press, 1967.

Feis, Herbert. *The Atomic Bomb and the End of World War II*. Princeton: Princeton Univ. Press, 1966.

————. *Between War and Peace: The Potsdam Conference*. Princeton: Princeton Univ. Press, 1960.

————. *Churchill, Roosevelt, and Stalin: The War They Waged and the Peace They Sought*. Princeton: Princeton Univ. Press, 1957.

————. *Contest Over Japan*. New York: W. W. Norton, 1967.

————. *From Trust to Terror: The Onset of the Cold War, 1945–1950*. New York: W. W. Norton, 1970.

————. *Japan Subdued: The Atomic Bomb and the End of the War in the Pacific*. Princeton: Princeton Univ. Press, 1961.

Ferrell, Robert. *George C. Marshall*. New York: Cooper Square Publishers, 1965.

Fischer, Louis. *The Road to Yalta: Soviet Foreign Relations, 1941–1945*. New York: Harper and Row, 1972.

Freeland, Richard M. *The Truman Doctrine and the Origins of McCarthyism: Foreign Policy, Domestic Politics, and Internal Security, 1946–1948*. New York: Alfred A. Knopf, 1970.

Gaddis, John L. *Russia, the Soviet Union, and the United States: An Interpretive History*. New York: John Wiley and Sons, 1978.

————. *Strategies of Containment: A Critical Appraisal of Postwar American National Security Policy*. New York: Oxford Univ. Press, 1982.

————. *The United States and the Origins of the Cold War, 1941–1947*. New York: Columbia Univ. Press, 1972.

Gardner, Lloyd C. *Architects of Illusion: Men and Ideas in American Foreign Policy, 1941–1949*. Chicago: Quadrangle Books, 1970.

Gerson, Louis L. *John Foster Dulles*. New York: Cooper Square Publishers, 1967.

Gimbel, John. *The Origins of the Marshall Plan*. Stanford, Calif.: Stanford Univ. Press, 1976.

Goldman, Eric F. *The Crucial Decade: America, 1945–1955*. New York: Alfred A. Knopf, 1956.

Gould-Adams, Richard. *John Foster Dulles: A Reappraisal*. New York: Appleton-Century-Crofts, 1962.

Graebner, Norman A. *The New Isolationism: A Study in Politics and Foreign Policy Since 1950*. New York: Ronald Press, 1956.

————, ed. *An Uncertain Tradition: American Secretaries of State in the Twentieth Century*. New York: McGraw-Hill, 1961.

Halberstam, David. *The Best and the Brightest*. New York: Random, 1972.

Halle, Louis J. *The Cold War As History*. New York: Harper and Row, 1967.

Harr, John Ensorr. *The Professional Diplomat*. Princeton: Princeton Univ. Press, 1969.

Heller, Dean and Heller, David. *John Foster Dulles: Soldier for Peace*. New York: Holt, Rinehart, and Winston, 1960.

Hilsman, Roger. *To Move A Nation: The Politics of Foreign Policy in the Administration of John F. Kennedy*. Garden City, N.Y.: Doubleday, 1967.

Ireland, Timothy P. *Creating the Entangling Alliance: The Origins of the North Atlantic Treaty Organization*. Westport, Conn.: Greenwood Press, 1981.

Jones, Joseph M. *The Fifteen Weeks*. New York: Harcourt, Brace, and World, 1955.

Kennan, George F. *American Diplomacy, 1900–1950*. New York: Mentor Books, 1951.

———. *Russia and the West Under Lenin and Stalin*. New York: New American Library, 1961.

Kolko, Gabriel. *The Politics of War: The World and United States Foreign Policy, 1943–1945*. New York: Vintage, 1968.

Kolko, Joyce and Kolko, Gabriel. *The Limits of Power: The World and United States Foreign Policy, 1945–1954*. New York: Harper and Row, 1972.

Kuniholm, Bruce R. *The Origins of the Cold War in the Near East: Great Power Conflict and Diplomacy in Iran, Turkey and Greece*. Princeton: Princeton Univ. Press, 1980.

LaFeber, Walter. *America, Russia, and the Cold War, 1945–1980*. New York: John Wiley and Sons, 1980.

Lash, Joseph P. *Eleanor: The Years Alone*. New York: W. W. Norton, 1972.

Lippmann, Walter. *The Cold War: A Study in U.S. Foreign Policy*. New York: Harper and Bros., 1947.

Lundestad, Geir. *America, Scandinavia, and the Cold War, 1945–1949*. New York: Columbia Univ. Press, 1980.

McLellan, David S. *Dean Acheson: The State Department Years*. New York: Dodd, Mead, 1976.

McNeill, William H. *America, Britain and Russia: Their Cooperation and Conflict, 1941–1946*. London: Oxford Univ. Press, 1953.

Maddux, Thomas R. *Years of Estrangement: American Relations with the Soviet Union, 1933–1941*. Tallahassee: Univ. Presses of Florida, 1980.

Manchester, William. *The Arms of Krupp, 1587–1968*. Boston: Little, Brown, 1968.

Mastny, Vojtech. *Russia's Road to the Cold War: Diplomacy, Warfare, and the Politics of Communism, 1941–1945*. New York: Columbia Univ. Press, 1979.

Mazuzan, George T. *Warren R. Austin at the U.N.: 1946–1953*. Kent, Ohio: Kent State Univ. Press, 1977.

Messer, Robert L. *The End of an Alliance: James F. Byrnes, Roosevelt, Truman, and the Origins of the Cold War*. Chapel Hill: The Univ. of North Carolina Press, 1982.

Mosley, Leonard. *On Borrowed Time: How World War II Began*. New York: Random, 1969.

Neumann, William L. *After Victory: Churchill, Roosevelt, and Stalin, and the Making of the Peace*. New York: Harper and Row, 1967.

Noble, G. Bernard. *Christian A. Herter*. New York: Cooper Square Publishers, 1970.

Notter, Harley A. *Postwar Foreign Policy Preparation, 1939–1945*. Washington, D.C.: GPO, 1949.

Osgood, Robert E. *NATO: The Entangling Alliance*. Chicago: The Univ. of Chicago Press, 1962.

Oshinsky, David M. *A Conspiracy So Immense: The World of Joe McCarthy*. New York: Free Press, 1983.

Paterson, Thomas G. *On Every Front: The Making of the Cold War*. New York: W. W. Norton, 1979.

————. *Soviet-American Confrontation: Postwar Reconstruction and the Origins of the Cold War*. Baltimore: The Johns Hopkins Univ. Press, 1973.

Patterson, James T. *Mr. Republican: A Biography of Robert Taft*. Boston: Houghton Mifflin, 1972.

Payne, Robert. *The Marshall Story: A Biography of General George C. Marshall*. New York: Prentice-Hall, 1951.

Phillips, Cabell. *The Truman Presidency: The History of a Triumphant Succession*. New York: Macmillan, 1966.

Pratt, Julius. *Cordell Hull*. 2 vols. New York: Cooper Square Publishers, 1964.

Pruessen, Ronald W. *John Foster Dulles: The Road to Power*. New York: The Free Press, 1982.

Price, Harry B. *The Marshall Plan and Its Meaning*. Ithaca, N.Y.: Cornell Univ. Press, 1955.

Reeves, Thomas C. *The Life and Times of Joe McCarthy: A Biography*. New York: Stein and Day, 1982.

Rosenau, James N. *The Nomination of "Chip" Bohlen*. New York: Henry Holt and Co., 1958.

Rostow, W. W. *The Dynamics of Soviet Society*. New York: W. W. Norton, 1967.

Rozek, Edward J. *Allied Wartime Diplomacy: A Pattern in Poland*. New York: John Wiley and Sons, 1958.

Schlesinger, Arthur M., Jr. *A Thousand Days: John F. Kennedy in the White House*. Boston: Houghton Mifflin, 1965.

Sherwood, Robert E. *Roosevelt and Hopkins: An Intimate History*. New York: Harper and Bros., 1948.

Simpson, Smith. *Anatomy of the State Department*. Boston: Houghton Mifflin, 1967.

Smith, Gaddis. *American Diplomacy During the Second World War, 1941–1945*. New York: John Wiley and Sons, 1965.

————. *Dean Acheson*. New York: Cooper Square Publishers, 1972.

Taubman, William. *Stalin's American Policy: From Entente to Detente to Cold War*. New York: W. W. Norton, 1982.

Thayer, Charles W. *Diplomat*. New York: Harper and Bros., 1959.

Theoharis, Athan. *Seeds of Repression: Harry S Truman and the Origins of*

McCarthyism. Chicago: Quadrangle Books, 1971.
————. *The Yalta Myths: An Issue in U.S. Politics, 1945–1955.* Columbia: Univ. of Missouri Press, 1970.
Thomas, Lately. *When Even Angels Wept: The Senator Joseph McCarthy Affair—A Story Without A Hero.* New York: William Morrow and Co., 1973.
Ulam, Adam. *Expansion and Coexistence: The History of Soviet Foreign Policy, 1917–1967.* New York: Praeger, 1968.
————. *The Rivals: America and Russia Since World War II.* New York: Viking, 1971.
Walker, Richard L. *E. R. Stettinius, Jr.* New York: Cooper Square Publishers, 1965.
Walton, Richard J. *Cold War and Counterrevolution: The Foreign Policy of John F. Kennedy.* New York: Viking, 1972.
————. *Henry Wallace, Harry Truman, and the Cold War.* New York: Viking, 1976.
Ward, Patricia Dawson. *The Threat of Peace: James F. Byrnes and the Council of Foreign Ministers, 1945–1946.* Kent, Ohio: Kent State Univ. Press, 1979.
Weil, Martin. *A Pretty Good Club: The Founding Fathers of the U.S. Foreign Service.* New York: W. W. Norton, 1978.
Weinstein, Allen. *Perjury: The Hiss-Chambers Case.* New York: Alfred A. Knopf, 1978.
Weintal, Edward, and Bartlett, Charles. *Facing the Brink: An Intimate Study of Crisis Diplomacy.* New York: Charles Scribner's Sons, 1967.
White, William S. *The Taft Story.* New York: Harper and Bros., 1954.
Williams, William A. *The Tragedy of American Diplomacy.* New York: Dell, 1962.
Yergin, Daniel. *Shattered Peace: The Origins of the Cold War and the National Security State.* Boston: Houghton Mifflin, 1977.

Secondary Works, Articles

Allen, Robert S. "State Department Quarterback." *Collier's,* 4 September 1948, pp. 17 and 61.
Bernstein, Barton J. "Courage and Commitment: The Missiles of October." *Foreign Service Journal* 52 (December 1975): 9–11, 24–27.
————. "The Week We Almost Went to War." *The Bulletin of the Atomic Scientists* 32 (February 1976): 12–21.
"The Bohlen Affair." *The Nation* 176 (4 April 1953): 279.
Burnham, James. "Was Bohlen a Blunder?" *Freeman* 3 (4 May 1953): 551–54.
Cook, Don. "Bohlen: Quintessential American Diplomat." *Los Angeles Times,* 8 January 1974, p. 7.
Daniel, Clifton. "Our Ambassador Behind the Iron Curtain." *The New York Times Magazine,* 24 July 1955, pp. 11, 22, 26.
"Dulles Betrayed." *Human Events,* 8 July 1959, p. 1.

Eliot, George Fielding. "Who Really Runs the World?" *The Survey* 85 (August 1949): 425–27.

Gaddis, John L. "Was the Truman Doctrine a Real Turning Point?" *Foreign Affairs* 52 (January 1974): 386–402.

Hammond, Paul Y. "NSC 68: Prologue to Rearmament." In *Strategy, Politics, and Defense Budgets,* pp. 267–378, ed. Warner R. Schilling, Paul Y. Hammond, and Glenn H. Snyder. New York: Columbia Univ. Press, 1962.

Harrington, Daniel F. "Kennan, Bohlen, and the Riga Axioms." *Diplomatic History* 2 (Fall 1978): 423–37.

Hogan, Michael J. "The Search for a 'Creative Peace': The United States, European Unity, and the Origins of the Marshall Plan." *Diplomatic History* 6 (Summer 1982): 267–85.

[Kennan, George F.] X. "The Sources of Soviet Conduct." *Foreign Affairs* 25 (July 1947): 566–82.

Maddux, Thomas R. "American Diplomats and the Soviet Experiment: The View from the Moscow Embassy, 1934–1939." *South Atlantic Quarterly* 74 (Autumn 1975): 468–87.

Mark, Eduard. "American Policy Toward Eastern Europe and the Origins of the Cold War, 1941–46: An Alternative Interpretation." *Journal of American History* 68 (September 1981): 313–36.

———. "Charles E. Bohlen and the Acceptable Limits of Soviet Hegemony in Eastern Europe: A Memorandum of 18 October, 1945." *Diplomatic History* 3 (Spring 1979): 201–13.

Messer, Robert L. "Paths Not Taken: The United States Department of State and Alternatives to Containment, 1945–1946." *Diplomatic History* 1 (Fall 1977): 297–319, 389–99.

Propas, Frederic L. "Creating a Hard Line Toward Russia: The Training of State Department Experts, 1927–1937." *Diplomatic History* 8 (Summer 1984): 209–26.

Schlesinger, Arthur, Jr. "Origins of the Cold War." *Foreign Affairs* 46 (October 1967): 22–52.

Schorr, Daniel. "Bohlen Returns to the Russian Challenge." *The New York Times Magazine,* 18 October 1959, pp. 14, 86–90.

Strom, Carl W. "The Office of Counselor of the Department of State." *The American Foreign Service Journal* 24 (December 1947): 14–15.

Sulzberger, C. L. "Foreign Affairs: Peacemaking a la Russe." *New York Times,* 26 June 1970, p. 40.

Walker, J. Samuel. "'No More Cold War': American Foreign Policy and the 1948 Peace Offensive." *Diplomatic History* 5 (Winter 1981): 75–91.

Wright, C. Ben. "'Mr. X' and Containment." *Slavic Review* 35 (March 1976): 1–31.

Dissertations

Bland, Larry I. "W. Averell Harriman: Businessman and Diplomat, 1891–1945." Ph.D. diss., University of Wisconsin, 1972.

Landa, Ronald D. "The Triumph and Tragedy of American Containment: When the Lines of the Cold War Were Drawn in Europe, 1947–48." Ph.D. diss., Georgetown University, 1971.

Mark, Eduard. "The Interpretation of Soviet Foreign Policy in the United States, 1928–1947." Ph.D. diss., University of Connecticut, 1978.

Wright, C. Ben. "George F. Kennan, Scholar-Diplomat: 1926–1946." Ph.D. diss., University of Wisconsin, 1972.

INDEX

T. Michael Ruddy, Associate Professor of History at Saint Louis University, received his doctorate at Kent State University and is the author of numerous articles on diplomatic history.